Barbarian Europe

The Making of the Past

Barbarian Europe

by Philip Dixon

ELSEVIER · PHAIDON

Advisory Board for
The Making of the Past

Frontispiece: the barbarian wars: a Roman soldier, with legionary sword and shield but an unusual plated helmet, fights barbarians armed with the curved knives of Dacians. From the memorial to the Roman dead of the Dacian wars. Early 2nd century A D. Adamklissi, Bulgaria.

ISBN 0 7290 0011 7

Elsevier Phaidon, an imprint of Phaidon Press Ltd.
Published in the United States by E.P. Dutton & Co. Inc., 201, Park Avenue South, New York, N.Y. 10003

Origination by Art Color Offset, Rome, Italy
Filmset by Keyspools Limited, Golborne, Lancs.
Printed and bound by Brepols, Turnhout - Belgium

Contents

Maps

Preface to the series

This book is a volume in the Making of the Past, a series describing the early history of the world as revealed by archaeology and related disciplines. The series is written by experts under the guidance of a distinguished panel of advisers and is designed for the layman, for young people, the student, the armchair traveler and the tourist. Its subject is a new history – the making of a new past, uncovered and reconstructed in recent years by skilled specialists. Since many of the authors of these volumes are themselves practicing archaeologists, leaders in a rapidly changing field, the series is completely authoritative and up-to-date. Each volume covers a specific period and region of the world and combines a detailed survey of the modern archaeology and sites of the area with an account of the early explorers, travelers, and archaeologists concerned with it. Later chapters of each book are devoted to a reconstruction in text and pictures of the newly revealed cultures and civilizations that make up the new history of the area.

Titles already published

The Egyptian Kingdoms
The Aegean Civilizations
The Spread of Islam
The Emergence of Greece

Biblical Lands
The New World
Man before History
The Greek World
The Rise of Civilization

Future titles

The First Empires
The Roman World
Ancient Japan
The Iranian Revival
Ancient China

The Kingdoms of Africa
Rome and Byzantium
Prehistoric Europe
India and Southeast Asia
Archaeology Today

Introduction

Few of the peoples in this book have ever been forgotten. Some had their own chroniclers, men who recorded their times and those of their ancestors. Others were the subjects of homilies or treatises prepared by Roman historians or churchmen. Even to their own writers the warriors of the past sometimes seemed savages; contemporary Romans saw them as awe-inspiring but only vaguely defined groups who threatened stable government in the provinces. The names of some have continued to the present day as terms of abuse – Hun, Goth or Vandal.

During the 5th century AD the barbarians, most of whom traced their origin back to the German-speaking tribes of the Baltic, broke through the Roman frontier defenses and in the course of two or three generations made themselves masters of almost the whole of western Europe. The Franks from beyond the Rhine occupied northern and central France; the Burgundians and other Germanic tribes annexed the Rhône valley and Switzerland. Spain and western France fell for a time to the Visigoths from eastern Europe, while Italy itself became the kingdom of the Ostrogoths from the fringe of Asia, later to fall prey to the Germanic Lombards. Britain, most northerly of the provinces of the Roman Empire, enjoyed a period of independence before passing under the control of migrants from northern Germany and Denmark. The area which had for so long presented at least a semblance of unity was now broken up into a series of antagonistic and often warring kingdoms. Political frontiers were insecure; whole provinces changed hands as the result of the success in battle of individual monarchs, and federations rarely survived the deaths of their founders. Into this complex of kingdoms poured fresh waves of barbarians, the Avars and Magyars from the east, and the Vikings from the north.

The period of the great Germanic migrations is sometimes called the Dark Ages, chiefly because of the inadequacy of the written record as a source for a continuous narrative. Some areas fare better than others: those provinces in which Roman civilization had set down its deepest roots were never wholly without chroniclers, or scribes willing to copy legal and administrative documents. But in the blackest periods of European illiteracy these areas, Italy, southern France or Spain, stand out like oases of historical knowledge in the middle of a prehistoric desert. In solving some of the problems the disciplines of archaeology and place-name study are of some help, though their results tend only to complicate an already puzzling picture. For the archaeologists the curse of a protohistoric period is everywhere visible, for in this period, when so much is already half-known from documentary sources, the temptation is irresistible to give to the data a more precise chronology or more specific context than they can truly sustain; the cause of the temptation, a natural enough desire to bring the material into correspondence with recorded events, is little enough justification for the tendentious arguments about the significance of discoveries, of which examples, not perhaps always intentional, are to be found in the following pages. The distribution of this archaeological material is complementary to that of the written record. With the possible exception of the Aegean area, the countries which flank the North Sea are archaeologically the most intensively studied in the world. The result is a mass of discrete observations whose synthesis has not yet been achieved, and which is little aided by written information, for these are the blackest regions of the Dark Ages.

Barbarian Europe is not the whole of the continent. The eastern half of the Roman Empire, with its capital at Constantinople, survived the fall of its western partner by nearly 1,000 years. Even if its frontiers were frequently broken by barbarian hordes, they were soon restored, and they formed an effective barrier to the expansion of barbarian kingdoms eastwards. The history of Greece, the Balkans and the eastern Mediterranean is thus part of the story of the Byzantine Empire, and has little to do with the Europe of the barbarians. While Constantinople stood, however, the empire had not fallen, and the possibility of a revival of the west by Byzantine conquest was never wholly abandoned. Meanwhile the barbarians themselves were changing. To an extent undreamed of by their first victims, the barbarian kingdoms – in their laws, material culture, religion and even speech – came to model themselves on the civilization they had had a hand in destroying. By the time the folk movements came to an end the borrowing had been acknowledged formally in a revival of the Roman Empire, but in a form that few Romans would have recognized.

Chronological Table

	BRITAIN	ITALY	IBERIA	GAUL	GERMANIA	S E EUROPE	MAJOR EVENTS

AD
Scotland Ireland and Wales — England — Normans
North Center South — Normans
West — East — Hungary

1066 Norman conquest of England

1000

1016 Knut, King of England

Saxon Empire

Sicily — Southern Italy — Normans

962 Otto I crowned Emperor

Magyars

911 Foundation of Normandy

900

Vikings

Galicia

Frankish Duchies

Saxon Empire

871 Alfred, King of Wessex

834 Vikings sack Dorestad

800

Franks — Lombards — Papal State

Franks

Bulgars

800 Charlemagne crowned Emperor

732 Arabs defeated at Poitiers

711 Arab conquest of Spain

700

Franks

Bretons

Aquitaine

Bulgars

Avars

639 Death of Dagobert I

Anglo-Saxons

Lombards

F r a n k s

600

568 Lombards invade Italy

Visigoths

Franks — Lombards

Gepids

526 Death of Theodoric the Great

Ostrogoths

Franks

Bavarians

Ostrogoths

481 Accession of Clovis

500

476 End of Western Roman Empire

Visigoths

451 Attila defeated

Huns

Vandals and Suebi

410 Alaric sacks Rome

400

Goths

376 Visigoths enter Roman Empire

Key to Regional Political Control

Roman	Byzantine	Celtic	Asiatic	Germanic	Arab

1. Romans and Barbarians

Roman cavalry and infantry in battle against Germans of the middle Danube. An Italian sarcophagus, c. 180–90 A D.

In the midwinter of the year 406 the river Rhine, the border between the Roman provinces of Germania and the unconquered tribes of central Europe, was frozen near the city of Mainz. The frontier garrisons were depleted, the attention of the commanders distracted by disturbances in Italy. On 31 December a horde of barbarians crossed the river and fell on the northwestern Roman provinces. The Roman allies in the Rhineland were unable to resist for long, and the cities of Mainz, Trier, Worms, Strasbourg, Tournai, Boulogne, Rheims and Amiens were sacked. A contemporary source reports that the invaders killed the hermits, burned the priests alive, raped the nuns, devastated the vineyards and cut down the olive trees; that may be hearsay, but, much later, the priest Salvian wrote of his memories of lacerated corpses in the streets of his native Trier, a former imperial capital. "The whole of Gaul," said the Gallic bishop Orientius, "smoked in a single funeral pyre." The Rhine frontier which had for centuries protected Gaul, Spain and northern Italy from attack was not rebuilt. For two years the invaders, Suebi,

Vandals and Alans, moved slowly across Gaul to Spain, where they carved for themselves kingdoms out of the former Roman provinces.

Opinions about the causes of the Roman collapse were first aired in the 5th century and are still being discussed. Some have seen the answer in terms of divine punishment – as a warning to Constantinople to reform its morals – or as the debilitating effects of Christianity. More recently, economic causes have been examined – impoverishment through unfavorable balances of trade, underutilization of resources, or declining agricultural productivity. Others have favored demographic movements – the devastations of plague or a decline in the birthrate leading to manpower shortage. Many of these are indeed credible factors in the steady decay of the power of both east and west, but the collapse of the Western Empire itself was incidental, a series of misjudgments and unfortunate coincidences. The decline and fall are seen through Roman eyes – inevitably, for almost all the eyewitnesses who have left records were Romans. But it is only half the story, for it concentrates on Roman stagnation and not upon the steadily growing numbers, unity and sophistication of the barbarians themselves.

The Roman Emperor Valerian kneels before his captor, the Shah Shapur I. After 260 AD, Naqsj-i-Rustam, Iran.

The defense of the empire. The empire in 400 had changed almost out of recognition in the four centuries since its initial consolidation under Augustus. During the 3rd century military and consequent financial pressures led to a period of anarchy and economic crisis. The recurrent threat came from the tribes of central Germany and the northern Balkans. Against them a series of emperors fought campaigns with varying success and at considerable cost maintained a strongly fortified frontier zone along the Rhine and the Danube. In the middle years of the 3rd century war with Persia led to a crushing defeat which coincided with rebellions in Gaul, Spain and Britain, and with the overrunning of the northern frontier by barbarian tribes. Under these pressures the economy collapsed and the empire seemed likely to break up. The subsequent reconstruction by Diocletian and his successors was far-reaching: a level of maximum prices for commodities was imposed, the administrative and military systems were reorganized, and heavy taxation was used to build up the army. The increasing complexities of government led slowly to the emergence of separate Eastern and Western Empires, their emperors nominally colleagues whose interests lay in the safeguarding of the Danube and Persian, and the German, frontiers respectively, a division which was underlined in 330 by the building of a "new Rome," the city of Constantinople, henceforth the capital of the Eastern Empire.

Signs of increasing difficulty in maintaining the *status quo* are clear. The province of Dacia (modern Romania) had been overrun in the 260s and was now officially abandoned. The frontier was brought south to the Danube. Further westwards a heavily fortified frontier lay between the upper Danube and the upper Rhine (to the east of Strasbourg), protecting a strategic enclave which was not naturally defended in the north. Like Dacia, this area came under pressure in the crises of the mid-3rd century; about 260 the much-weakened garrisons were compelled to withdraw, and the lands were seized by the barbarian Alamanni. Despite efforts to unseat them, the Alamanni retained control and prospered: according to Ammianus, the Roman army which campaigned in the area in 357 saw "villas rich in livestock and crops." Within the empire, by contrast, some areas were in decay: we hear of shrinkage of settlement in the Balkans, of huge areas of land formerly cultivated but now abandoned in Campania, of repeated and generally frustrated attempts by the government to enlist recruits and to compel landowners and city authorities to carry out their obligations in taxes and public duties, and increasingly of complaints of tax burdens and extortion. How representative this is of general decline we do not know, for the necessary statistical documents do not survive, but it is quite clear that it was a perpetual struggle to keep the army up to strength, and shortage of men was a growing preoccupation with successive governments.

Under the early emperors the armies were frontier troops, stationed in a complex network of fortresses along the border line. Despite the large numbers of men under arms (by the end of the 3rd century probably over 400,000) the requirements outstripped supply, for the frontiers were enormous – that in Europe alone was over 1,500 miles in length – and the detachments in any single sector were correspondingly small. As long as Rome's enemies were fragmented, this static defense line proved adequate; but against the larger confederacies, which were a feature of the barbarian wars of the 3rd century and later, the old system broke down. The reserves were insufficient to reinforce points of conflict without withdrawing troops from other frontier stations, and thus inviting the collapse of further sectors of the defenses, while the troops on the spot were too scattered to withstand concerted attacks. The situation demanded new strategy, and by the beginning of the 4th century the army had been reshaped. The front-line troops were reduced in importance: it was their task to report enemy movements and to delay invaders. The best regiments were pulled back into the provinces and grouped into mobile field armies who could be rushed into action against fast-moving barbarian attacks. Defense was now flexible and more economical, but the system could, and as we shall see did, break down when attacks were made over a large area, and the demands on manpower were still huge. As a direct result the reorganized army relied more and more on the use of barbarian soldiers.

This was indeed not altogether a new policy. In the early empire auxiliary regiments were normally raised from native tribes on the periphery of the Roman world, at first serving under their own chieftains but later, as a precaution, under Roman officers. During the troubled 3rd century their numbers grew as emperors found themselves forced to enroll barbarians from among the very tribes who threatened the frontiers. By the 4th century the greater part of the army was composed of barbarian troops. The army lists name units of Franks, Alamanni, Goths, Vandals, Heruli, Quadi, Marcomanni and Alans, and these and similar tribes provided the backbone of the established regiments. Barbarian commanders now became more common. Sometimes these men were chieftains who brought their tribal levies into the army. One may have been Erocus, "King of the Alamanni," in Constantius' entourage at York in 306; or Fraomer, king of a branch of the Alamanni from near Mainz, who in 372 appears as a Roman officer of Alamannic troops in Britain. They were not confined to the lesser posts: in the 4th century soldiers of barbarian origin rose to the top ranks, and a notable feature of the late empire is the domination of the government by generals like Arbogastes or Bauto (both in origin Franks) or Stilicho (half a Vandal).

Two further changes in Roman relations with barbarian tribes paralleled this development. Deserted areas near the frontiers were resettled with barbarian prisoners who farmed the lands and provided a new source of recruits; more important, some tribes were allowed to settle within the empire under their own rulers, as "federates," in return for treaty obligations of military service. This break with tradition may have been thought of as no more than a temporary expedient: when Julian admitted the Franks to Belgium he was preoccupied with civil tension and the threat of war with Persia; similar arrangements apparently made by Magnus Maximus with the tribes in northern Britain in the early 380s immediately preceded his invasion of Gaul and usurpation of the imperial throne. The result in each case was to set up within the frontiers buffer-states to whom fell part of the duty of defending the empire.

It is not clear how much resentment these policies caused. The dress and manners of barbarians were imitated by some, and perhaps for that very reason were parodied by Roman writers; signs of racial tension do appear. Significantly, these are clearest after the military reversals of the late 4th century: after the disaster of 378 at the hands of the Visigoths, those Goths who served in the army at Constantinople were massacred, as a precaution. A riot at Thessalonica in 390 led to the murder of the Gothic commander of the garrison and official reprisals in which thousands were reported killed. In 408, during the crisis of the Visigothic invasions of Italy, the families of the barbarian troops stationed in north Italy were massacred. These are violent reactions: the typical attitude is more likely to have been grudging acquiescence in the necessity of using the barbarians, and a personal determination to have as little to do with them oneself as possible. An unlooked-for effect of this growing contact was that when the invaders finally broke the frontiers their aim was to share the benefits of Roman civilization, not to destroy it.

The barbarian tribes. The identification of the tribes beyond the imperial frontiers is notoriously difficult, and the difficulties increase in proportion to the distance from the frontier to the tribal homelands. Travelers' tales are well known to be tall. We can read in Classical authors like Herodotus of northern seas populated by griffins or of tribes whose names and characteristics have been taken from poetry and literature by that time nearly 1,000 years old.

Such as it is, then, our evidence suggests that during the last centuries BC and the first centuries of our era barbarians migrated from northern and central Europe southeastwards, from modern Germany and Poland through Czechoslovakia to southern Russia. Folklore places the ultimate origins of almost all the invaders of the empire in Scandinavia and the Baltic area, and attempts have been made to link the tribal names of the 4th century with those recorded in the 1st century or even before. Archaeology too has been pressed into service, and areas in which similar styles of decoration in pottery or metalwork occur have been identified as the territories of particular tribes. The aim is probably misguided. Too little is known of the criteria used by our sources to distinguish individual tribal groups: in the events of the migrations politics rather than cultures were important, and in those cases where we know something of the politics the tribes were not discrete units but confederacies, ready, if need arose, to split up and reform themselves into fresh groupings. These all-important federations do not appear in the archaeological record: here the emphasis is on continuity of occupation of settlement sites, and on time-honored practices of agriculture and manufacture within narrowly defined regions which can seldom with any plausibility be tied to the tribal names we know.

But two changes which may have a bearing on early migrations can be traced. From about 100 AD the marshlands along the southern fringes of the North Sea were increasingly colonized, and further inland during the same period the greater size of the cremation cemeteries and the development of large villages indicate growth of population and imply a need for expansion as barbarian pressure on the Roman frontiers increased during the 2nd and 3rd centuries.

From the 4th century onwards the broad outlines of the political framework of barbarian Europe are clear enough. In the Danish peninsula and the adjoining area of northern Germany were the territories of the Jutes, the Angles, the Saxons and the Frisians; to the east, in the valley of the Elbe, were the Lombards. Between these tribes and the empire lay two large confederacies, both creations of the 3rd century: on the lower Rhine the Franks were a longstanding threat to Gaul before the Roman commanders of the mid-4th century reluctantly allowed them

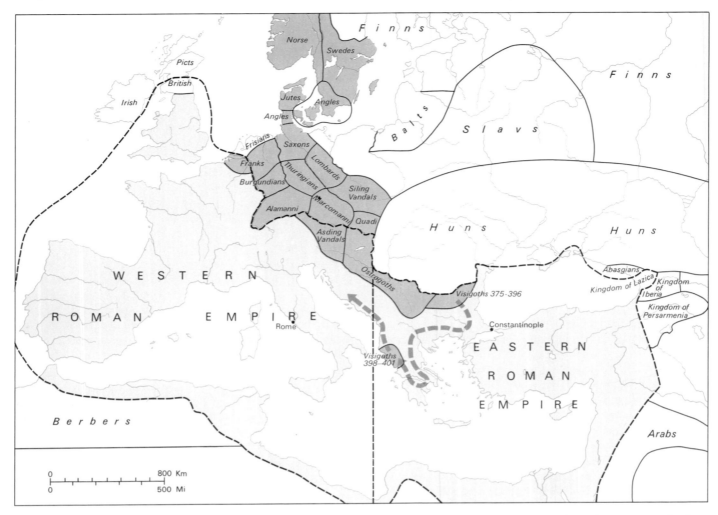

The Roman world on the eve of the barbarian migrations. The Visigoths have moved through Yugoslavia; other tribes occupy lands on the frontiers.

to settle in parts of Belgium and entered into treaty relationship with them; to the south, the Alamanni, a group whose name (literally "all people") spells out their confederacy, had in 259–60 broken through the upper Rhine frontier and now held firmly onto the fertile enclave between the Rhine and the Danube.

On the Danube itself the 4th-century Roman garrisons were confronted by the Goths. Their traditions place their original homeland in southern Sweden (Gotland), from which their migrations had taken them into Poland by the beginning of the 2nd century AD. During this century and the next they pushed towards the Black Sea. Here they split into two groups: the Ostrogoths occupied the lands between the Dniester and the Dnieper, and the Visigoths took over the province of Dacia (modern Romania) after its evacuation by the Romans about 270. The Gepids, their neighbors in Poland (and formerly in Sweden, if their legends can be trusted), now occupied eastern Hungary, where their lands marched with those of the long-established south German tribes, principally the

Quadi and the Marcomanni, still in the area ascribed to them by Tacitus at the end of the 1st century AD.

Information on the settlement further from the frontier is less trustworthy. The Vandals, said to have come from Jutland, had by the time of Tacitus penetrated to the head of the Oder basin. One group, the Siling Vandals, remained in Silesia; another, called the Asding Vandals, in the 3rd century moved southwards to the Danube frontier of the empire. A further tribe from the Baltic, the Burgundians, took a similar route, and by the 4th century were settled next to the Alamanni at the head of the Weser.

However confused the details, the general arrangement of the Germanic peoples is known. They spoke variants of the same language, and frequently cooperated with each other, but the unity of these tribal conglomerates must not be overemphasized: branches of the same peole were often at loggerheads; individual tribesmen (and even tribal levies) are found fighting for opposing armies. A confederacy could be led by several chieftains, whose power depended on their own, sometimes transitory, prestige. Their leadership might last only for a stated term: some were indeed elected by the tribal assemblies as war leaders to counter a particular crisis. Men of recognized royal stock, called "kings" by the Romans, are quite shadowy figures. They seem to have had some religious functions and some may have had the duty of interpreting the law: the paramount chieftain of the Visigoths was referred to by the Romans as the *Iudex* or Judge. In Tacitus' time a king might be a war leader, but generally only by election; his successor was chosen from among all the suitable candidates of royal blood. Partition of tribal areas among two or more successors of a king is well attested, and indeed was the custom in the Frankish kingdom throughout the early Middle Ages. This lack of a single supreme authority and absence of central organization made much simpler the task of the Roman garrisons to hold back the barbarian hordes.

The decline of the west. The mobility of groups or of whole peoples which has been described makes it clear that the great migrations of the late 4th and 5th centuries were merely a continuation of a long process of movement beyond the frontiers. The decisive factors which changed the character of barbarian pressure on the empire from ill-sustained raiding to mass immigration were the advance of the Huns and their destruction of the thriving Gothic kingdoms.

Roman descriptions of the Huns range from stock phrases, applicable to all nomads, to outright mythology. They were identified as the Horsemen of the Apocalypse, as Magog, as the offspring of devils who overcame their enemies by magic. More prosaically, but no more accurately, they were identified with the long-vanished tribes of the far north, the Scythians, Cimmerians or Massagetae, and it was asserted that they ate no cooked food, drank blood, lived and slept on their horses, and were so ugly one would think them two-legged beasts. "The Roman army," said St Jerome, "is terrified by the very sight of them." Of their origins little is known. Racially, they presented to Roman observers characteristics we would now call Mongoloid, such as flat noses, small eyes, weak profiles and lack of facial hair. Their graves, however, show a mixed population, with some, perhaps only slight, Mongol traits. The language they spoke survives only in the form of personal names, and interpretations are controversial: some elements of Iranian, or Germanic have been traced – both presumably borrowings from their subjects – but the majority of the names appear to be a form of Turkish. Very little is known of their history before they reached the fringes of the Roman world in the 370s.

In the 1st century BC movements eastwards from central to eastern Asia ended in the formation of a confederation of tribes in Mongolia. Their neighbors, the Chinese, who were in frequent conflict with them, called them the Hsiung-nu. Many have equated them with the Huns, and pointed to the Chinese victories of the 4th century as spurs to a westward migration of Hunnish survivors. The theory is open to many objections, but some support is given by a scattered distribution of cast-bronze cooking vessels, on average about 18 inches in height, the Hunnic cauldrons. Within Europe the use of these barbaric cauldrons spread along the coast of the Black Sea into Hungary and from there through Germany westwards. Most are chance finds without context; a few come from 5th-century Roman sites on the Danube frontier, presumably relics of Hun auxiliaries in the Roman army. Quite apart from their distinctive and exotic appearance, those whose metal content has been analyzed have shown an extraordinarily high proportion of copper in the alloy, a crude technology quite unlike anything else in Europe. All are agreed to be of Hunnic manufacture, and findspots of similar vessels in Asia can be traced eastwards through the Altai mountains to prototypes on the northern border of China, the area of the Hsiung-nu confederation.

About 370 the Huns overran the Alans, another nomadic group in the Don area, and together they fell on the kingdom of the Ostrogoths. Weakened perhaps by the revolt of subject Alans, the kingdom collapsed. Their neighbors the Visigoths tried to check the Huns at the river Dniester but were outflanked and retreated south-westwards. After a further reverse (the Goths it is said were saved only by the slowness of the Huns through weight of their booty) thousands of Visigoths fled to the Danube.

A contemporary Roman writer, Ammianus Marcellinus, presents the scene vividly. The commanders of the Danube frontier troops had taken little notice of reports of troubles far to the north, for this sort of rumor was seldom significant to the empire. Then men began to appear on the far bank of the river and begged to be allowed to cross. Their numbers grew steadily, until the bank was crowded by an immense multitude of Gothic refugees seeking shelter inside the empire. Word was brought to the Eastern Emperor Valens, far off in Syria. He and his advisers considered the Goths a much-needed source of recruits to the army, and since the Danube provinces were underpopulated land could be found for them. Thus in the autumn of 375/6 permission was granted to the Goths to cross the Danube.

The official plan of controlled and dispersed settlement under the supervision of Roman officials failed completely. The Goths (200,000 according to one source – more realistically Ammianus says that trying to count them was like counting the sands on the shore of Libya) came across on improvised rafts and passed in confusion into the Roman province of Moesia, where profiteers were soon at work selling dog meat to the starving Goths in exchange for Goths as slaves.

As the number of refugees increased and their temper worsened the Roman troops withdrew to the mountain passes between Moesia and Thrace, from which they were dislodged by an outflanking movement of Huns and

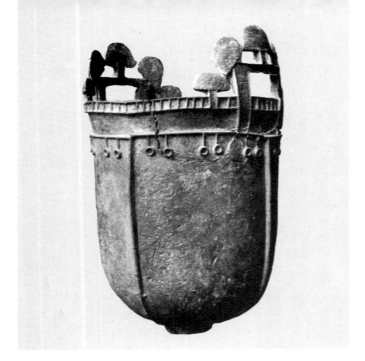

Alans, with whom the Goths in desperation had made alliance.

Nothing now prevented an invasion of Thrace, and at Adrianople on the road to Constantinople in 378 the Goths met and, with the aid of Ostrogothic cavalry, decisively defeated the army of the Emperor Valens, who was himself killed in the battle. Gratian, Emperor of the West, who was hurrying too late to his colleague's assistance, was forced to deploy his army against fresh barbarians, probably Huns, who threatened the Roman provinces higher up the Danube. The situation seemed desperate to the church father Gregory: "The cities are devastated, myriads of people are killed, the earth is soaked with blood, and a foreign people is running through the land as if it were theirs." But skillful generalship and disharmony among the barbarians saved the Romans. Valens' successor, the general Theodosius, in 382 came to terms with the Visigoths, who were allowed to settle south of the Danube in areas originally intended for them, but now under their own tribal organization, and with their own rulers, to serve, in the eyes of one contemporary, "as an unconquerable defense against the assaults of the Huns."

While the east settled back to some sort of order,

Above: a stewpot cast by Huns for Huns, a typical example of a Hunnic cauldron of the 4th or 5th century from Hungary.
Below: the path of the barbarians: the European distribution of Hunnic cauldrons (after O. Maenchen-Helfer) and south Russian plate brooches (after E. T. Leeds and H. Kühn).

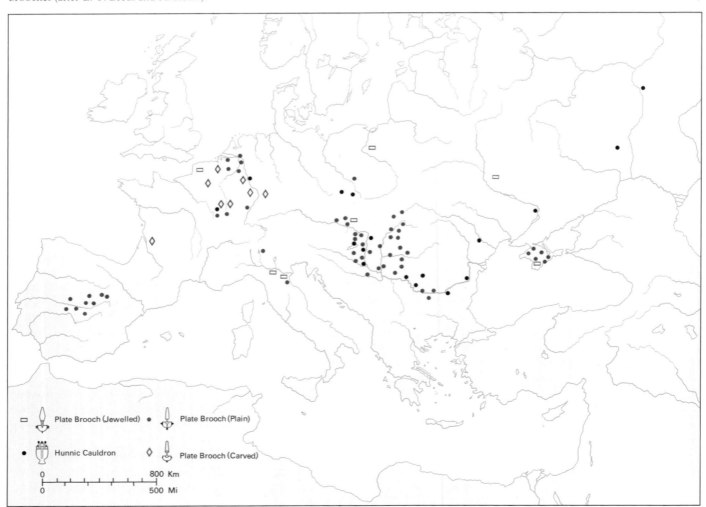

Theodosius the Great, emperor 379–95, whose election to the throne was a result of the disaster at Adrianople, and who spent his reign defending the east against the barbarians. Silver mass dish from Spain, c. 390.

disturbances began in the west. Early in 383 Magnus Maximus, commander of the army in Britain, brought his troops into Gaul in opposition to the Emperor Gratian. The emperor, who was about to begin a campaign against the Alamanni, led his army to meet Maximus near Paris. Before they came to battle most of his troops deserted, and Gratian himself was killed in the retreat. Maximus now set up his administration in the center of the Rhine frontier in the fortress-city of Trier. His coup may have been prompted by a desire to replace the rule of Gratian with a strong military regime, and he lost little time in repressing the Franks and bringing Gaul and Spain to heel; but he did not hesitate to use barbarians when it promised advantage. In 383 he encouraged a German tribe, the Jugunthi, to cross the frontier and ravage Raetia (modern Bavaria and Tyrol) in order to harass the advisers of Gratian's brother and successor, the young Emperor Valentinian.

The sequel is a sign of the times, for Valentinian's general, the Frank Bauto, had to call in Huns and Alans, already settled in Hungary, against the Jugunthi. These barbarian allies crushed the Jugunthi, but continued riding

westwards towards Gaul. Bauto, like many another would-be employer of mercenaries, was forced to pay them to retreat as well as to advance. The final overthrow of Maximus similarly depended on foreign troops. After a period of wary peace between Trier and the imperial government based in Milan, in 387 Maximus crossed the Alps and deposed Valentinian. The action compelled Theodosius, the Emperor of the East, to move; since the Visigothic settlement he had been preoccupied with new troubles with the north and with Persia. Now he collected an army almost wholly composed of barbarians – Goths, Huns and Alans.

The intention was soon achieved: Maximus was killed and Valentinian restored as emperor. But defectors from Theodosius' army, mostly Visigoths, turned in growing number to brigandage in Macedonia and were joined by fresh hordes of barbarians from across the Danube. In late spring 392 the bishop of Constantinople wrote, "The barbarians have left their own territory and many times have overrun huge tracts of our lands, set fire to the countryside and seized the towns; but instead of returning to their homes, like drunken revelers they mock at us."

Ivory diptych (dedicated by a consul to commemorate his year of office), believed to show the barbarian general Stilicho and his family. Italian, c. 395.

Theodosius' campaigns proved inconclusive, and by the end of the year he had to contend with another usurper in the west, for Valentinian was dead – some said by his own hand – and his erstwhile general, the Frank Arbogastes, proclaimed as emperor Eugenius, a comparatively harmless teacher of rhetoric. The second army of the east against the west, like the first, relied on barbarians, Alans, Huns, even Arabs, and (according to an admittedly biased source) more than 20,000 Visigoths.

By late 394 the usurper had been captured and executed, his followers dispersed and Theodosius was emperor of both east and west; but the respite was brief, for in January 395 Theodosius died. He divided the empire between his young sons, Arcadius and Honorius, and entrusted the sons to the guardianship of his niece's husband, the Vandal Stilicho. In the event, Stilicho's protectorship was acknowledged only in the western half of the empire by the younger brother, Honorius, and the consequent disunity of the empire ruined the west.

Alaric and the sack of Rome. The late Theodosius' army was still mostly in northern Italy, but the Visigothic contingent, led by their king Alaric, had returned eastwards and was now pillaging Thessaly. An expedition to Thessaly proved unsuccessful, for Stilicho failed to catch

Alaric and was compelled at the end of his campaign to return most of his troops to Arcadius' advisers in Constantinople, who were faced with Hunnic raiding and were suspicious of Stilicho's ambitions. The Visigoths meanwhile moved southwards and began pillaging the Peloponnese. In 397 Stilicho advanced against them once more and surrounded Alaric's forces near Olympia. Somehow (hostile critics said through Stilicho's indolence) Alaric managed to escape to Epirus (Yugoslavia). The eastern government chose to regard Stilicho's activities as aggressive, for the Peloponnese was well within their own half of the empire. Stilicho was declared a public enemy of the east and, presumably to thwart an alliance with Stilicho, Alaric was appointed Constantinople's commander in the northwestern Balkans. However useful the gambit may have seemed at the time to Constantinople (and a reaction soon set in with another massacre of Gothic troops in that city), for the west it proved disastrous. The Visigoths were now legally established close to Italy's borders, and were as free as before to do what they pleased.

In the autumn of 401 Alaric launched a sudden attack on northern Italy. After an indecisive battle south of Turin he withdrew, under agreement, to Epirus. Stilicho's policy for lack of resources was one of compromise. The government was chronically short of troops, and he was now forced to bring back regiments from Bavaria, the Rhine and Britain to defend Italy. When in 405 another Gothic king tried to follow Alaric's example by crossing the Alps (unsuccessfully, thanks to Hunnic auxiliaries), his defeated army was promptly enlisted among the ranks of the victors.

New territories and fresh recruits were needed, a problem that could be overcome, Stilicho decided, by the annexation to his own western government of some of the Danube provinces of the Eastern Empire. Terms for the expedition were arranged with Alaric, but the preparations were overtaken by the events of the winter of 406/7, when the Rhine frontier collapsed under the attacks of the Vandals, the Suebi and the Huns' former allies the Alans. It was a critical situation made worse by further developments: the British armies, now cut off from Italy by the invasions, were already in revolt and had elected a series of their own emperors. Two survived only months; the third, Constantine, brought his army into Gaul at the very beginning of 407 and set up his court in southern France at Arles. In the next year Constantine absorbed the provinces of Spain into his new Gallic empire. As a final blow, Alaric advanced to the borders of Italy where he waited for Stilicho to join him for the long-proposed campaign in the Balkans. The western government was in no position to honor the arrangements (and there is no evidence that Alaric really expected them to); on the pretext of a broken contract, Alaric demanded massive compensation for his fruitless march from Epirus. The money was found despite considerable opposition from the Italian aristoc-

Center: Honorius, younger son of Theodosius the Great, and his successor in the western half of the empire (395–423).

Right: Constantine III, once a private soldier in Britain, who in 407 led an army into Gaul and for four years maintained a precarious empire in rivalry to Honorius' government.

racy; but the incident increased Roman antagonism both to the barbarians and to Stilicho's policy of diplomacy. A revolt in the army mustering against Constantine gave Stilicho's rivals their chance: Honorius agreed to his assassination in August 408, and his supporters were purged.

Alaric's approaches to the new regime were rebuffed in a mood of anti-barbarian feeling. The result was a second invasion of Italy: Rome itself was blockaded by the Visigoths through the winter of 408/9, and the siege was raised only by the payment of a large ransom. Honorius' court, safely stationed in the fortress-city of Ravenna, which was now the favorite refuge of the government, was unable to interfere (and was, indeed, for a time compelled to recognize the claims to Gaul of the usurper Constantine) but still refused to come to terms with Alaric. Alaric's aim seems to have been simply a supply of cash to maintain his prestige and shipments of grain to feed his people, but the negotiations dragged on until the middle of 410. When they finally broke down, Alaric sacked Rome and in the hope of crossing to the corn-lands of Africa marched to southern Italy, where he died at the end of the year, giving the government in Ravenna a much-needed breathing space to worry about the problems north of the Alps. The fall of Rome by now had little military significance, for the government was still safe in Ravenna. The damage to prestige, however, was enormous, and the shock of the violence done to the city of St Peter, which was to inspire St Augustine's *City of God*, provided material for numerous sermons.

Dissolution of the empire. In the previous winter, 409/10, the Vandals, Suebi and Alans, who had been pillaging Gaul for over two years, broke through Constantine's garrisons in the Pyrenees and began to devastate Spain. In the face of the threat, Constantine's new empire dissolved; his general in Spain proclaimed his own protégé emperor, came to terms with the barbarians and in 411 led a combined army of his troops and Vandals against Constantine. The latter sent for assistance from the Franks and the Alamanni, but now found himself blockaded in his capital, Arles, by the Spanish forces. Meanwhile an expedition against Constantine (postponed since

408) was being mounted by Ravenna; after a confused campaign the imperial troops defeated in turn the rival armies of Spain and of the Rhineland, and took over the siege of Arles. Constantine was soon captured and executed, but the pacification of the Rhineland itself was achieved with help from an unexpected source. Athaulf, brother and successor of Alaric, led the Visigoths out of Italy and crushed the revolt.

At the end of ten years' fighting, then, the Western Empire seemed to have recovered its equilibrium. But the situation in 412 was very different from that of 401. The province of Britain was now independent and the imperial government showed little interest in regaining control; northwestern France was in a state of revolt that seemed endemic; northern Spain was in the hands of Suebi, Alans and Vandals; and the Visigoths held the balance of power in central and southern Gaul. Athaulf, it is true, from time to time proclaimed himself champion of the empire, but he now established himself in southern Gaul, and there was soon in conflict with Honorius. A blockade and famine drove the Visigoths into Spain, where Athaulf was murdered in 415. His successors were unable to make the crossing to the rich grain lands of Africa but were so successful in ousting the Alans and Vandals from central Spain that the imperial government became alarmed at their growing power. In 417 the Visigoths were invited back into Gaul, and at the beginning of 418 the province of Aquitaine was formally ceded to them as a federate kingdom with its capital at Toulouse. The alliance had much to recommend it: to the Romans, a promise of some stability and military assistance; to the Visigoths, a place to settle after more than 20 years of movement under Alaric and Athaulf. But the settlement of Aquitaine, like the abandonment of Britain, was in practice a recognition of the breakdown of the old empire.

Gaul had suffered pillage for more than ten years. "All the land between the Alps and the Pyrenees . . . has been devastated," wrote St Jerome in 409, though he was far away in Bethlehem, and certainly exaggerated. Namatianus' eyewitness account of Italy in 417 is more telling: the public buildings of Rome, as we know from inscriptions, were already being restored after Alaric's sack; in the countryside reconstruction was clearly slow, for travel was still difficult: the bridges were wrecked and the inns were in ruins. The invasions, then, had been disruptive. The barbarian settlement itself was, somewhat surprisingly, less so. The migrants were eager to carry on local agricultural custom and often visibly scrupulous in finding the boundaries to estates and observing the rights of property. Dispossessed landowners appear in the records, men living in poverty, in retirement or exile, but the settlement was generally viewed by the barbarians themselves as the billeting or quartering of their men upon a fraction (a third, sometimes two-thirds) of a property whose owner kept the remainder. The word used of such a barbarian settler was *hospes*, guest, with only slight irony; his relationship with his host was perhaps not ideal but was preferable to wholesale clearance, examples of which are comparatively rare.

One of these exiles is remembered in a long autobiographical poem. Paulinus, an Aquitanian, the grandson of a most influential imperial adviser and himself briefly embroiled in imperial politics, had lost his possessions by a combination of bad judgment and robbery, and had fled to Marseilles. Living there in poverty, he received, to his delight, a sum of money, a windfall from a Goth who wanted to buy a piece of land which Paulinus had once owned and who had taken the trouble to seek him out. His case was not unique, for the laws codified by the barbarians to regulate their new kingdoms carefully deal with Roman tenurial and personal rights, as well as their obligations.

Within the very heart of the Visigothic kingdom some landowners kept their estates. North of Bordeaux, Leontius, an Aquitanian nobleman, still lived in a great mansion overlooking the estuary, with storehouses, porticoes and frescoes and all the necessities of civilized life. The life of the upper classes, however, now differed from that of their 4th-century predecessors, for Leontius' mansion had walls and towers. Bishop Sidonius of Clermont-Ferrand refers to the similar "hill-fortresses" of one of his friends in central Gaul, and when the prefect Dardanus retired from official life he moved into an inaccessible valley in the Maritime Alps, protected by walls and gates. The middle classes, too, found their lives changed. Even those not directly involved in barbarian settlements saw, as the empire declined, the disappearance of their former opportunities to make their reputations and fortunes in the imperial civil or military service. Their careers and interests now had to be local, and the gradual eclipse of this once important bureaucratic class is a significant feature of the change from imperial to medieval society.

Considerable changes took place, then, but for some a stable and orderly way of life prevailed. The Visigothic court at Toulouse surprised visitors by its dignity. "Greek elegance, Gallic plenty, Italian briskness," Bishop Sidonius observes. Real symbiosis, however, was impossible, for the Goths were heretics.

While they were still outside the empire, missionary work among the Goths had been begun by the Gothic bishop Ulfila, an adherent of Arius, an Alexandrine priest whose creed recognized the divinity of God the father, but not that of Christ himself. When they entered the empire the Goths were strongly influenced by Arian groups in the middle Danube, and the form of Christianity to which both the Goths and the Vandals were converted was Arianism. Some of the 4th-century emperors were Arians, but the doctrine had been denounced by the Council of Nicaea in 325, and against it ever-sterner measures were taken during the 4th century. These religious differences seem to have troubled the Goths little: outside Africa persecutions by Arians of Catholics were rare and the Catholic Church was generally tolerated. But the accident of Arian conversion prevented the absorption of the barbarians into the much more numerous Romanized population and reinforced the personal distaste of the provincials for their conquerors.

Europe becomes isolated. The foundation of the Visigothic kingdom of Toulouse marks the end of the first stage of the fall of the west, and during an interlude of comparative peace in Italy and southern Gaul the resumption of traditional modes of behavior seemed possible. In Spain the Suebi and Vandals were still unchecked and here the new allies, Visigoths and Romans, campaigned in 419 and subsequent years. At the end of the 420s a new threat arose. Under their king Gaiseric the Vandals crossed the straits of Gibraltar and proceeded along the North African coast. Africa was the home of a thriving religious and intellectual community, and had for centuries supplied Europe, and Rome in particular, with corn and oil, but the imperial government seemed powerless as the Vandals took city after city. When St Augustine died in Hippo in 430 the barbarians were already camped outside its walls; by the end of the decade they had captured the capital, Carthage, and worse was to come (at least in the eyes of our ecclesiastical sources) for the Vandals began a savage persecution of the powerful and wealthy Catholic Church of Africa, who remembered the period as "a century of tyranny and captivity" whose end was greeted with tears of joy.

The Vandals were the only barbarian people to create a navy, and its effect was out of all proportion to their numbers. An edict from Constantinople shows how serious such a threat appeared: in 419 a Crimean bishop had asked pardon for some of his flock "who have betrayed to the barbarians the art of shipbuilding, hitherto unknown to them." The emperor agreed, but decreed that repetition of the offense would be a capital crime. In the event the judgment was sound, for as master of Carthage Gaiseric controlled the famous Carthaginian shipyards, and lost no time in setting them to work. During the next summer his fleet ravaged Sicily, and the Vandals, despite all the efforts of Rome and Constantinople, were able to launch attacks at will on the coastline of the Mediterranean. For a while

Mediterranean trade all but disappeared, and in the view of some historians never recovered; by the time that the pirates were finally dispersed in the 6th century, the merchants had established other, safer markets nearer home.

The activities of the Vandals which fragmented the Mediterranean world were paralleled by events in Gaul. The Visigoths proved uncertain allies and supported Ravenna only when it suited them. In 425 during the succession crisis after the death of Honorius they besieged Arles; ten years later they attacked Narbonne. Both were attempts to gain possession of part of the Mediterranean coastline and were strongly resisted. But the ability of the imperial court to influence events in Gaul was now steadily declining. The northwest was still in the hands of its peasant rebels, the Bacaudae of Brittany, the northeast had been abandoned to the former federates, the Franks, and central Gaul was dominated by Aëtius, a Roman general whose allegiance to Ravenna was only nominal.

In his youth, in the first decade of the 5th century, Aëtius had spent some time as a hostage among the Huns. Some have described the Huns as his friends; it would be truer to say that Aëtius recognized the value of his contacts with the Huns in furthering his own policies, but that the link was certainly commercial. Hunnic mercenaries were nothing new. They were nomads whose tribal units were small and accustomed to independent action: in the 370s some fought with Ostrogoths against attacks of Huns and Alans; others joined the Visigoths against the Romans; Huns were called in by Honorius against the Goths, and Stilicho himself had a Hunnic bodyguard. Aëtius was seen by contemporaries to be remarkable not for his use of such allies, but for the way in which he seemed able to raise fresh levies when he wanted them.

Aëtius came to prominence in the succession crisis of the 420s, when he arrived, too late, with a Hunnic army to help John, the usurper of Honorius' throne. With such assistance Aëtius was too powerful to be eliminated, and the new imperial government sent him to Gaul with their blessing. We hear of him in 428 defeating the Franks on the Rhine, in 430 the Juthungi on the Danube and the Visigoths near Arles, in 432 the Franks again. An attempt in that year to dispose of him was a failure, for Aëtius hired more Huns and compelled the government to recognize his authority in Gaul: during the next 20 years his position was secure. In 436 his lieutenant Litorius with the aid of Hunnic mercenaries suppressed the peasant revolt of the northwest, while Aëtius himself decimated the Burgundians, unruly federates who were pushing across the middle Rhine. In 437 the troops were brought south again, where the Visigoths had taken advantage of Roman preoccupations and were blockading Narbonne. After a series of successful campaigns Litorius' Hunnic army was annihilated outside the walls of Toulouse. In Marseilles the priest Salvian commented sardonically, "The Visigoths put their trust in God, but we put ours in Huns." Both

sides were exhausted, and in 439 another peace treaty was arranged.

The breakdown of order in Gaul is obvious enough during this decade, and in the next few years Aëtius was forced towards an ominous new policy. In 440 he established a tribe of Alans in deserted land on the Rhône south of Lyons; in 442 more Alans were installed in central Gaul near Orléans, and in 443 the remnants of the Burgundians were settled to the east of Lyons, in Savoy. A few years later Bishop Sidonius expressed his disgust at the newcomers, "Long-haired hordes . . . the greedy Burgundian who spreads his hair with rancid butter . . . reeking of garlic and foul onions." Aëtius was perhaps establishing his own federates, as substitutes for his former Hunnic mercenaries, for the Alans of Orléans were at once in action against the peasants of Brittany. About Aëtius himself historians' opinions vary. He has been considered a feudal magnate, the first of a new order in medieval Europe, effectively defending Gaul from barbarian absorption. Conversely, he has been regarded as the upkeeper of the obsolete and now vanishing dominion of the Gallo-Roman aristocracy, his career as one of brutal and senseless oppression, in the end ruinous. But he had predecessors in his role, men like Maximus and Constantine, the usurpers. What distinguishes him from them is that to exercise his power in Gaul it was no longer necessary to declare opposition to Italy; he was able to act as viceroy almost with impunity. The change is a measure of the dissolution of imperial authority during the 5th century, as is Aëtius' end – not through an imperial army, but by a knife.

Attila and the Huns. The activities of the Huns outside the empire during the first 30 years of the 5th century are remarkably obscure. Gibbon and others suggested that the Gothic invasion of Italy in 405 and that of the Vandals and their allies into Gaul in 406 were provoked by Hunnic movements in eastern Germany. The assumption may be true, but other campaigns are more certain: at the end of the 4th century Huns ravaged Mesopotamia and Syria; a few years later they began their devastations of Thrace. Their pressure on the Danube frontier during this period has a lasting memorial, for in the face of the threat the eastern imperial capital was defended by massive new walls.

During the 440s the pattern changes. Before, the Huns were a nuisance, but, like the barbarians they had replaced, they could at some cost be driven off; now they seemed irresistible. The reason for the change was the supremacy of Attila. He and his brother Bleda were co-rulers of the Huns of the northern Balkans. Probably in 445 Attila murdered Bleda and was accepted as king by the whole of his confederacy of tribes. In 447 he crossed the Danube, devastated Thrace, defeated the imperial armies and marched on Constantinople. The eastern emperor submitted to terms – the immediate payment of massive arrears of tribute and the evacuation of the Danube

Above: part of the new land defenses of Constantinople, built by Theodosius II between 413 and 439. Two tiers of great walls run for a distance of four miles across the peninsula and protected a city whose area was nearly six square miles.

Below: the Huns of Attila with their booty ride through Europe: a 19th-century contribution to the Hunnic myth, by the Spaniard Ulpiano Checa y Sanz (1860–1916).

frontier and of a broad belt to the south of it. Attila transferred his attention to the Western Empire. He probably hoped for an immediate cash settlement and regular tribute, for Aëtius and the imperial government had been conciliatory some years earlier under similar coercion.

The answers were unfavorable, for in 451 he led his army into Gaul. He announced, it is alleged, that he came as Rome's ally and intended only the suppression of the Visigoths. The story has been so embroidered by our sources with accounts of intrigues by Gaiseric and the Vandals, by the emperor's sister and by Aëtius himself, that the motives and even the events are in doubt. Somewhere near Troyes between Paris and Dijon Attila was defeated by Aëtius' motley army of Gauls, federates and Visigoths. He retired to Hungary to recoup, and in 452 descended on Italy; initially successful, the Huns were weakened by disease and threatened by an expeditionary force which Aëtius had arranged with Constantinople. With his prestige considerably impaired Attila was forced to accept a truce and again withdrew to Hungary, where he died early in 453.

At his death the confederacy broke up into quarreling and disunited groups commanded by his sons. Roman opinion was gleeful, but rather shocked at the suddenness of the change. Had they been interested in Hunnic internal affairs at other periods, we should probably be able to see this disunity as the normal state and the empire of Attila as the exception. But the next event was completely unexpected, for in 454 some of the Germanic subject tribes took advantage of the succession crisis (and perhaps of the loss of confidence after Attila's setbacks) to stage a revolt. An army of Huns was smashed, somewhere in Romania, and Hunnic power in Europe collapsed completely.

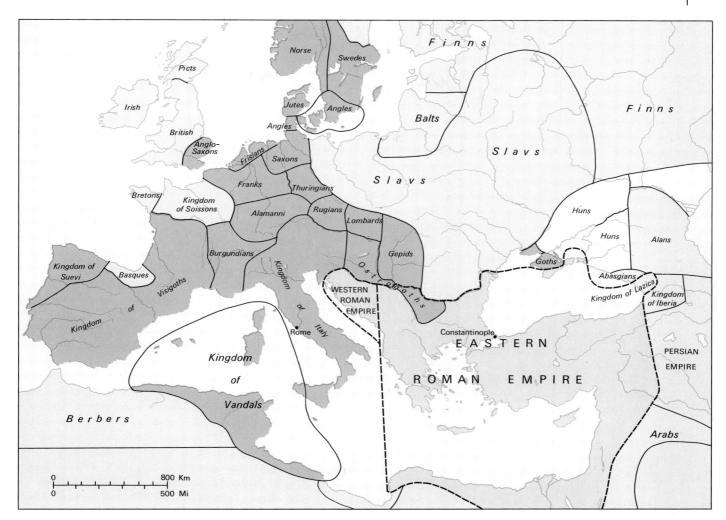

Europe in 476 AD. By the time of the deposition of the last western emperor only the remnant of Yugoslavia and the Kingdom of Soissons were under even nominal Roman control.

Individual Huns continued serving as mercenaries, some prominently, and pockets of survivors remained in Hungary and the Balkans; but most of the Huns withdrew to the steppes east of the Black Sea, where they remained until swamped by fresh nomads from the east.

The eclipse of Rome. The final disintegration of the Western Empire took less than a generation. Aëtius did not survive Attila long. In 454 the Emperor Valentinian arranged his assassination. The precarious control maintained in Gaul since 418 was lost: about 455 the Franks annexed northeastern Gaul and the Alamanni extended their territories into Alsace and the Alps, almost unnoticed, for the attention of Italy was engaged by the sack of Rome by King Gaiseric's Vandals. A series of short-lived emperors tried and failed to check Gaiseric's attacks, while in Gaul Aëtius' successor, the general Aegidius, found himself unable to fight both the barbarians and his home government. The Visigoths profited by the con-fusion: in the 450s they penetrated Spain, in the 460s they seized Narbonne and in the 470s they took over Arles, Marseilles and the territory of Clermont-Ferrand in the heart of Gaul. Now Aegidius' son and successor Syagrius found himself enclosed in the center of northwestern France, in his own independent and rather shadowy kingdom of Soissons, until swallowed up in 486 by the expansion of the Franks.

In Italy the last of the barbarian soldiers' puppet emperors, Romulus Augustulus, had already been deposed by Odoacer, a Skirian general, who told the eastern emperor that it would not be necessary to nominate a successor, and took over the government himself. Odoacer's rule lasted 12 years, from 476 to 488, and the man who was to conquer him, Theodoric the Ostrogoth, like Alaric the Visigoth, was encouraged on his way by the eastern government, who found the continued presence in the Balkans of their new Ostrogothic federates an embarrassment. The foundation of Theodoric's kingdom of Italy marks the end of imperial pretense in the Roman west. A little more than a century had passed since the Visigothic refugees fled from the Huns across the Danube.

2. The Discovery of the Barbarians

A continuous literary tradition links the writers of antiquity with the present day, and those who felt the need could, at almost any period, turn to the sources and read of the activities of their ancestors at the foundation of Europe. In the 14th century Geoffrey Chaucer could write in his *Pardoner's Tale*:

> Looke, Attilla, the grete conquerour,
> Deyde in his sleep, with shame and dishonour,
> Bledynge ay at his nose in dronkenesse,
> A capitayn sholde lyve in sobrenesse

and trust at least some of his audience to understand the reference. More recent historical research has added much. We now know far more about the background, about the economic or cultural pressures that influenced, some would say dictated, decisions. Chieftains and princes seem more rational and less wayward than they did, for example, to Chaucer, or even to Gibbon. Their figures become rounded, at the very time that the same studies tend to deny them any real choice in their actions.

From people to objects. Faced with this rich variety of sources, of chronicles, of biographies, of sacred and secular letters, of laws, of land charters – of written information of all kinds – a great many historians of the early Middle Ages have tended to ignore the possible importance of archaeology. In 1910 the historian Sir Charles Oman expressed an accepted view of Anglo-Saxon England: "The spade, so useful in the Roman period, helps us little here." This attitude, even then, after several generations of discoveries, is understandable. Unlike the dramatic unearthing of a new civilization (such as that which at the same time was being exposed in Greece and Crete) the mundane vestiges of the barbarians seemed scarcely important – simply footnotes to established history. They were given attention when they illustrated known facts, and seemed perhaps most significant when they were the relics of named and recorded people.

This is an old-established habit of mind. The 11th-century Tower of London was long called "Caesar's Tower," a distinction shared with several other Norman buildings; against such manifest absurdities the skepticism of antiquarians such as Sir Thomas Browne was a corrective: "Vulgar chronology will have *Norwich* Castle as old as *Julius Caesar*; but his distance from these parts, and its *Gothick* form of structure, abridgeth such Antiquity." But attributions to the more shadowy figures of the Dark Ages were easier to believe. In England King Arthur stood high in popular imagination, and the antiquaries, with fewer records for the period at their disposal, were more easily persuaded: John Leland, antiquary and traveler, passing a prehistoric hillfort in Somerset in 1532, noted "Camallate, sumtyme a famose

town or castelle," and we have no idea whether he was following a local tradition about King Arthur's Camelot, or simply drawing his own conclusions from the local place-names.

Relics of the famous were well known in the Middle Ages. Most of the genuine ones had been known since the time to which they belonged, but a few were rediscovered, and one such is among the first recorded Dark Age excavations. In 1190 the monks of Glastonbury in Somerset announced the discovery of the bones of King Arthur and his queen in a grave beside the abbey church. To judge from a late 13th-century account by a Glastonbury monk of the exhumation there had clearly been some previous tradition about the site, and modern excavations have revealed not only the hole from which the bodies were removed, but also traces of further graves, wooden oratories and a mausoleum quite likely to be of 6th- or 7th-century date. The monks identified the bones as those of King Arthur because of an inscription. In the upper part of the grave, fixed to the underside of a stone, was a small lead cross inscribed in Latin: "Here lies buried famous King Arthur in the island of Avalon." The cross has been lost since the 18th century, and our only record of it is the early 17th-century drawing published by Camden.

Camden's drawing (1607) is the sole record of the appearance of the lead cross discovered at Glastonbury in the 1190s.

Some have declared the cross a 12th-century forgery by the Glastonbury monks, and the disinterment a ruse to improve their finances. Profit from pilgrims was indeed the result, but the archaic style of the letters of the inscription tells against the skeptic, for medieval forgery of deeds and charters was widespread but generally inept. For many years the letter forms on the cross have been taken to be of the 10th century, and it has often been said that the cross was placed at the top of the grave during an otherwise suspected raising of the level of the church graveyard in the late 10th century. Proof that the hero Arthur was dead and buried (and so unlikely to come again) would have been politically useful to any government with disaffected subjects. The discovery may thus have been inspired, and its consequent publicity welcome to both 10th- and 12th-century monarchs. But, as in so much else connected with King Arthur, doubts remain: the cross, indeed, on the basis of the letter forms, has recently been attributed to the 6th century once again. Whatever the truth of this, the discovery shows at least the comparatively early date of an Arthurian association with Glastonbury.

Because of the link with a similarly grand historic figure the discovery in 1653 of the grave of the 5th-century Frankish King Childeric at Tournai in Belgium received widespread attention. Sir Thomas Browne recorded his reactions: "The Monument of *Childerick* . . . casually discovered three years past at Tournay, restoring unto the world much gold richly adorning his sword, two hundred Rubies, many hundred Imperial Coyns, three hundred golden Bees, the bones and horseshoe of his horse enterred with him, according to the barbourous magnificence of those dayes in their sepulchral Obsequies." Omitted from his list is the significant item, a gold ring engraved "Of king Childeric"; for at Tournai, as at Glastonbury, the identification was made as a result of an inscription. Browne was writing in 1658, five, not three years after the actual discovery, and his words may have been inspired less by the opening of the tomb than by the impressive publication of the finds in 1655, with full descriptions and fine drawings – drawings which now provide the only evidence for most of the objects, for all but a few were stolen in 1831 and have never been recovered.

Similar discoveries, poorer or more anonymous than the graves of Arthur or Childeric, received less publicity. In the 1540s John Leland passed by Bedford and recorded "Betwixt Kinges Crose yn the midle way to Newenham and the castel were found many bones of men buried." At about the same time a Kentish burial mound was being excavated "by the care of Mr Thomas Diggs and charge of Sir Christopher Hales, and a large urn found under it." Both discoveries, to judge from the contemporary accounts and from more recent finds, were Anglo-Saxon, but this was not at all clear at the time; in the words of James Douglas, the late 18th-century antiquary, "the inscription and the medal [coin] are the only facts which

Almost all the contents of the grave of Childeric, including the king's gold signet ring, were stolen from the Imperial Art Gallery in Paris in 1831. Casts of the ring survive, and the barbarity of its workmanship is seen clearly in this modern replica.

can obviate error, and produce the substitutes for deficiency of ancient records." Lacking this evidence, graves containing only coarse pottery and corroded metalwork seemed undatable.

"Our Brittish, Saxon or Danish Forefathers."

The difficulty of dating permeates the fullest and most elegant of the 17th-century accounts of such unspectacular discoveries, Sir Thomas Browne's treatise on mortality, *Hydriotaphia* (1658). Browne's interest was aroused by excavations in Norfolk: "In a Field of old *Walsingham*, not many months past, were digged up between fourty and fifty Urnes, deposited in a dry and sandy soile not a yard deep, not farre from one another: Not all strictly of one figure, but most answering these described [that is to say, illustrated]: Some containing two pounds of bones, distinguishable in skulls, ribs, jawes, thigh-bones, and teeth, with fresh impressions of their combustion." The

illustration which accompanies this account is the first published drawing of Anglo-Saxon cremation urns. Browne acknowledged that, as far as concerns the "precise Antiquity of these Reliques, nothing [is] of more uncertainty" and noted that some might consider them "belonging unto our *Brittish*, *Saxon* or *Danish* Forefathers." Later he conceded "that Urnes conceived of no *Romane* Originall are often digged up both in Norway and Denmark," but his final verdict was that "these sad and sepulchral Pitchers" were of Roman manufacture, and he begged his British readers to forgive their former conquerors "remembering the early civility they brought upon these Countreys, and forgetting long passed mischiefs: we mercifully preserve their bones, and pisse not upon their ashes."

British, Roman, Saxon or Danish – the possible choice in the 17th and 18th centuries was wide, and the circumstances of discovery made progress difficult. Finds

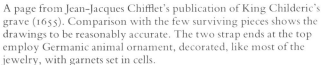

A page from Jean-Jacques Chifflet's publication of King Childeric's grave (1655). Comparison with the few surviving pieces shows the drawings to be reasonably accurate. The two strap ends at the top employ Germanic animal ornament, decorated, like most of the jewelry, with garnets set in cells.

The Walsingham urns from Sir Thomas Browne's *Hydriotaphia* (1658), the first recognizably Saxon pottery to be published. Browne noted that some might consider them as "belonging unto our *Brittish*, *Saxon* or *Danish* Forefathers" but his final verdict was that "these sad and sepulchral Pitchers" were of Roman manufacture.

were made accidentally, by ditch diggers or plowmen, and further investigations of a site were haphazard. Objects were lost or scattered, and groups from graves of different dates casually jumbled together. At North Elmham in Norfolk, for example, in 1711 "some Labourers were repairing the Fence at the South side of the Close, and in the bottom of the Ditch accidentally pitch'd upon a Pot, which they expected to have been full of Money, and fell to ransacking; but finding nothing but Dust and Ashes, went to their Work again, and digging on found two or three more . . . The Report of which put some Persons of more Curiosity upon a further search; and digging further under the hedge and afterwards further into the Close, found great quantities of them, and several very near together." But the finds were distributed without record, and few can now be identified.

An advance came after the middle of the 18th century, through the excavations of two clergymen, Bryan Faussett and James Douglas. Both concentrated their attention for more than 20 years on opening small inhumation mounds on the downs of Kent. These made ideal sites for such rudimentary digging, for they were visible from the surface and relatively limited in scale. Faussett considered these barrows the relics of Romans, as did most of his contemporaries; one went so far as to compare the topography of the Chartham cemetery near Canterbury with Caesar's description of his landing in Britain and to call the mounds the burial places of the Roman dead of that campaign; he identified a grave which he regarded as unusually rich as that of Q. Laberius Drusus, an officer whose death Caesar records.

The Revd. James Douglas recorded this speculation and was frankly contemptuous ("As to the whole of the . . . conjecture, they are really too puerile for a comment"). To Douglas belongs the credit for recognizing the remains as Anglo-Saxon. He was among the first to present his results in a form of use to future scholars, for in 1793 he published a handsome folio volume, *Nenia Britannica: or a sepulchral history of Great Britain*, illustrated by reproductions of his own aquatint drawings. He saw the need for the accurate presentation of "these *data*," for "an assertion or misrepresentation of the contents of a barrow has laid the foundations for a system, and succeeding antiquaries have followed each other on the same mistaken principles." To counteract such frailty he made a selection from the huge number of barrows he had opened, and dealt with each in turn, illustrating and describing in detail every object, and generally noting its position in the grave. Despite its age the result is surprisingly like a modern excavation report, and Douglas was able to point out not only the similarity of the contents of the graves, and so to assume their contemporaneity, but could draw attention to associated Roman and Byzantine coins of the 5th and 6th centuries. "Deducing the date of the lowest [latest] of these coins, it will be found reasonable to proceed to a still lower [later] date of their deposit." He noted that one such

barrow actually cut through the Roman Watling Street, and concluded "The Roman claim to these sepulchres, notwithstanding their coins have been found, must be totally out of the question."

He was right, but the dispute about the date continued, for the pottery in the Kentish inhumation burials was in shape and decoration unlike the "sad and sepulchral pitchers" of the cremation cemeteries in the Midlands and East Anglia. Brooches of the types that by this time were turning up in increasing numbers in Germany and Denmark, and were generally acknowledged to be barbarian, were so far not recognized among the cremations, and still are extremely rare. Douglas' work, therefore, did not solve the problem outside Kent, and even there was not completely understood. Another candidate for the ownership of the vessels, the Ancient Briton, was now becoming more popular, thanks to the activities of Dr William Stukeley. During the first half of the 18th century Stukeley had been assiduous in his study of the prehistoric monuments of southern England, and his influence continued long after his death. Douglas himself had protested at the habit of considering all relics "British" or "Celtic," and mentions Stukeley and "the effusions of his fancy" only in criticism: "It was the misfortune of the ingenious Doctor to see most of our ancient monuments with the magnifying lens of Celtic optics." The invective had little effect, and for over half a century "British" remained a popular description of the pottery.

19th-century controversies. During the first half of the 19th century there was a notable increase over much of Europe in the numbers of people interested in local history and archaeology, culminating in the proliferation of national and local archaeological societies. The new generation found their evidence accumulating rapidly, as the result of industrial expansion. Hitherto undisturbed land was being swallowed up by houses, gravel working and railroad construction. Not all the excavations were useful; as the secretary of the Society of Antiquaries commented in 1847, "Railroad excavations, although they often lead to curious discoveries, are not the process most favourable to antiquarian research." But in the years around 1850 the controversy of dating was finally settled by a series of notes and articles in the journals of the newly formed British national societies. Recent discoveries at Kingston-on-Soar in Nottinghamshire provided the ammunition. In 1846 the Kingston urns were illustrated as being of the "Primeval Period," that is, British.

In the same year in another journal it was minuted that "Mr C. Roach Smith read a note from Professor Henslow, accompanying a number of drawings of urns discovered near Derby. Some of the urns are of peculiar form, and may be late Roman, or even Saxon. They will probably form the subject of an article in a future number of the Journal." These were the Kingston urns, and the next year Henslow's article appeared. He was indignant: "My limited knowledge of antiquities does not enable me to speak at all decidedly on this subject" but "I can see no reason for doubting their having been deposited by the aboriginal Britons." Roach Smith himself must have inserted the disputed date into Henslow's original note, for he is found maintaining his position in a review notice of the same year, 1847: "With the Derby urns was found a fragment of one of those peculiar fibulae [brooches] now certified as Saxon. The ornamental stamps upon them also accorded with the patterns of decorated specimens obtained from authenticated Saxon interments; facts which induced us to conclude that these urns were of late rather than early origin." So far, so good, but Roach Smith was editing for publication the notes left by the long-dead Revd. Bryan Faussett of Kent, who, it must be recalled, had believed in the Roman origin of the Kentish relics. Roach Smith had no intention of denying Faussett's views and to allow Roman manufacture *and* Saxon influence he reached a most unhappy compromise; he concluded that the Kingston urns "belonged to the latter part of the Romano-British period," and fell back on the support of general opinion: some of the associated objects are often found with "unquestioned Roman remains."

Few if any now agreed with him. Thomas Wright, a friend of Roach Smith who had a couple of years earlier expressed some very sensible views on Anglo-Saxon churches, and who (as Editor) had seen Henslow's in-

The "aboriginal British" urns from Kingston-on-Soar in a drawing prepared to illustrate Henslow's article in the *Journal of the British Archaeological Association* for 1847.

The photograph shows one of the few surviving Kingston urns, shown as Fig. 2 in Henslow's drawing (*below*), with stamped ornament and small shoulder bosses. Mid-6th century.

dignant article before publication, wrote a paper which, ironically, he printed in the Journal in 1847 immediately before what he politely described as "the following valuable communication by Professor Henslow." Wright chose to ignore Roach Smith's attribution of the objects to the Romano-British; he congratulated him on recognizing them as early Saxon, and compared the Kingston material with other objects "decidedly Saxon."

Henslow's reaction to this second apt anticipation of his paper seems unfortunately not to have been recorded.

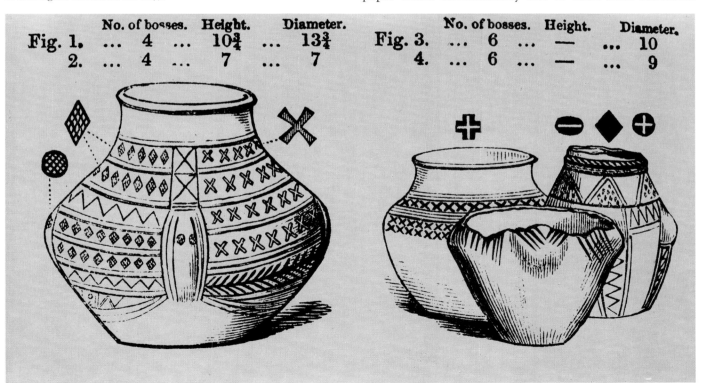

	No. of bosses.	Height.	Diameter.
Fig. 1.	4	10¾	13¾
2.	4	7	7

	No. of bosses.	Height.	Diameter.
Fig. 3.	6	—	10
4.	6	—	9

Roach Smith continued to fight a discreet rearguard action. In 1855 he published Bryan Faussett's records of his excavations; to this Wright contributed a map of England on which the Anglo-Saxon cemeteries then known, 81 in all, were plotted against known Saxon towns – perhaps the first such distribution map. Smith followed the current trends in his introduction, for he attributed the objects to the Saxons; but he added, perhaps by now wistfully: "It is a just question if, after all, these urns might not be assigned to the latest Romano-British population." The tide, however, had now turned; metalwork and pottery were generally acknowledged to be of post-Roman date, and in the same year, 1855, J. Y. Akerman published *Remains of Pagan Saxondum*, a hodgepodge of haphazardly collected material, but all of it now stated to be "Saxon."

The material culture of the barbarians in England had at last been identified, and the effects of the discovery had profound significance on the continent. For centuries in Denmark and northern Germany the casual unearthing of urns and metalwork by laborers and builders had matched the development in England. These finds were seldom if ever thought Roman, for the area was known to have lain outside the empire. Though they were obviously of "native" origin it was quite unclear to *which* natives they belonged. In Britain a Roman occupation served to divide the population, somewhat unrealistically, into Iron Age Celts and Romano-Britons; but on the continent the barbarians seemed an amorphous group whose history was only dimly glimpsed in the accounts of Roman writers.

Until the middle of the 19th century German archaeologists had frequently attributed the Saxon culture of eastern Germany to the aboriginal Slavs. The view was widespread, and was the equivalent of Stukeley's description of Anglo-Saxon pottery as primeval British; the notion had grown of a general pre-Roman culture in Europe, sometimes loosely referred to as "Scythian." With the identification of English Saxon material this was now scarcely tenable, and the link between the continent and the new ideas in England was soon provided by John Kemble, an Englishman working in Hanover. In 1855 he came across Akerman's *Remains of Pagan Saxondum* and was immediately struck by the similarities between English and German objects. In a pioneer paper published in 1856 he described and illustrated German urns, including some from the great cemetery at Perlberg. Kemble concluded "Keltic they are not, or they would not be found in Lüneburg; Slavonic they are not, or they would not be found in Warwickshire: one only race remains – they are Saxon in the one place as well as the other ... We can henceforth use indifferently the discoveries of Englishmen and North Germans for the elucidation of our national treasures."

The advice was soon followed. The cremation cemeteries of north Germany, like those in England, contained very few objects, such as Roman coins, that could be independently dated; but now English evidence could fill the gap, for it was well known that the Saxons had come to England in about 450 A D: the Venerable Bede, after all, had said so, and other authorities give dates that are not dissimilar. Thus objects found commonly in German graves but not in England must have been in use before 450, and those common in both countries must have been made after 450 but before the 7th century, when the English became Christians and the pagan practice of cremation was forbidden. In no more than a decade the controversy had been settled, and a new framework established for dating the pottery and metalwork of the barbarians. In the meantime fresh evidence for the Anglo-Saxons had appeared, for it had been unexpectedly found that some of their churches were still standing.

The church at Reculver, Kent, threatened by cliff erosion, was demolished in 1805 by its vicar, who had no idea of its antiquity. The ruins, which still stand at the edge of the cliff, belong to the minster built in 669. Engraving by H. Adelard.

The discovery of the churches. A few buildings, such as Charlemagne's palace at Aachen or the palaces and great churches of Italy, were never forgotten. Charlemagne himself could pray at the shrine of St Peter amid the Roman walls, or examine the cloak (*capella*) of St Martin in the building which took its name, "Chapel," from the relic. Those who came afterwards could stand in Charlemagne's own Chapel and look at his throne, or even, like Otto III in the year 1000, breach the floor to find his bones. Antiquaries might (and did) ignore these great buildings. They could hardly discover them. In the structural remains of the past the Romanists were first on the scene, and Roman remains were the object of the early antiquaries from Camden onwards: when the 7th-century crypt of Hexham Abbey was opened in 1726 it was visited by Stukeley and others, to transcribe the inscriptions on the Roman slabs reused in its walls.

The problem, like that of the pottery and metalwork, was a matter of dating. Misled by the name for medieval buildings with pointed arches (Gothic, apparently first used in 16th-century Italy), antiquarians ascribed these styles to the Goths, often quaintly. In the 18th century Bishop Warburton wrote: "This northern people [the Goths] having been accustomed to worship the Diety in groves, when their religion required covered edifices, they ingeniously projected to make them resemble groves as nearly as the distance of architecture would permit." Hence pointed arches and leaf ornament. But a somewhat romantic revival movement was now beginning: from the middle of the 18th century architects were at work imitating and refining the "Gothick" styles they saw about them in medieval buildings. By the first decade of the 19th century, through a combination of written record and the evidence of structure, a scheme of styles and periods had been agreed, now reversing the emphasis and

extending from no earlier than the 11th century to modern times. In 1819 one of the leading figures in the movement, the architect Thomas Rickman, in the second edition of his very aptly named volume, *An Attempt to Discriminate the Styles of Architecture*, drew attention to a church at Barton-on-Humber, Lincolnshire. In the tower two styles were obvious: the lower part, which was marked by unusual triangular-headed windows and decorative stone ribbing, had been raised in height by the addition of an upper story; but this upper part was "Norman, and certainly not late Norman." Rickman concluded that the lower stories were of great antiquity, and wondered whether they might be Saxon. He went out to look for similar buildings, and by 1834 was able to present a list of 20 that were "supposed Anglo-Saxon."

Barton-on-Humber. The drawing by Jewitt (*left*), published in the 5th edition of Rickman's *Styles of Architecture* (1848), is accurate in detail but (a warning against reliance on drawings) it ignores the western annex which is shown in the modern photograph (*right*) and which formed part of the Saxon church.

Alfric's translation of the Pentateuch in the British Museum. This Anglo-Saxon illuminated manuscript of c. 1000 AD was used in 1846 by Thomas Wright to show that some architectural details in surviving churches predated Romanesque styles.

Firm conclusions could not yet be drawn, but Thomas Wright, whom we noticed earlier as a disputant in the matter of the Saxon origin of urns, now entered the field. In 1845 he published drawings taken from a Saxon illuminated manuscript of the late 10th or early 11th century. The architectural detail so clearly matched that of Rickman's churches that the identification was certain, and in succeeding years the Hexham crypt (ignored for well over a century since its first discovery) was correctly dated, and further examples added to Rickman's original list.

Some of the newly found buildings were surprisingly complete. One such, at Bradford-on-Avon in Wiltshire, had long been surrounded by later buildings and was partly in use as a cottage and partly as a charity school; about 1857 the discovery of carved angels beneath the plaster of the building, till then assumed to be secular, aroused the curiosity of the local vicar; his view that he had found an 8th-century Saxon chapel was not immediately accepted – one expert, John Parker, dated the structure to the 12th century – but an increasing awareness of the styles appropriate to Saxon and Norman building (supported by documentary references perhaps relevant to this church) was finally convincing. The subsequent clearance in the 1870s of centuries of accretion revealed that much of the fabric was still intact.

The significance of old masonry in many surviving parish churches was now being recognized. In 1834 Rickman had listed 20 Saxon buildings; the present total,

the result of years of patient investigation, is over 400. But the establishment of even relative chronology has progressed more slowly.

The plunderers and the typologists. Discoveries in the early 19th century were numerous, and knowledge and understanding of the barbarians grew rapidly. But in contrast with the spectacular developments of the period from 1830 to 1850, the second half of the century was disappointing. The reason was perhaps the failure to improve on the poor standard of the earlier excavations. At Toddington in Bedfordshire, for example, gravel working uncovered a large cemetery in 1819: "A person who was daily on the spot . . . considers that there were some thousand bodies buried there, from the large quantities of black earth which were thrown out with the gravel, in solid masses." At Eye in Suffolk in the previous year about 150 urns had been turned up in no more than four days' working. These were the chance finds of industrial activity, but deliberate excavations too showed little appreciation of the needs of careful records. Very few indeed made plans of their diggings, and the drawing with which in 1793 Douglas illustrated his report was far in advance of its time. But how far even this was a true record is unclear, for the skeleton itself is certainly derived from a standing model, perhaps from an anatomical textbook, and the speed of digging far exceeded any capabilities of accurate measurement.

Writing of a barrow cemetery near Deal, Douglas noted: "In December, 1782, I visited this range, having read of these barrows in Dr Stukeley's work; and finding them not all explored, I opened about fourteen of the remainder." During the 1760s and 1770s Bryan Faussett had opened no fewer than 728 barrows and associated graves. They were seldom described in detail, a typical specimen being a barrow at Kingston Down, Kent: "Tumulus and grave much as the last. The bones were very much decayed; the coffin did not appear to have passed the fire. Nothing but some nails and the blade of a knife." For the time such speed and cursory publication were normal – the prehistoric burial mounds of southern England during this period suffered from similar haste – but it says much for the lack of progress in techniques during the 19th century that Roach Smith felt it useful to publish these uninformative jottings a full 80 years after the excavations. Little advance even in studies of the finds could be made when the objects themselves sometimes failed to survive. Excavators or their patrons freely gave away finds to friends or local notables, and the treasure-hunters were soon on the scene: when the Viking ship-burial at Borre in Norway was found in 1852 most of the rich goods disappeared during the excavations.

Douglas had recognized the need for preserving the groups of associated material together, but the collecting instincts of the antiquaries hindered their studies. Pots and brooches were gathered and sold regardless of their context: a fossil collector in Cambridgeshire wrote in 1874

Bradford-on-Avon. The chapel as drawn in 1869 by the architect J. T. Irvine, and its present condition after the removal of the cottages and sheds which had obscured it for centuries.

of "3 urns, the smallest very nice . . . They was found in Stoney Hill with the skelitons and other things. I shall want ten shillings for the urns. I have got four heads two are Pretty good and two are Broaken and some Leg Bones I have got a Bullick face with the horns on it Perfect." A little later, rescue excavations on the site of the new Girton College, Cambridge, exposed a large cemetery which was tolerably well recorded, but it was still not thought necessary to note which brooches and which pots were found together. At Sancton near York during this period the great cremation cemetery suffered from the same disregard for associations, and similar examples could be multiplied across Britain and Europe.

As a result scholars towards the end of the 19th century were faced with a huge and disordered body of material which was difficult to analyze. Individual pieces could be compared and contrasted with each other, but little sensible could be said about their historical context, for this had been generally lost during the course of their excavation. The solution seemed to be offered by the theories of growth and change propounded for living things by Charles Darwin, and demonstrated, in the study

of musketry, by Pitt Rivers. A group of objects of the same general type could be placed in series and the notion of fashion-change used, like that of natural selection, to arrange the pieces in an order beginning with the typologically earliest and ending with the typologically latest. The criteria for the order varied: the general assumption seems to have been that designs begin "pure," then "mature," suffer from a process of adaptation to become "degenerate," and thereafter may be modified into distinctly different designs which in their turn are varied through time. This process, whose formulation was perhaps the most significant single contribution of the 19th century to archaeology, can be seen at work in historically known periods, for it lies behind the 19th-century definitions of architectural style, and behind instinctive reactions to the new and the obsolete in contemporary fashions.

Following the work of his compatriot, the great prehistorian Oscar Montelius (1843–1921), the Swedish scholar Bernhard Salin (1861–1931) analyzed the animal motifs used in migration-period art. The illustration is based on his drawing of animal heads used in Salin Style I (late 5th and 6th century).

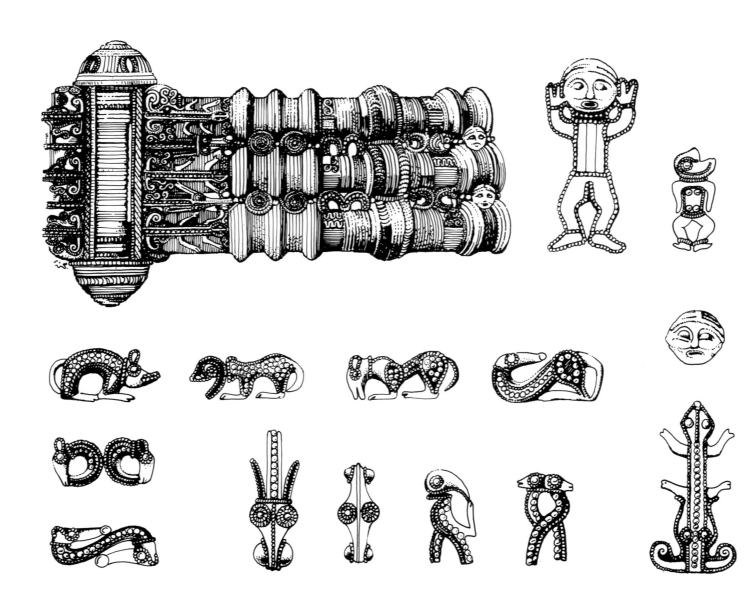

The most obvious changes of taste were visible in the decoration of brooches, and to them and related metal-work scholars turned their attention. The last years of the 19th and the first decades of the 20th century were the great age of the typologists; objects were placed in relative sequence dependent on sometimes minute variations of design, and the broad framework provided by recorded events served as a peg to which the relative chronologies of fashion-change could be attached. Thanks to the extensive compilations of the Scandinavian scholars Bernhard Salin (1861–1931) and Nils Åberg (1888–1957) brooches were no longer described merely as "late Roman" or "Saxon"; it now seemed possible to attribute a piece to its logical position in a series which began in the 4th and ended in the 6th or 7th century. There might be some disagreements; the same piece might be attributed by some to the late 4th century and by others to the mid-5th. But these were minor discrepancies, with their origin in conflicting views of the speed of change, and seldom disagreement in principle.

With the greater precision in dating came increasing sophistication in the interpretation of the significance of objects. The English scholar E. T. Leeds long afterwards in 1951 wrote, "Brooches are the most distinctive class of relics by which the material stability of a population in a given area . . . can be judged." "Material stability" has frequently been interpreted as "political stability," and not many would now agree wholeheartedly, but in its time the opinion was widely held. In 1855 Roach Smith drew attention in passing to regional differences in burial customs and the design of brooches within England. The next decades saw the unification of modern Germany and the growth of vocal nationalism: influenced by con-temporary moods, the study of the culture and national origins of the Germanic peoples increased in popularity. As more material was uncovered it became possible to devise spheres of culture, geographical areas within which objects of similar design were found, and then to declare these the tribal areas of known peoples, the Vandals, the Alamanni, the Angles and others.

The archaeological picture was based almost entirely on brooches. Pottery, perhaps because of its relative plainness, had received scant attention since the 1850s: publication of excavation reports concentrated on the metalwork, and often described merely a small selection of the ceramic material. Other aspects of the life of the barbarians were similarly neglected; in 1913 when E. T. Leeds published his *Archaeology of the Anglo-Saxon Settlements*, in which he drew together for English readers the new ideas on the typology and dating of brooches, "not a single instance of an early Anglo-Saxon occupation area vouched for by the discovery of sherds or the like . . . [had] ever been brought to light in this country." The result was not, despite its title, a study of *settlements*, but a new and more telling arrangement of cemetery material.

Settlement, society and landscape. Leeds himself was first to change this situation. In a gravel pit at Sutton Courtenay near Oxford, workmen came across Saxon material in shallow scoops in the ground. In a series of rescue excavations between 1921 and 1937 Leeds revealed the remnants of a village of small huts whose floors were recessed into the gravel. The discovery, soon followed by others in England and on the continent, raised fresh problems, for the huts measured less than 12 feet square, and the sophistication of barbarian metalwork could not appropriately be associated with these flimsy shelters; the point was put strongly in 1948: "It is impossible to imagine a man of the type buried in the Taplow barrow having no more adequate domestic amenities in life than those provided by a wattled hut of the Sutton Courtenay model." More pointedly perhaps "a man of the type buried at Sutton Hoo" might have been added, for in 1939 on the eve of World War II the excavation of a ship-burial mound in Suffolk had demonstrated the lavish state to be expected of a Saxon chieftain. More careful excavation of cemeteries pointed in the same direction, for the variety of social levels in a single graveyard could no longer be

The careful techniques of modern excavation are slower and more expensive than those of the past but are likely to reveal more information about the date or nature of sites. Cleanliness and precision are the ideal. Here an Anglo-Saxon skeleton in the cemetery at Ruskington, Lincolnshire, is being cleaned before recording.

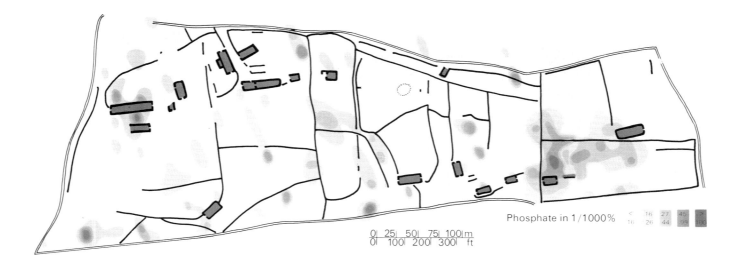

Phosphate in 1/1000%

0 25 50 75 100 m
0 100 200 300 ft

The plan of Vallhagar shows the soil-phosphate variations in relation to buildings which allowed the excavator to identify areas in heavy use by animals. Concentration of phosphates (from animal dung and urine) indicates milking and byre areas. After M. Stenberger.

ignored. Continental scholars had led the way: in the 1910s an Alamannic cemetery had been found to contain rich graves surrounded by clusters of poorer burials – the householder and his household – and further excavations in Germany and England gave confirmation. At Finglesham, Kent, for example, a small inhumation cemetery, in use for perhaps a century, produced three rich graves and 29 containing few or no objects – glimpses of a complex social structure.

The new settlement archaeology provided fresh evidence. From the late 1950s large rectangular wooden houses were being found in addition to the sunken-floor huts; indeed on some sites it seemed likely that the huts were subsidiary buildings, store huts or workshops, or the dwellings of peasants beside the timber halls of their masters. Settlements clearly differed considerably in their size and structure, and slower and more cautious excavations have now revealed changes in the settlement patterns of individual villages: houses are abandoned, village centers and the layout of occupations shift; individual houses grow larger and richer, and others decline; food remains suggest fluctuations in the relative importance of cereals and animal husbandry; imports mark the significance of trade. All are factors in our understanding of the social and economic pressures which influence the origin and growth of communities. The inland village was dependent on its fields; here the finds are few and their significance more debatable, for the links between a settlement and the land it owned are archaeologically tenuous. Still more vaguely defined is the crucial question of the relationship between one community and the next.

These details of peasant life recovered by excavation are almost all unrecorded in our documentary sources until the end of the first millennium AD, and the significance of archaeology in their study is acknowledged; more controversially, excavated material has been used to correct or refute historical accounts, especially the obscure and garbled stories of the barbarian migrations. For the first time buildings belonging to the period of transition from "Roman" to "Saxon" have been recognized in towns; the declining economy of the 5th century has been traced, and attempts have been made to show how much or how little impact was made in the Roman provinces by the barbarian invasions. In the face of the increasing complexity of information it is becoming more difficult to accept the straightforward traditional accounts of events. Important developments were taking place which contemporary writers did not recognize or did not bother to record.

Some of these discoveries have been spectacular – the unearthing in 1953–57 of an Anglian palace at Yeavering in Northumberland; the discovery in the early 1960s of princely graves at Cologne or Morken in the Rhineland; the excavation of extensive and complex villages, such as Warendorf on the Ems (1950s) or Wijster in the Netherlands (1958–61); the recovery of a group of Viking ships from the seabed at Roskilde (1962); or, most ambitious of all, the current attempt to excavate the total area of the most important trading center in the Carolingian Empire, the great town of Dorestad. Most, however, have attracted little attention – simply a few post sockets or fragments of domestic rubbish, or new interpretations of the significance of earlier findings. In the end these mundane relics prove the more important, for taken together they allow a reconstruction of settlement and society largely independent of the written record. Our historical accounts, for so long the only sources of information about the successors to the empire, present generalizations from a partial, sometimes biased, viewpoint; though its results are often hotly disputed, the value of the spade can no longer be denied.

Arthur and the Britons

Few fictions have enjoyed greater popularity than the story of King Arthur, his round table, and the quest of his knights for the Holy Grail, the cup from which (by a medieval rationalization of a pagan myth) Jesus drank at the Last Supper. In its time the story has inspired playwrights, poets, innumerable painters, musicians and film directors and television producers, to their own recreations of the great court of Camelot. Much of the detail comes from a romance, Geoffrey of Monmouth's *History of the Kings of Britain* (c. 1135), a collection of legends (bulked out by the writer's imagination) which convinced its readers by its circumstantial detail and careful incorporation of genuine material. After the uncritical acceptance of the legend during the Middle Ages, the story of Arthur languished in a more skeptical age until in the present century it has been restored to favor in a new form: as a memory of the last successful resistance of the Romano-British to the Anglo-Saxon invaders.

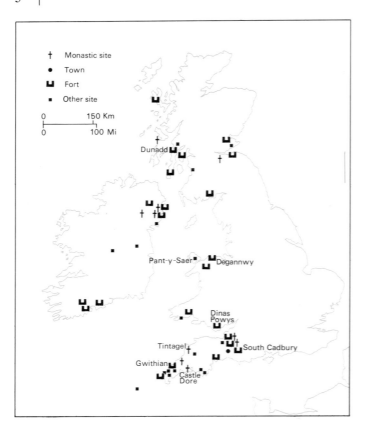

Monastic site

Town

Fort

Other site

0   150 Km

0   100 Mi

Dunadd

Pant-y-Saer Degannwy

Dinas Powys

Tintagel South Cadbury

Gwithian

Castle Dore

Previous page: King Arthur, mortally wounded, sits while his sword, Excalibur, is returned by Sir Bedevere to the Lady of the Lake. A 14th-century illustration from *The Story of Lancelot of the Lake and the Death of King Arthur.* British Museum.

In the poem *Gododdin* of c. 600 a man is called a hero "though he was no Arthur." Context is lacking, and for details of Arthur's "career" we have to wait until the compilation attributed to Nenius (9th century). By now Arthur has been given a series of victories against the Anglo-Saxons, one of which, the battle of Mons Badonicus, can be reliably dated to c. 500. Among the legends of medieval romance are stories which locate Arthur in specific places, one of them the rock of Tintagel on the coast of Cornwall (*right*), associated with Arthur's birth. In the 1930s excavations in the ruins of the 12th- and 13th-century castle revealed the foundations of a Celtic monastery established about 500, and identified vessels which had been imported into Britain from the later Roman potteries of Europe. Work in the last 40 years has shown that similar pottery was reaching a variety of sites, monastic and secular, in the west of Britain (*left*, after C. Thomas).

Below: Arthur and his knights sit at the Round Table at which Sir Galahad is about to take his seat. 14th-century French manuscript. Bibliothèque Nationale, Paris.

The most impressive of the excavated sites is South Cadbury Castle, a prehistoric hillfort in southwest England, sometimes identified (on the unhelpful authority of John Leland) as Arthur's Camelot. Imported pottery like that from Tintagel and fragments of Merovingian glass, turned up by the plow, provided the incentive for a major excavation program from 1966 to 1970. The hilltop proved to have been occupied, perhaps spasmodically, about the 3rd millennium BC. The great ramparts belonged to an Iron Age fortress some 18 acres in area, virtually abandoned in the Roman period. but reoccupied in two post-Roman phases. The last of these belonged to a *burh* built perhaps about 1000 AD, and used in the time of Aethelred against the Danes. The earlier reoccupation, its defenses sandwiched between the Aethelredan walls and the decayed Iron Age ramparts, was associated with reused Roman building stones and imported pottery. This phase of the site, to be dated to some point between the 5th and the 7th centuries, is the Arthurian period at Cadbury. Its identification as Camelot is less than serious, for Camelot belongs to the legends of the Middle Ages. Much more important, South Cadbury is by far the largest and most complex of the Dark Age sites so far discovered in the British-controlled regions of Britain and provides us with an example of one of the immediate successors to the Romanized towns of the southwest, a fortified center of population (and of resistance to the Anglo-Saxon invaders) which has little to do with the ideals of *Romanitas* and much more contact with the Celtic world the Romans did so much to suppress.

Cut through the collapsed debris of the last Iron Age gate at Cadbury the excavators found the postholes of a timber gate tower, a plain rectangular structure with posts at its corners and grooves for horizontal sills recessed into the 6th-century road surfaces (*right*: the digger is working at the nearer edge of the gate area). The reconstruction of this structure is necessarily speculative. The drawing (*left*, after L. Alcock) shows the outer face of the entrance and its accompanying defenses of stone and timber looking towards the camera position in the excavation photograph. The upper parts of the gate, with a guardchamber and fighting platform, can be paralleled among Roman frontier works, but their form is quite uncertain.

The excavated area in the interior of the fort revealed a mass of postholes and pits, mostly belonging to the Iron Age and earlier occupations. One group of postholes has been distinguished from the rest and dated to the 6th century on the evidence of imported pottery found in a beam slot apparently associated with the group. The plan, an irregular rectangle measuring 63 by 34 feet, is seen as the remains of a major structure of the Dark Age reoccupation, prominently placed at the center of the fort, and therefore perhaps the principal building of this period (*above*, based on L. Alcock). Two rows of posts in the interior were probably the main roof supports, carrying a high upper-roof structure of coupled rafters. The resultant barn-like hall, in this case subdivided by a partition to provide more private accommodation, was the farmhouse type common in prehistoric northern Europe, whose existence has been suspected among the Celtic peoples of Wales and Ireland.

Castle Dore, on flat ground in southern Cornwall, was a prehistoric fortification (its interior about an acre in extent) of much smaller size than South Cadbury. Its reoccupation is not precisely dated. Small-scale excavations in the 1930s produced undistinguished sherds of pottery believed to be post-Roman, but no certain imported wares. Its ascription to the Dark Ages relies on the legend of King Mark of Cornwall, traditionally located at Castle Dore, and his son Tristan. A mile to the south of the stronghold stands the 5th- or 6th-century memorial stone to *Drustanus filius Cunomori*, Tristan son of Cynfawr. The excavations showed that part, at least, of the defenses had been restored (D) and that roughly built circular huts had been put up beside the entrance passage (A). In the interior of the fort stood a building (B) identified as the "palace" of King Mark (after C. A. R. Radford and P. Rahtz), usually visualized as two huge aisled halls, with small subsidiary buildings. The limited scale of the digging and the irregularity and infrequency of the component postholes make these most unconvincing structures, but that they were Dark Age timber houses of some sort seems clear. Further traces of buildings were found to the northeast (C).

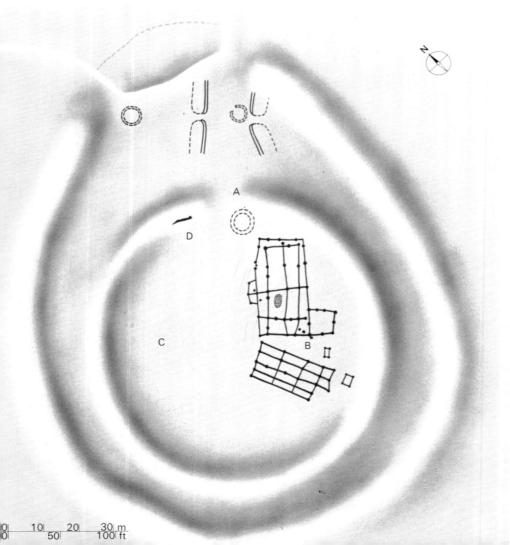

Monasteries and princely sites in western Britain, such as Tintagel, Cadbury or Castle Dore, are considerably outnumbered by the remains of settlements of lower social status, "native settlements" or "hut groups." Comparatively few of these have been excavated, and the finds, crude pottery and bone and stone implements, make their dating particularly difficult. Some, indeed, have been ascribed to the Dark Ages chiefly because of their lack of distinctive Roman pottery. At Pant-y-Saer, on the island of Anglesey, North Wales (reconstruction *right*, after C. W. Phillips and R. C. H. M. *Anglesey*), an enclosed homestead group of normal Roman-period and Dark Age type consisted of a massive drystone wall, pierced by a narrow entrance (C), enclosing two circular huts (A), one with a low bench around its walls, the other with two rectangular annexes and a fragment of a courtyard wall. The pottery belonged to the customary "native" tradition, but in the larger of the two annexes (B) a large silver brooch was found (*below right*) which is similar to types current in eastern Scotland from the 5th to the 7th centuries, and so establishes use of this site during the post-Roman period. The precise function of the hut group is unclear: the two circular huts may have belonged to separate units, but their difference in layout and in associated buildings suggests that they had different purposes within a single family holding. The smaller hut may have been domestic and the larger unit workshop and agricultural buildings. The brooch indicates some wealth, and it is tempting to see in such a site the descendants of the rural villas of the Roman period.

Right: silver penannular brooch from Pant-y-Saer, Anglesey. Probably 6th century. National Museum of Wales.

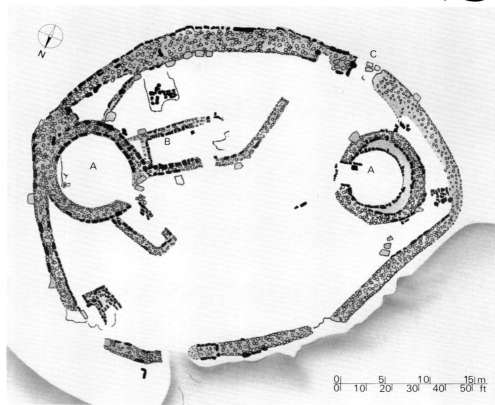

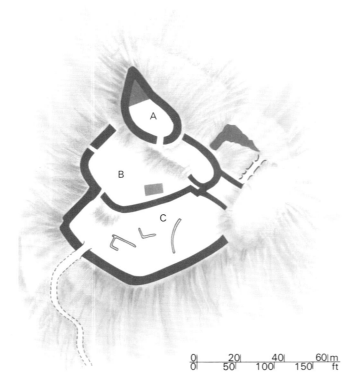

Some of the imported pottery had its origin in the Byzantine Empire. The majority seems to have been made in SW Gaul, and the areas to which it was traded were not confined to those in British occupation. A wide belt of sites flanking the Irish Sea has produced Gallic sherds, and the trade reached into the territories controlled by the enemies of both British and Anglo-Saxons, the Scotti of northern Ireland and western Scotland and the Picti of eastern Scotland. At Dunadd, Argyll, this imported pottery has been recognized at a powerful Scottish fortress besieged in 683 and 736, one of a series of similar sites known because of their plan as "nuclear" forts (*left*, after J. H. Crawe). At the top of a steep hill stands a tiny citadel 100 feet by 40 (A). Massive stone walls run out from this nucleus to enclose a middle courtyard (B) and a lower enclosure (C), in which stand the ruins of recent houses. The excavations of 1929 (shown shaded, *left*) revealed that little evidence for internal arrangement had survived the investigation of the site in 1905. The photograph (*above*) shows the hill of Dunadd as it is seen today.

The result of the archaeological investigation of the Arthurian period has been to diminish the significance of Arthur himself. His shadowy figure lurks at the edges of the historical picture and his name appears in the titles of surveys of the period; but the studies of the relics of the 5th- and 6th-century British are providing a version of the history of post-Roman Britain which no longer relies on the still-disputed legends of Arthur's resistance to the invaders.

3. The Angles, the Saxons and the Jutes

Beyond the Roman frontier of the lower Rhine, between the sand dunes and marshland of the North Sea coast of Germany and Jutland and the forests and moors of the hinterland, lived tribes who until the 4th century AD are almost unnoticed in our surviving Roman sources. While the Goths and Vandals were migrating southwards and eastwards to Russia and the Danube frontier, they remained in the north, comparatively remote from the Mediterranean world. The Romans of the later empire knew their principal groups as the Frisii of the north Dutch coast, the Saxones of the north German plain, and the Anglii of eastern Jutland.

Much of their earlier history is extremely obscure. The Angles and their neighbors in northern Jutland and the Baltic islands believed that they were united under monarchs as early as the 2nd century, and preserved legends of the wars of heroes and great kings. According to their own traditions the Saxons had no such leaders, but lived in small groups under chieftains. Archaeologists have not yet located Anglian palaces, but, during the past half-century, the uncovering of settlement sites along the North Sea coast has revealed much about the life of lesser people and of their chieftains: the pattern during the Roman period is of slow growth of small agricultural communities.

Hadrian's Wall, for 300 years a frontier between Romans and barbarians, still runs across the Northumbrian hills.

The interior of a model of a three-aisled farmhouse from the Roman Iron Age site at Tofting near Schleswig. Beyond the cross passage and partition lie the hearth and living quarters.

Part of the radially planned village at Feddersen Wierde, West Germany, in the 3rd and early 4th centuries, showing houses, sheds and enclosure ditches. After W. Haarnagel.

Settlements and cemeteries. One such site, at Wijster some 25 miles south of Groningen in the Netherlands, was excavated in the late 1950s and early 1960s. A small group of farm buildings, perhaps no more than a single farm, was occupied in the mid-2nd century A D. The farmhouses of this and subsequent phases were long rectangular buildings whose roofs were supported on two rows of internal posts. The interior, open from the ground to the roof, was thus divided longitudinally into three parts; the type (known in northern Europe from the Bronze Age until modern times) is generally known as the "three-aisled" house, and in a great many cases provided accommodation at one end for the family and at the other for their livestock. Small square or rectangular buildings served as granaries and storerooms; other huts (frequently with their floors recessed into the ground to provide extra headroom) were used for industrial and weaving activities. Some sunken-floor huts in which hearths indicate occupation are likely to have been the hovels of dependants. The settlement at Wijster grew slowly, and by the early 3rd century may have amounted to three farms. After c. 225 an influx of settlers is apparent: the hamlet now contained at least 12 houses. During the 4th century the settlement developed into a regularly planned village, laid out in fenced enclosures separated by roadways. Occupation of the settlement and burials in the adjacent cemetery both finish in the first half of the 5th century.

Excavations on an even larger scale at Feddersen Wierde, in the Saxon lands on the Weser near Bremerhaven, have since 1955 revealed a complex sequence of building. Like Wijster the site began as a farmstead – in this case in the late 1st century BC. Steady growth led to a series of small *terpen* or artificial mounds on each of which stood a three-aisled house and farmbuildings. During the 1st century A D these mounds were leveled up to produce a large *terp* on which a radially planned village of at least 30 houses was erected. As the settlement grew during the succeeding centuries until its abandonment about 450, its planning was domi-

nated by a single large house, separated from the rest by a palisade and ditch which also enclosed workshops, granaries and stalls for animals. It is difficult not to see in this group of buildings the residence of a local chieftain, and its survival through three centuries is clear evidence for some stability in social and economic life in the Roman period.

The cemeteries tell the same story. At Wehden, between the Weser and the Elbe and not far from Feddersen Wierde, the earliest cremation urns belong to the 2nd century A D and the latest to about 500. At Westerwanna on the lower Elbe the earliest vessels date from about 100 AD and the pottery styles show continuous development until the abandonment of the cemetery in the 6th century. In almost all cases the largest number of urns in the cemeteries belong to the 3rd and 4th centuries, the period of greatest expansion in the coastal settlements.

Against this background of continuity the study of the changes of fashions in artifacts permits some conclusions about the shifts of cultural influence in the area. Broad distinctions can be made: the urns of central Jutland and the adjacent Baltic areas tend to be globular with either short upright rims or tall conical necks; decoration is rectangular, with horizontal lines or corrugations on the neck of the pot, and with vertical lines on the shoulders, emphasized during the 4th and 5th centuries by small bosses. These types are usually called "Anglian," and the pottery of northern Jutland, the territory of the historical Jutes, has a general similarity to that of the Anglian areas, often with rather roughly made, shouldered vessels and grooved ornament.

The pottery in use on the German coast contrasts in shape: here are found urns with tall hollow necks and prominent rims, and wide-mouthed angular bowls. In the 3rd and 4th centuries the decoration of these southern pots has affinities with that of the Anglian areas. During the 4th century differences become more marked, for vessels are ornamented with incised chevrons and semicircular curves, and the decoration begins to include the use of simple repetitive impressed stamps and rosettes made by finger-tipping – styles that echo the late Roman pottery of the Rhineland. These designs can be attributed to the Saxons, but it is significant that the great "Saxon" urn fields of old Saxony (the region of the rivers Elbe and Weser) are by no means as uniform as those of "Anglian" central and northern Jutland.

Side by side with the "Saxon" stamped and rosetted pots are found vessels with globular bodies and corrugated necks which would not be out of place in Anglian Fünen, 200 miles to the north. The notion has accordingly won acceptance that the influence of Anglian designs spread southwards and westwards to Holstein and to Hamburg and Stade on the Elbe. To the west, in the tract of land between the Elbe and the Weser, mixed "Anglo-Saxon" cultures were forming as early as the beginning of the 3rd century, tending to show a predominance of "Anglian" traits beside the Elbe and "Saxon" a little further westwards along the estuary of the Weser.

Changes in pottery style are not directly linked to changes in population, and it would be mistaken to assume from variations of ceramic tradition an otherwise unrecorded migration of Angles southwards; but there are other signs of incursions into the North Sea coastlands, for hoards of coins, buried for safekeeping and never recovered, were being concealed here at the end of the 2nd century. As the Scandinavian scholar Sture Bolin remarked, "The more numerous the hoards the greater the disturbance and the greater the distress." A little later, perhaps towards the middle of the 3rd century, there are signs of the encroachment of the sea on the coastline, compelling the raising of some settlements on artificial mounds and the abandonment or reduction in size of others, their inhabitants migrating, presumably to other less inhospitable homes, and so increasing the mixture of cultural traditions.

Migration and consequent overpopulation had their effect on the empire during the second half of the 3rd century: attacks on the northern frontiers multiplied. Romans usually described their opponents as "Franks," seldom yet as "Saxons," but they meant the inhabitants of the coastal plain, and the invaders of the lower Rhine included Frisians. Some of these barbarians remained on

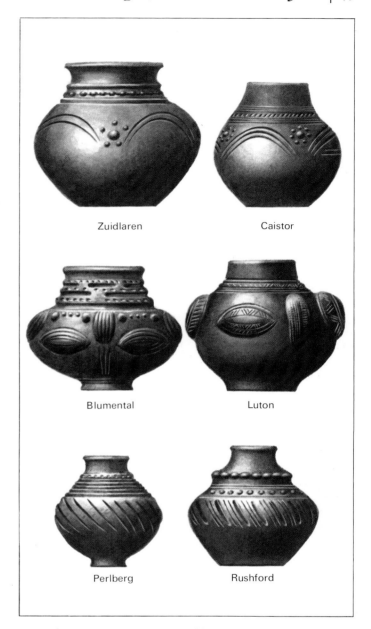

Zuidlaren

Caistor

Blumental

Luton

Perlberg

Rushford

Similarities in design between pots from England (*right*) and the continent (*left*). After J. N. L. Myres.

the lands near the mouth of the Rhine and in Belgium, and the pressure for space may have been reduced for two or three generations. During this period, until the later 4th century, those settlements which have been excavated show signs of prosperity. The situation is clearest at Wijster where the final village with its planned layout was associated with quantities of goods imported from the empire.

Trade contacts. Trade with the empire was by no means new, even though, in Julius Caesar's view, one German tribe at least encouraged the presence of Roman traders in order to sell to them Roman goods captured in war. In the early empire the Marcomanni of Bohemia acted as middlemen in a network of trading which brought Roman bronze and silver vessels, glassware and pottery to the Baltic coasts. Archaeology bears witness to one of the products of the north taken in return by the Romans – the amber of the Baltic. Other goods, economically more significant but perishable and not to be found by excavation, are suggested in the literary sources – furs and other animal products, cattle and dogs, and slaves. Individual Roman objects may have been the result of war and looting: in this class fall inscribed vessels intended as dedications to Roman temples but found in Norway and Sweden.

More clearly the result of friendly contact are the thousands of Roman coins found scattered or in hoards outside the empire. At first confined to those parts of Germany nearest to the frontiers, by the 2nd century Roman silver currency is found as far away as Sweden. Part of the trade financed by this silver passed from the Danube and Black Sea across the Gothic lands of central Europe to Scandinavia, and brought to Sweden products from southeastern Europe. But bronzework, painted glassware and fine red pottery from the Roman factories of the Rhine and Gaul traveled to Germany and Jutland by a different route. The 3rd- and 4th-century coin hoards of

Roman glass vessels imported into Scandinavia during the 3rd century and found in graves at Nordrup and Himlingøje, Denmark.

Holland and northern Germany indicate traffic from the mouth of the Rhine along the Frisian coast and so to Jutland and the Baltic.

Jutes and Angles. Within Jutland itself archaeologists have so far failed to produce evidence comparable to that of the large and continuously occupied settlements of the southern North Sea coasts. Excavated villages, indeed, are not uncommon: on the North Sea coast of northern Jutland, for example, the partial uncovering of an extensive settlement at Ginderup revealed nearly three dozen aisled houses belonging to seven successive levels. Some 30 miles to the south another excavated settlement, the fishing village of Nørre Fjand, consisted in all of over 60 houses and other buildings, not all contemporary. Both villages, however, seem to have been deserted before the end of the 3rd century, and of the many settlements wholly or partially traced in Denmark only Drengsted in north Schleswig has produced evidence, so far unpublished, of occupation during the period when the great migrations were beginning in the 4th and early 5th centuries. Excavations at Grøntoft on the west coast of Jutland have provided a possible explanation, for the village was found to have shifted its site at least five times in some 700 years up to the 3rd century; successive settlements were not therefore superimposed, and the absence so far of villages of 4th- or 5th-century date may thus be a chance failure of discovery.

But more than 20 years ago the Danish scholar P. V. Glob suggested that the heaths of Jutland, increasingly populated during the Early Iron Age and Roman Iron Age, were becoming impoverished and their cattle enfeebled by the disease called "vosk" resulting from mineral deficiency. As the land became poorer, its occupants moved away to better lands in the east and south. More is now known about local variations in the effects of climate and soils on agriculture, and such an all-embracing theory is today less fashionable; but some abandonment of settlement seems probable. However, the marginal land affected by impoverishment of this sort, untouched by modern agriculture, is precisely where archaeologists have tended to concentrate their efforts, and the results of settlement archaeology probably apply chiefly to moorland Jutland.

In the rest of the peninsula there are clear signs of continuing life: the evidence here comes from buried hoards of coin or bullion, or from the contents of graves. Findspots are most frequent towards the eastern seaboard and on the Baltic islands, especially in the Anglian region and that of the related cultures to the north of Angeln. Most significant are the deposits where ritual offerings of weapons and armor, Roman and native ornaments, pottery food-containers, clothing, and even complete ships were thrown into the peatbogs. The most famous, at Nydam in the Anglian culture-province, was excavated as long ago as the 1860s. Sacrifices here began in the 2nd

The Nydam ship: an enormous rowing boat of the 4th or early 5th century taken from a peatbog in south Jutland in the 1860s. The finds became an issue in the Danish-Prussian war of 1863–65, and were surrendered by the Danes as part of the peace treaty.

century AD and continued, probably intermittently, until about 450, with a mass of material of the mid- to late 4th century.

Deposits of this period were found in other 19th-century excavations in the bogs at Kragehul and Vimose on the island of Fünen. In recent years a further bog, at Ejsbøl on the mainland opposite Fünen, has been found to contain a large 4th- and a small mid-5th-century deposit. In view of the military character of the sacrifices – swords, spears, bows and arrows, and armor – it seems likely that the gods were being placated by thank offerings after campaigns, perhaps against the empire, for many of the objects were Roman. Considering the vagaries of success we should not be surprised that these deposits were neither regular nor of uniform quantities of objects. More important in assessing continuity than these irregularities is the repeated use of the same peatbogs as cult-centers serving the religious needs of local communities over a period in almost all cases extending from the middle of the 2nd to the middle of the 5th century. Despite the lack of excavated villages, then, there are no signs in the east of the 4th-century dislocation found in the settlements of the North Sea coast of Jutland.

The migration begins. Movements from here, however, were already under way. We have seen how the Anglian linear pottery styles were influencing the development of design on the North Sea coast of Germany, and were producing an archaeological culture which was stylistically and, presumably, also racially mixed "Anglo-Saxon." Now, in the later 4th century, a new type of brooch was becoming fashionable. Its origin was the common plain bow-brooch of the Roman period, a safety pin in which a curved band of metal separated the coiled wire spring from the catch plate which held the pin. The spring, functional rather than decorative, was now concealed by a rectangular plate from whose sides protruded ornamental knobs, and the catch plate was hidden behind an elongated foot on which rudimentary decoration was possible. The earliest examples of this type, the cruciform brooch, are attributed to east Holstein, and from there it spread northwards to Angeln and the Baltic, eastwards

towards the Polish frontier, and westwards among the mixed culture of the Elbe-Weser region.

The diffusion of brooches may have been caused, to be sure, by contact and imitation, but invasions are suspected. In 1951 the Dutch scholar P. C. Boeles drew attention to disturbances further westwards on the Frisian coast during the first half of the 5th century. He saw a break in the occupation of Frisia: the local culture was replaced by one including Saxon urns and brooch types from the Elbe and Weser. A new burial rite, inhumation, appeared among the older cremation cemeteries, and the most extensively investigated settlement in the area, the mound-village of Ezinge, was destroyed and rebuilt by the invaders.

Some change in the pottery and brooches is indeed apparent, and the mixed cemeteries seem to be a new development. The evidence from Ezinge, however, is inconclusive. For nearly 1,000 years the design of the houses on this developing *terp* was of the normal three-

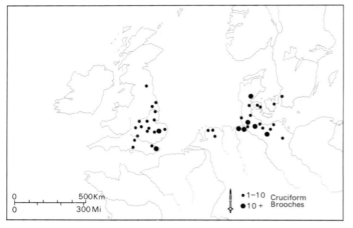

Left: the distribution of cruciform brooches of the 5th century. After A. Genrich with additions.

Below: cruciform brooches of the 6th century from Cambridgeshire. They retain the form of head-plate knob found in earlier examples, but have elaborated the foot of the brooch into prominent animal heads.

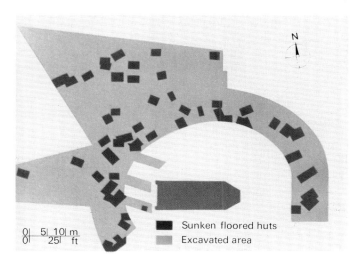

The upper levels of the mound at Ezinge, Netherlands, showing the sunken-floor huts which replaced earlier types c. 400 A D.

aisled plan. At some time near 400 AD at least the excavated part of the settlement was destroyed by fire. No aisled houses could be traced in the subsequent re-occupation; instead, cut through the ashes were the floors of more than 60 sunken-floor huts belonging to several phases. When the site was excavated in the 1930s such buildings were regarded as typical of the Anglo-Saxons, and thus proof of a forcible seizure of the area. More recent excavations, however, as we have seen at Wijster, have shown that the sunken-floor hut was neither a purely Anglo-Saxon type nor confined to the migration period; in their homelands, indeed, the dwelling houses of such invaders might well be three-aisled buildings similar to those of the Frisians.

The dramatic destruction of Ezinge, then, need not have been a result of Anglian or Saxon invasion, however likely such events might be; but a fragment of Old English saga, the *Fight at Finn's Burg*, is localized in this area. Finn Focwalding, chief of the Frisians, is visited by his wife's brother Hnaef, a Danish leader. A fight breaks out, its cause unstated, and Hnaef is killed, but the Danes, now led by Hengest, remain masters of Finn's hall and agree to a truce with the Frisians. The feud has not been settled, and Hengest, with reinforcements, kills Finn and his followers and returns to Denmark. The saga was old and well known by the 8th century, when a précis of it appears in the epic poem *Beowulf*. How old is uncertain, but the situation accords with a period of expansion into Frisia in the first half of the 5th century.

During these years widespread disruption has been traced along the North Sea coast. The settlement sites were abandoned: no later villages succeeded the 4th-century complexes at Wijster, Feddersen Wierde or Gristede. The cremation cemeteries of the Elbe and Weser, in which for three centuries thousands had been buried, dwindle suddenly into insignificance not long after 400, and contain mere handfuls of later 5th-century urns. At precisely this time in the Danish bogs most of the votive deposits stop abruptly; the few that continue reveal by comparison mere trickles of objects. "We are not surprised," the Dutch scholar Van Es has said. "The Anglo-Saxon invaders of England must have come from somewhere." Some of the North Sea peoples joined in the Frankish and Gothic movements into Gaul; one result of their activity may have been the introduction to the North Sea coast of exuberantly decorated metalwork with motifs of Classical origin, for it has recently been suggested plausibly that this was the work of Roman craftsmen brought back with their conquerors to the Elbe and Weser. Some of the coastal peoples remained in their new lands on the edge of Gaul. Others, perhaps the majority, turned their attention across the sea to the Roman province of Britain.

The end of Roman Britain. Saxon pirates were no strangers to the coasts of Britain, and against them during the late 3rd and 4th centuries a chain of forts had been built, manned by troops under the command of the "Count of the Saxon Shore." But the most urgent threat came from the north, where Hadrian's Wall and its associated outposts formed one of the strongest frontiers in the empire. In the 4th century the enemy were the Picts, a confederation like the Franks or the Alamanni, who occupied eastern Scotland, and pressed on the allied, or at least more quiescent, tribes immediately to the north of the Roman defenses. At about this time the presence of a further danger can be inferred from the construction of coastal fortresses in the west, at Cardiff and Lancaster, and of smaller forts in north Wales: these were intended to thwart pirate raids by the Scotti of Ireland.

During the earlier 4th century the raiding was localized. In the 360s attacks multiplied, and in 367 an attack by Picts, Scots and the savage Attacotti (perhaps of western Scotland) coincided with a thrust along the coast and against the Rhine frontier by Saxons and Franks. The operation was thought to have been jointly planned – the contemporary historian Ammianus Marcellinus used the words "barbarian conspiracy" – and proved remarkably successful: one of the generals of the army in Britain was killed, and the other captured. At some cost the defenses were reconstructed but the new arrangements worked for no more than a decade: in 383 Magnus Maximus, probably commander of the British army, began his ultimately unsuccessful usurpation of the Western Empire. He took with him into Gaul substantial detachments of his army, but the province was perhaps not left unprotected, for in the quasi-legendary genealogies of the British chieftains of Wales Maximus appears as an ancestor and, as "Macsen Wledig," he survived as a hero until the Middle Ages; in southern Scotland at about this time are recorded rulers with Latin names. Both phenomena are perhaps vestiges of alliances with native rulers; such a federate solution (as we have seen in the cases of the Franks

Elaborate equal-armed brooches of the 5th century are found in the Elbe-Weser area and Frisia. In England these and later types are spread from East Anglia to Wiltshire. *Above:* a gilt-bronze example from Collinbourne Ducis, Wiltshire; *below:* from Haslingfield near Cambridge.

and the Visigoths) would be in accord with the current official strategies of frontier defense.

After the suppression of Maximus the imperial government turned its attention to the northern barbarians – the poet Claudian's panegyric of 400 AD names Picts, Scots and Saxons as the enemy now tamed by Stilicho. But in the mounting crises of the 400s the advantage was lost, for the defense of Italy against Alaric and his Visigoths required men. In 401 a legion which, in the words of another of Claudian's poems, had been "bridling the Scots and inspecting the auspices in the entrails of Picts" was brought "from the ends of Britain" to confront the Goths. The army of Britain, steadily depleted by a government whose prime concern remained the security of northern Italy, responded by setting up a series of emperors of its own. The first two, a soldier (perhaps a general) and a leading civilian, proved unsatisfactory and were eliminated by their erstwhile supporters. The third, the soldier Constantine, was elected in 407, just after the Vandals, Suebi and Alans swept across the Rhine and into Gaul. There had been recent troubles in Britain: in 405, according to Irish sources, the king of Ireland had been killed fighting in the English Channel, and Irish settlement

in south Wales and Cornwall may date from this period. But Constantine, as we saw, took his troops into Gaul, and set up the capital of his short-lived empire far away at Arles; we have no record of any measures taken by him against Scots or Picts.

In 410 Saxons attacked Britain: the information, from a nearly contemporary chronicler, is perhaps reliable, and the event may have resulted in the last official connection between the imperial government and the island. The Emperor Honorius (presumably in response to a request for aid) wrote to the cities of Britain and told them to look to their own defense. In its original form the letter may have been more helpful than this curt record suggests: already in April 406 Honorius had written to the provinces at large, to recommend policies of self-help and offering freedom to slaves who responded to the call. Now in the disturbances of Constantine's usurpation some further encouragement to loyalists in Britain would be timely. If the letter was indeed addressed to "the cities" the normal provincial government was in rebellion or had disappeared, and official sanction for any military action civilians might take would be necessary to safeguard the provincials against future charges of treason and public riot. There is certainly no reason to believe that the imperial government saw the break with Britain as more than temporary. Indeed, a 5th-century army list which still records the now-vanished troops and their obsolete stations in the former province implies that the imperial bureaucracy was ready for the reestablishment of normal government. The steady erosion of Roman control over Gaul during the 5th century made such an ambition less and less realistic.

Britain independent. "The Romans," according to the 6th-century Byzantine historian Procopius, "were never able to regain Britain, which from then onwards was governed by tyrants." It is likely enough that the new leaders were great landowners, men now chosen by their fellow citizens because of their patronage and established position under the old imperial system. It is likely too that the titles they adopted derived from the old administration, based at least in the first generation on civilian magistracies rather than hereditary kingships. Each may have controlled only the territory of his native city. One may have become paramount over his colleagues from other cantonal capitals – a suggestion made more plausible by the predominance given to one Vortigern in our texts. Factions may have developed; there are hints of religious and social disputes. But our picture of the internal politics of the troubled half-century after 410 relies heavily on guesswork. This is unfortunate, for in this period occurred several interesting changes. The Pictish threat which had for so long oppressed Roman Britain was diminishing; the Scotti, now converted to Christianity through the efforts of their former hostage St Patrick, were turning their attention away from the province and beginning their

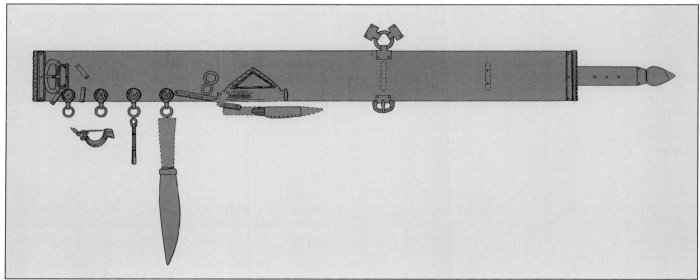

settlements on the west coast of the land to which they gave their name, Scotland. A British military revival seems likely, and is suggested in the words written a century later by the British monk Gildas: "The island grew rich; the abundance of goods exceeded the memory of any former times. But, with prosperity, [decadent] luxury increased."

The gap in written evidence is partially filled by archaeology. Along the Roman frontier from Romania to Yorkshire belt buckles and fittings of similar designs have been recognized as part of the equipment of the late Roman army. Many occur in the graves of men buried in barbarian fashion with their weapons, and few have been found outside the frontier zone. Manufactured perhaps principally in the workshops of the Danube and the Rhine, they date from the second half of the 4th century. Cruder

Top: the belt-fittings from a warrior's grave discovered in 1874 at Dorchester, Oxfordshire, are typical examples of late Roman military uniform, used to attach straps and small pieces of equipment to a broad belt stiffened by plates. Though usually found in Roman contexts, the belts are often assumed to have belonged to Germanic allies.

Center: a late Roman military belt with strap distributors, stiffeners and attachment plates. Reconstructed from a grave at Rhenen, Netherlands. After J. Ypey.

and more stylized versions found in England are best seen as derived types, made for use by local units. For how long their production continued is unclear: one, found in a woman's grave with brooches of the early 6th century, may have been a century old when buried. The locally produced British brooches belong certainly to the late 4th

The medieval castle of Pevensey, Sussex, sits inside the massive walls of the Roman fortress of Anderida, once on the sea coast, built to defend the Saxon shore. In 491, according to the *Anglo-Saxon Chronicle*, "Aelle and Cissa besieged *Andredesceaster* and killed all the inhabitants; there was not even one Briton left there."

century, are likely to have been still in military use in the first quarter of the 5th century, and may have remained current for a few years later than that. Their findspots are illuminating, for they occur in or near towns of southern England, in a few *villae* (Roman country houses) chiefly in the south and west, and in association with Germanic settlement in southeastern England. It seems, in fact, that they were worn by troops stationed to protect the south of England from barbarian attack.

That Germans were among such troops is to be expected, for soldiers of barbarian origin permeated the imperial army. Roman pottery in the east of England which seems to imitate north German designs was perhaps intended for such a barbarian market. Women's graves with Germanic ornaments have been found in association with some of the warrior burials: thus settled communities of Germanic peoples are implied. But the presence of these barbarians in Roman service has tended to blur the archaeological distinction between imperial soldiers and barbarian invaders. Whatever their origins such troops could be expected to defend their new homes against external aggression, and the Picts, not the Saxons or Angles, were the principal danger. Against an allied army

of Picts and Saxon pirates St Germanus of Auxerre, a Gallic bishop in Britain on church affairs, but formerly a soldier, won a victory in 429. Picts were still the expected threat when a generation later a body of Angles was brought in and settled as federates in Kent in the southeast of England.

Hengest and Horsa. Long afterwards, the compilers of the great *Anglo-Saxon Chronicle* placed the arrival of their ancestors in England in the years after 449. According to the tradition three shiploads of mercenaries, invited by the British King Vortigern, landed in Kent, where territory was ceded to them. After successful campaigns against the Picts, the mercenaries, under the command of two brothers, Hengest and Horsa, turned on their employers and, with fresh immigrants, overran the southeast of England. Hengest is not a common name, and it may be more than a coincidence that the leader of the Danish group in Frisia in the *Fight at Finn's Burg* was also called Hengest, for in Canterbury, Kent, pottery of Frisian origin has been excavated, while tradition, some pottery and perhaps some metalwork design link Kent to Jutland. But the Kentish settlement, whether of the mid-5th century or (as Gallic chroniclers imply) of the 430s, need not have been the earliest establishment of German tribes within England: at Sancton, Yorkshire, and Caistor-by-Norwich, Norfolk, the discovery of cremation urns of late 4th-century types suggests that here, not later than the early 5th century, were settled barbarians in sufficiently large groups to preserve their own burial customs.

A pattern in the settlements can thus be traced. Towards the end of the 4th century are found military graves with Germanic associations; their occupants should be seen as upholders of the Roman establishment. At about the same time, or a little later, further eastwards on the English North Sea coast are signs of barbarians whose links with the empire were weaker: in their burial ritual, their pottery and their metalwork they echo the styles of free Germany and Jutland. Like the continental federates, Visigoths or Franks, their role was at first defensive; one may assume that they, like their continental counterparts, became increasingly independent during the course of the 5th century, as Roman ability to coerce declined, until the time when they felt able to end the pretense and assert their overlordship.

In Gaul the change took place in the 450s and 460s, when, with Aëtius dead, the Visigoths and the Franks began their annexation of parts of that province. In Britain a similar attempt may have taken place a few years earlier: Gallic chroniclers record that at the beginning of the 440s Britain "passed into the hands of the Saxons." The report was somewhat exaggerated, but a few years later (according to the 6th-century British writer Gildas) the Britons wrote for help to Gaul: "The barbarians drive us to the sea and the sea thrusts us back to the barbarians. Between these two modes of death we are either killed or drowned." The date of the letter was probably 446 or 447, and the recipient of the appeal almost certainly Aëtius, who had his own problems with the barbarians in Gaul, and was soon to be in conflict with Attila and the Huns. No help came to Britain from him, and in the next few years the *Anglo-Saxon Chronicle* records a series of British defeats at the hands of Hengest and Horsa. The sources, Gallic, Saxon and British, seem to be referring to the same events, the revolt of the new Kentish federates and their conquest of parts of southeastern England. The result was felt in Gaul, for here in the 460s large and organized bodies of British exiles joined the Gallic provincials against the Visigoths and Saxons, and settled down in eastern Brittany and Normandy, where they are recalled by the modern place-name Bretteville. By the end of the century they had been absorbed into the expanding kingdom of the Franks.

The British recovery. But in marked contrast to the rapidity of the collapse of Gaul, the progress of the barbarian invaders of Britain was slow. At the end of nearly half a century of conflict (by which time the Franks had achieved the subjugation of Gaul from the Rhine to the Pyrenees) battles were still being fought in Sussex and Hampshire less than 100 miles from the Kentish settlements. The reasons for this comparative failure are uncertain. The Anglo-Saxon invaders may have been too few in numbers to make easy settlement of territories they overran; the British resistance seems to have been stubborn.

At the end of this period of limited conquest and frequent small-scale raiding the invaders were decisively defeated, at a date close to 500, at the siege of Mons Badonicus – a battle which later tradition associates with the name of Arthur. The spot has not been certainly identified, but seems to have lain towards southwestern England, perhaps near Bath or at one of the Dorset hillforts named Badbury, far to the west of previously recorded conflict. A campaign so far from home is likely to have involved large numbers, and their defeat halted the invasions. Forty-four years later Gildas calls this battle of Mount Badon "almost the most recent and not the least slaughter" of the Anglo-Saxons, and could describe the comparative peace which the victory had brought, a peace which the Britons were still enjoying.

Archaeology provides some confirmation. Between the Elbe and the Weser, while the migrations were beginning, a taste had grown for pottery with protuberant bosses and impressed ornament. As the style developed during the late 5th and the 6th centuries the design was dominated by a riot of stamped and molded decoration. Those types which can be attributed to the second half of the 5th century are found in England in cemeteries from Yorkshire in the north to Surrey in the south, and extend westwards into the upper Thames basin, into Oxfordshire and Berkshire. The latest type, which should belong to the half-century after Mount Badon, is found in the east of England but is absent from the upper Thames: here indeed it is difficult to find any Anglo-Saxon artifacts at all which could be dated to the first half of the 6th century. It seems, in fact, that occupation of this area was interrupted in those very years of peace described by Gildas. There is a hint too that an agreed division of the country was made by treaty, for in the next generation Gildas regrets that some of the shrines of the saints are now inaccessible because of the "grievous partition made with the barbarians."

The peace seems to have been more grievous for the barbarians than the British. Metalwork of Kentish and Anglian types has been reported from cemeteries from western France to Belgium. Many place-names in northeastern France seem to be of English origin. An explanation is given by the Byzantine historian Procopius, a contemporary of Gildas: "overpopulation was so great in Britain that large numbers every year migrated with their families to the Franks, who settled them in deserted parts of their land." Less reliably, the 9th-century German monk Rudolf of Fulda tells of a landing by Saxons in the Elbe estuary and of subsequent conquest; the date of the dimly remembered incident, 531 AD, corresponds with Procopius' account. These Anglo-Saxon settlements of northern Gaul and the resettlement of the Saxon ancestral homelands of the Elbe are both part of the same movement: after the apparent failure of the conquest of Britain at the beginning of the 6th century many of the immigrants were abandoning the attempt and returning to the continent.

A group of English saucer brooches in the Ashmolean Museum, Oxford. The early geometric ones are found inland in the south Midlands; the later, zoomorphic forms (top left and far left in the picture) come from the east coast. Late 5th and 6th century.

Anglo-Saxon consolidation. Such evacuations were premature, for after a series of campaigns (probably made unduly lengthy by the compilers of the *Anglo-Saxon Chronicle*) the English expanded in the middle of the 6th century into Wiltshire in southern England, and so began the last and successful phase of invasion. The victorious general's name, Cynric, is not Germanic but Celtic; he may have been a British tyrant, commander of a local war band, and the bare record of his battles in the *Chronicle* certainly conceals a more confused situation than the simple opposition of British and Anglo-Saxon forces.

The historical account of these years of invasion relies heavily on Bede, a Northumbrian monk of the 8th century who was without doubt the greatest historian of the Middle Ages. In a famous passage he named the invaders as "from three of the strongest nations of Germany, the Saxons, the Angles and the Jutes," located their homelands and identified their descendants: from the Saxons came the nations of the East, South and West Saxons; from the Angles were derived the East Angles, Middle Angles, Mercians and Northumbrians; from the Jutes came the people of Kent and of the Isle of Wight. Bede saw the origins of the English in terms of the settled kingdoms of his own day. The 5th-century movements on the continent, however, had introduced into the North Sea coastlands peoples drawn from many sources. The subsequent crossing to Britain began piecemeal, and the migrant groups brought with them material cultures whose elements were thoroughly mixed, for when the migrants were buried in their new homelands, pottery and brooches at home in the Saxon areas of the Elbe were placed next to artifacts paralleled in Angeln and Fünen:

"Saxon" objects of the initial phases of the migration are as much at home in East Anglia as are "Anglian" artifacts in Wessex.

Large and organized groups of settlers, with uniform culture, may have crossed, and too little is yet known of the contemporary occupation sites to allow firm conclusions about their nature. Discoveries so far, however, suggest that the early settlements were small and fragmented. By far the largest known, the village of Mucking at the mouth of the Thames in Essex, consisted of no more than 200 sunken-floor huts, not all contemporary, and one or more rectangular houses. But even Mucking may be exceptional. Its origin seems to have been in a military settlement guarding the Thames, which has produced several examples of late Roman military metalwork; it may well have developed, as its excavator has recently suggested, as a "transit camp" during the migrations. Probably more typical of the new settlements is the hamlet of West Stow in Suffolk, where the total excavation of the site exposed some six rectangular houses and groups of sunken-floor huts – identified as the property of only six family units. That the migrants settled down in small groups is further suggested by the cemeteries, few of which contain more than 200 burials belonging to any one century: even allowing 40 years to a generation, they must, in striking contrast to the great urnfields of Germany, have been serving local populations to be numbered in tens rather than hundreds.

Outside the densest areas of English settlement on the east coast, such small groups must have been dominated by their British neighbors. Some, as in the days of the empire, served as mercenaries, for about 540 Gildas repeats an apparently contemporary protest that the Britons should not rely for their defense on *foederati*, their barbarian allies. We know of Cynric's activities in Wiltshire about 550 because the later Saxon kings of Wessex viewed him as the founder of their dynasty and preserved his traditions. Elsewhere local movements like these have been forgotten, and the origins of the great Midland kingdoms are undocumented. In the far north in the middle of the 6th century the rock of Bamburgh was fortified by a warlord, Ida, "from whom sprang the royal race of the Northumbrians." Ida's new realm was small, a strip of the northeast coastal plain, and was maintained with difficulty in the face of British opposition. The Anglo-Saxons of Yorkshire, by now settled for a century and a half, remained until the 580s subject to the British kings of York, and seem to have played no part in the struggle until their overlords were killed by the descendants of Ida.

From such small beginnings in the middle decades of the 6th century the newly founded principalities expanded rapidly at the expense of British or English neighbors. The written records are West Saxon and emphasize the important role of the local leaders, Cynric and his successor Ceawlin. But there are hints that the impetus came from East Anglia, for pottery types at home in

Norfolk and Suffolk spread during the later 6th century across the upper Thames and Midlands to Gloucestershire and Warwickshire in the west. Overpopulation in the East Anglian coastlands may have been extreme. Long afterwards Bede reported that because of the migrations the Angeln district of Jutland "is said to remain empty up to the present day." No grave groups or even chance surface-finds of this period have yet been reported from this area, and we have already seen how the Danish ritual deposits in bogs tail off during the 5th century: only one, Kragehul on Fünen, postdates 500 AD, and its late deposit may have been a reoccupation. By 550 Procopius can call this tract, between the Baltic Slavs and the Varni of north Jutland, a desert. Its people moved to England and among the migrants was the Anglian royal family itself: kings of Angeln were counted among the ancestors of the Mercian monarchy.

Cynric's victories were won against the British. In 568 his successor Ceawlin defeated English forces led by an Aethelbehrt, presumably the king of Kent of that name. In the 570s together with Cutha (described as his brother) Ceawlin absorbed into his kingdom the Saxon and British regions of the south Midlands and upper Thames. In 577 an allied army including Ceawlin defeated and killed "three British kings" far to the west, and captured the cities of Gloucester, Cirencester and Bath.

Right: Frankish claw beaker found in association with late cruciform brooches in a grave at Mucking, Essex. Mid-6th century.

Below: the settlement at West Stow, Suffolk, a village founded in the early 5th century and surviving about 250 years. The sunken-floor huts represent a series of phases, and the halls too may belong to different periods. After S. E. West.

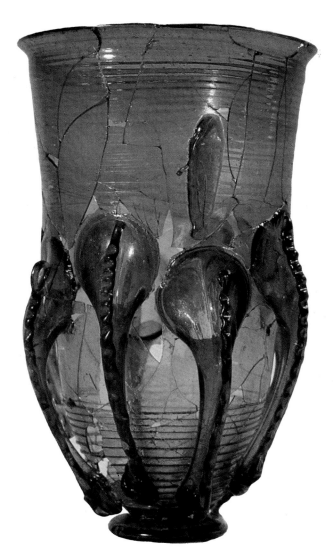

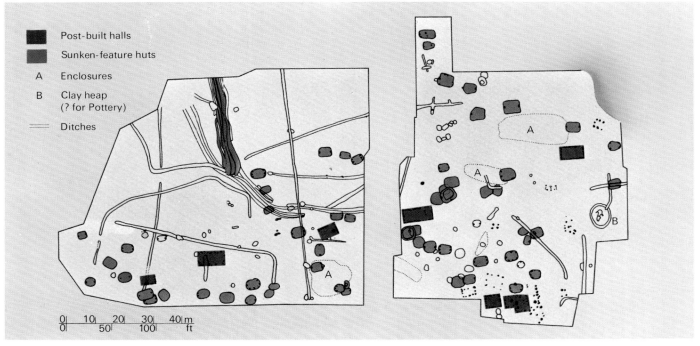

Post-built halls
Sunken-feature huts
A   Enclosures
B   Clay heap (? for Pottery)
===   Ditches

The British collapse. While the archaeological evidence for the Anglo-Saxon expansion in these years grows steadily, that for British survival so far east is scarce, for excavations in the cities captured in 577 have failed to locate any traces of occupation after the 5th century. The problem, indeed, is general, for the artifacts by which archaeologists of the Roman period are accustomed to identify the Romano-British cultures disappear early in the 5th century. A mere handful of coins entered Britain after 400; by 425 the Roman pottery industry had disappeared, its decline perhaps economic during the break-up of the old social and governmental systems. The factory products were replaced by handmade pottery, difficult to date or even to distinguish from plain pre-Roman or Saxon types. So far only a few Roman cities have provided evidence of the continuity of any sort of use through the 5th century: at St Albans, to the north of London, large building works of mid-5th-century date; at Wroxeter, on the Welsh border, the slight impressions left by timber buildings above the latest Roman levels; at Canterbury, in Kent, sunken-floor huts beside Roman streets, and elsewhere even less than this. An anonymous Saxon poet later recorded his impressions of a Roman city, perhaps Bath:

> Snapped rooftrees, towers fallen,
> the work of the Giants, the stonesmiths,
> mouldereth. Rime scoureth gate towers,
> rime on mortar.
> Shattered the showershields, roofs ruined,
> age under-ate them . . .

Decay was advanced by the early 6th century. Gildas complained "Our cities are still not occupied as they were; even today they are dismal and deserted ruins." Though he may have exaggerated, it is noticeable that almost all the pottery imported to the British in these early post-Roman centuries has been found not in the cities but in the monasteries and small hill-fortresses of the Celtic west. The centers of influence were changing.

In little more than a generation, from 550 to 580, British power collapsed, and no contemporary native writings have survived to explain its fall. Gildas died before the final conquest, probably in 572, and his only extant treatise belongs to an earlier age, the troubled peace of the 530s and 540s. But his words foreshadow the disaster: the British were ruled by tyrants "sunk in murder and adultery," who had turned from God to "the Enemy of all mankind." Amid his homily he talks of feuding, of dynastic rivalry prompting assassination, of fragmentation of the *Cymry* ("fellow citizens," as the Welsh still call themselves) into petty monarchies impotent to resist the determined attacks by the English invaders when they began in the years after 560.

By the beginning of the 7th century the boundaries of the new English kingdoms – the kingdoms of Bede – were formed. The old settlement areas of the east – East Anglia,

The framework of a house from the latest levels of the Roman city of Wroxeter. Even with more sophisticated carpentry than this reconstruction attempts, the structure would seem primitive indeed beside the ruins of the Roman public buildings.

Kent, and the lands of the East Saxons (Essex) and South Saxons (Sussex) – remained significant but were of small extent. The new territories, the kingdoms of the Northumbrians, the midland kingdom of Mercia, and the southern kingdom of the West Saxons in Wessex, were by comparison huge and the bulk of their population must have been British under English domination. Even in Kent the law provided for serf classes; in Wessex the inferior classes included substantial landowners: the English name by which they were described is "foreigner," *Wealh* or *Wylisc* – "Welsh."

Those British who remained free from Anglo-Saxon control were now confined to the highland zones of the southwest, Wales and the northwest; during the course of the next century their horizons shrank and cooperation between them against the English became exceptional; in time even their languages developed separately. Refugees from the lowlands are known, some perhaps bringing to southwest Scotland and thence to Wales the tradition of the north British conflict of about 600 AD with the rising kingdom of Northumbria – the epic poem *The Gododdin*, in which "300 men rode out and there was slaughter. Though they were slain they slew, and they shall be honored till the end of the world." *The Gododdin* owes little to the Roman world: its society is a warrior aristocracy whose standards of excellence differed little from those of the Anglo-Saxons they opposed. In mainland Europe the barbarian settlement was rapid, and the conquerors, many already Christian, inherited and preserved Roman administration, law and language. But during the prolonged invasion of Britain such continuity was broken and the veneer of Roman civilization was lost. The emergence of an England that was both barbarian and pagan was an unlooked-for result of the long-successful resistance to the invaders.

Settlements and Houses

The houses of barbarian Europe were built largely of timber, and their traces in the ground are correspondingly slight. Archaeologists are normally confronted by rows and clusters of postholes, gullies to hold the bases of fences or walls, and dark shadows which mark the spot where timbers have rotted away. Few sites are so deeply stratified that floor levels survive to separate structures of different dates, and the cutting of one posthole by another, which allows the excavator to sort out the phasing of his site, is an occurrence more to be desired than to be expected.

Even when the ground plans and phasing have been established, the study is incomplete without an assessment of the function of the site. Such interpretation requires the imaginative reconstruction from the surviving postholes of long-vanished upper parts of the building, a process whose methods have not been, and perhaps

cannot be, precisely formulated without controversy. Some clues come from a few structures the lower parts of whose walls have been preserved from decay in waterlogged ground. Other, more disputable evidence comes from the earliest surviving buildings in an area (normally of the 12th century or later) for it can be held that they stand at the end of a development in traditional styles, earlier examples of which are now represented only by postholes.

Among the first of barbarian houses to be identified was the sunken-floor hut or *Grubenhaus*. A hollow measuring some 10 or 12 feet by 8 feet was cut to a depth of 2 or 3 feet, and an upper structure arranged on posts resting at the edge of the recess. The traditional reconstruction (*below*, from West Stow, Suffolk) is of primitive appearance, a dug-out with little headroom, floor space or comfort.

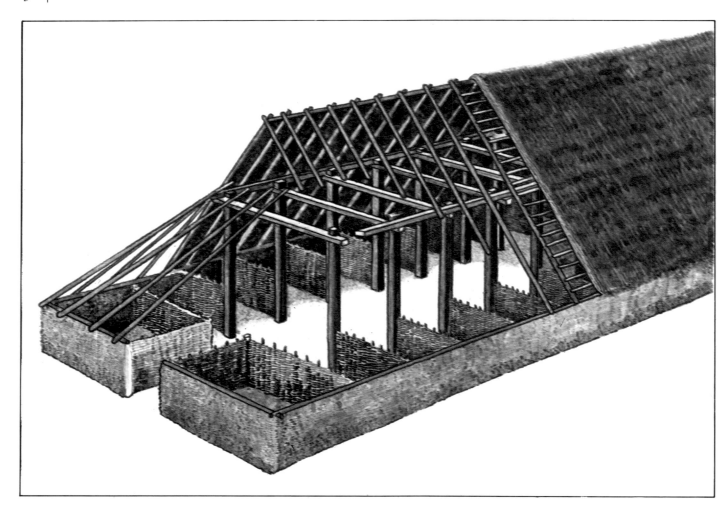

Examples of sunken-floor huts have been found at sites within Germany throughout the Roman Iron Age, and are common during the migration period in much of northern Europe, but they lie outside the main stream of traditional building. From the 4th millennium B C throughout prehistory (and in parts of Germany until the present century) the common house plan in central and northern Europe has been a large rectangular hall, sometimes more than 100 feet in length, whose roof rested on two or more rows of posts. A reconstruction of this type from Feddersen Wierde, near Bremerhaven, Germany (*above*, after plan by W. Haarnegel), shows the lower end of a longhouse with partitions for animals. As in the case of several of the Feddersen houses, the walls and stalls were preserved as high as the eaves.

Left: some of the "sunken-floor" huts at West Stow, Suffolk, showed clearly that they had been larger than the hollow in the ground. In these cases the hollow seems to have been a cellar or cavity below a wooden floor. The reconstructed "hut" is now a much grander building than the traditional dug-out.

Right: the West Stow hut, no longer "sunken-floored" but "sunken-featured," during reconstruction. How many *Grubenhäuser* at other sites should be interpreted in this way is uncertain, and some were certainly hovels, perhaps used only as workshops.

Below: the Dutch village at Wijster (occupied from the 2nd to the 5th century A D) contains several variants of the normal aisled plan. The "cattle-ends" of the buildings are of normal design; at the "house-end" the arrangement of postholes shows that some modifications to the upper roof structure were incorporated. The simplest (*left* and *center*) lacks one pair of roof supports beside the hearth. A distinct version (*right*) omits almost all internal supports at the house-end, replacing them by double postholes beside the walls. Van Es's suggestion that these are crucks (crooked timbers joining at the ridge) makes the upper roof reconstruction difficult, and the drawing shows the tiebeam supported by curving braces, the "base-crucks" of medieval buildings. After plans by W. Van Es.

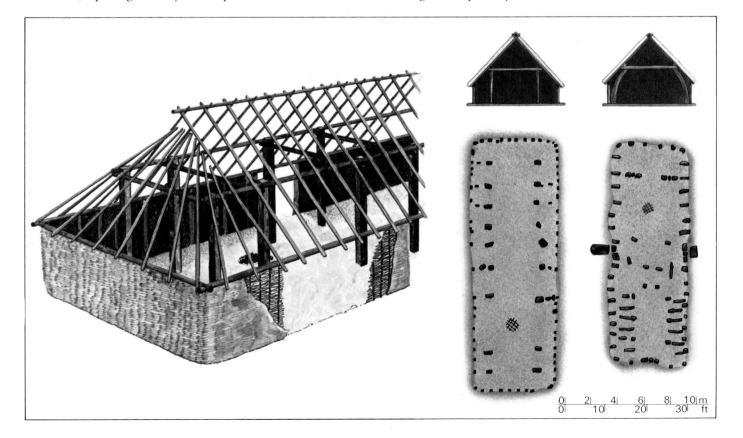

For many years only *Grubenhäuser* were discovered in England, but recent excavations have revealed rectangular halls and complex village layouts comparable to those on the continent. At Chalton, Hampshire, part of a village of several periods includes only two *Grubenhäuser* among its post-built halls. Some of the buildings form groups enclosed by fences (*above*). The excavator's phasing of the site shown on the plan (*left*, after P. Addyman and T. Champion) is still hypothetical.

Right: the post-built halls at Chalton (reconstructed here), at West Stow, and at the village currently being excavated at Catholme, Staffordshire, differed markedly from continental houses. So far no aisled houses have been found in England, for the English halls had substantial wall-posts and no internal supports. The evidence from Wijster suggests that attempts were being made in the 4th century to clear the floor area of some houses of their encumbering aisle posts, and small unaisled buildings are known on the continent. But the abrupt break with tradition in the English halls, and the regularity of their planning, make it possible that they are representative not of Germanic but of Romano-British building traditions. After R. Warmington.

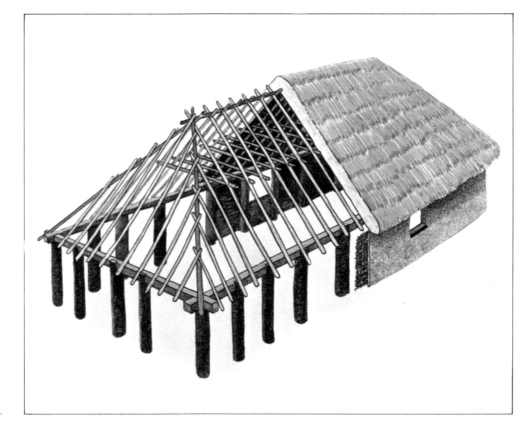

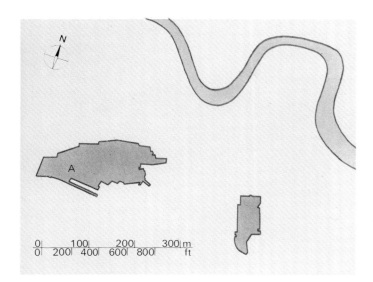

The scale and complexity of the settlements of Germany are shown clearly by the excavations at the 7th- and 8th-century site of Warendorf, on the River Ems in Westphalia. The general plan (*left*) shows the old course of the Ems and the excavated areas of the village. All areas revealed similar density of occupation, and so the settlement is likely to have been continuous from east to west for a distance of at least a quarter of a mile. Part of the excavation (A), shown in the larger plan (*below*), demonstrates the difficulty of distinguishing phases in such a site: in each phase this area contained one major hall and several smaller buildings, surrounded by sheds, workshops and polygonal arrangements of postholes that were perhaps the bases of raised haystacks. After W. Winkelmann.

Below: the houses at Warendorf were radically different from older aisled buildings. Their walls (and their ridges) were curved, perhaps to lessen wind resistance, and their interiors were free of roof supports. To prevent collapse under the weight of the roof the walls were buttressed with angled braces. The drawings show two alternative interpretations, one in which the thatching is continued to the ground and the other, more probable, in which the braces and walls are left exposed. After W. Winkelmann.

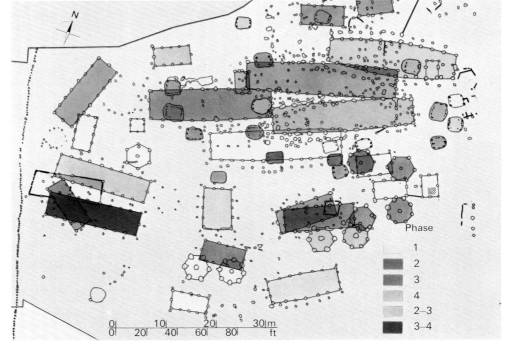

Phase

1
2
3
4
2–3
3–4

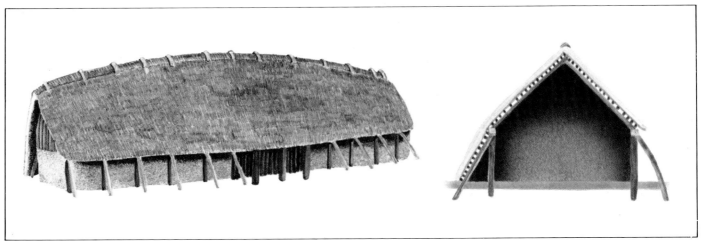

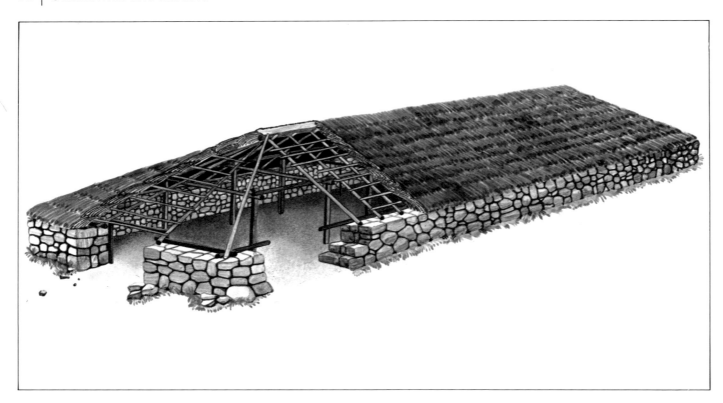

Opposite above: a house from the settlement (2nd to 6th century) at Vallhagar on the island of Gotland, Sweden. It is typical of Scandinavian farmhouses in modifying the aisled house design by the introduction of massive drystone walls. The roof covering is shown as turf, necessitating a shallow pitch. After M. Stenberger.

Opposite below: the impressive size of the timber halls is conveyed by the rebuilding of one of the 31 barrack blocks excavated at the Danish army camp at Trelleborg, Sjaelland (c. 1000 AD). The Trelleborg rebuilding illustrates a difficulty of such experimental archaeology, for although the design is structurally feasible – it is, after all, still standing – more recent work has shown that the outer posts were angled braces like those at Warendorf and that the building was probably lower, and without its veranda.

Below: the barbarian village: an idealized representation of the 7th-century Frankish settlement at Gladbach near Cologne, Germany. *Grubenhäuser* cluster around small unaisled halls in a community of half a dozen family units, set among its fields amid the uncleared forests.

4. The Successor Kingdoms

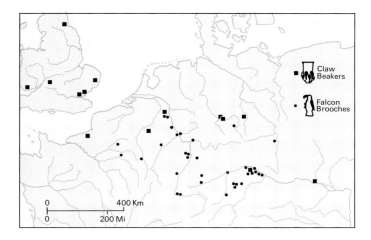

The distribution of claw beakers and falcon brooches during the 5th and 6th centuries. After U. Koch.

While the province of Britain slipped further and further away from the Mediterranean world, the traditions and politics of that world too were changing. Four principal kingdoms succeeded to the power of the Western Empire, the Gothic kingdoms of Spain and Italy, the Lombard kingdom which replaced the Goths in Italy, and the Frankish kingdom of Gaul and Germany. The history of the 5th and 6th centuries is the story of their conflicts with each other and with the still formidable Byzantine Empire of Constantinople.

The Franks. Although the Franks lived close to the Roman frontier of the Rhine, and after the disasters of the 3rd century even occupied lands within the empire, remarkably little is known of their activities before the middle of the 5th century. Some Franks, as Roman federates, tried to defend the Rhineland in 406, and with the abandonment of the frontier they and others formed their own almost autonomous states in the north. Against these groups Aëtius fought in 428 and perhaps in 432, with little effect; during the 440s the priest Salvian, in exile near Marseilles, describes the ruin of the once prosperous Rhine towns, Mainz, Cologne and his native Trier.

The confederation of the Franks was at best a loose union. During the 4th century one branch was distinguished as "Salian," "salty" or "sea-shore," and appears to have occupied Belgium. Other branches settled in the Rhine valley, and by modern writers are described as "Ripuarian" (or "riverbank") Franks, a name with no ancient authority. Soon after 450 some details become clearer. The town of Cambrai in northern France had been captured and formed the center of a petty kingdom. Another principality centered on the Roman city of

Opposite: the Roman glass industry of the Rhineland continued without interruption under the Frankish kings. The most spectacular of its products, like this example from Castle Eden, County Durham, are the mold-blown claw beakers of the 6th century.

Cologne, and a further group under a war-leader, Childeric, son of the half-legendary Merovech (from whom the royal family took its name, "Merovingian"), were fighting on behalf of the surviving Roman administration; for Aegidius, governor of the remains of the province, and his successor Count Paul, used Childeric and his troops against the Visigoths on the Loire.

Childeric died about 481 at Tournai in Belgium, a town about 30 miles north of Cambrai which was perhaps the center of his own small kingdom; there, in 1653, his grave was accidentally uncovered in the middle of a Roman cemetery. Childeric's signet ring, inscribed "CHILDERICI REGIS" – "[seal] of King Childeric" – shows that he called himself a king, and the contents of his grave reveal something of the wealth that might be amassed by a successful, but not yet national, chieftain: his jewelry and the ornaments of his swords were of gold, their surfaces formed into a series of cells built up around intricately cut garnets. This polychrome decoration has its earliest parallels in the east, on the Black Sea coasts and in the Eastern Empire. After Childeric's time it became widely popular among the Franks and their neighbors. But what is remarkable about the objects from Tournai is that they are the earliest securely dated examples of the style and yet they display the metalworking techniques fully developed in the form that they follow almost unchanged for two centuries. That they were imports from more sophisticated areas, perhaps from the empire, is possible; but two pieces, published in 1655 but now lost, were strap ends manufactured in exactly the same polychrome technique as the other jewelry, though shaped in imitation of contemporary Germanic animal ornament. These at least were presumably of local origin, and the other objects from the tomb are likely to be local produces.

Childeric's son Clovis (more properly Chlodovechus, that is Ludwig or Louis) succeeded his father in Tournai, and with his accession the Franks emerge from obscurity, for their history was recorded by a Gallo-Roman aristocrat, Georgius Florentius, known by his ecclesiastical name of Gregory, bishop of Tours.

Gregory of Tours. Gregory was born about 540 in the city of Clermont-Ferrand in central France. His family was distinguished by its traditions of public service, both as imperial senators and as churchmen: he counted four saints among his ancestors (he too was to be canonized) and in 573, on the death of his cousin St Eufronius of Tours, he was elected bishop of Tours in his stead, taking his place in what has not unjustly been described as his "family seat." As Gregory himself notes, all but five of the 18 bishops of Tours who preceded him were his relatives. The responsibilities of these bishops were many. They administered huge church estates; they looked after the spiritual, and frequently the bodily, welfare of their citizens, and they saw to the structure of their churches and the establishment of new foundations. During the initial phases of the migrations, when the secular powers were in decline, the bishops (many of whom had left careers as soldiers or officials) provided much-needed stability for their communities.

After the collapse of the upper Danube frontier two priests, St Severinus and St Constantius, bishop of Lauriacum, with the aid of provincials and a heterogeneous group of barbarian allies, established in lower Austria an almost autonomous military theocracy. The influence of the bishops continued after the establishment of the barbarian kingdoms, for they were the natural leaders of the Catholic populace, and Gregory himself acted as intermediary between Frankish kings, asserted the rights of the Church, and defended his community against royal officers. Gregory's *Ten Books of History*, which we call the *History of the Franks*, were written in the midst of this busy official career. Their purpose was to record contemporary events before they were forgotten, for he had heard that "there is no one who can write a book about what is now happening"; his detail is accordingly fullest for the years of his own manhood, the period from 575 to 591, and his information about Frankish origins is scanty and probably unreliable. But the accession of Clovis son of Childeric is a turning-point in his narrative, for Clovis impressed Gregory with his determination, however bloodthirsty, and his success as the first Catholic king of the Franks, "for he walked before Him with an upright heart, and did what was pleasing in His sight."

The Frankish expansion. For knowledge of Clovis' eventful reign we depend almost entirely on Gregory's narrative. This, unfortunately, contains at least one major error (a battle of 507 misdated to 495/6) and in compiling his account Gregory has either coalesced into one event campaigns fought over a number of years or has altered the order of events towards the end of Clovis' reign, and is thus able to present the Frankish wars of aggression as Catholic crusades against the heretics. Which view is to be preferred is still much disputed, and it affects the interpretation of this important phase of Frankish conquest. Some details, however, are not in doubt.

Clovis was about 16 years old in 481 when he succeeded

The Gothic kingdoms at their greatest extent under Theodoric of Italy; the Franks were still expanding into southern Gaul and the Eastern Empire had not begun its conquests.

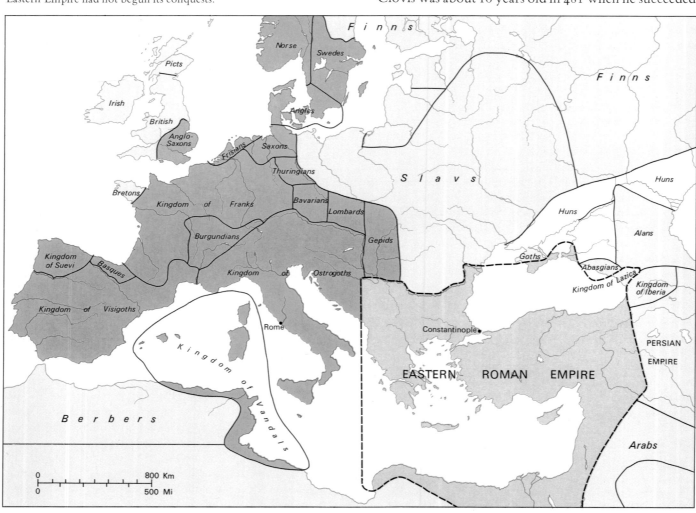

his father to the throne of Tournai. Some five years later, together with his kinsman Ragnachar, king of nearby Cambrai, he attacked Syagrius, the son of the former Roman general Aegidius, who now controlled the "kingdom" of Soissons, the last remnant of Roman Gaul. Syagrius fled to the Visigothic kingdom of Toulouse, only to be handed back to Clovis and murdered in secret, the first recorded of many such assassinations. The kingdom of Soissons was absorbed by the Franks. Subsequently – the date in Gregory's account is vague – Clovis suborned King Ragnachar's nobles, defeated him in battle, murdered him and his brothers, and took over the kingdom of Cambrai. "In this way," says Gregory, "he managed to kill many other kings and his kindred whom he suspected of conspiracy . . . and spread his dominion over all Gaul."

The suppression of Syagrius left Clovis in control of the north, and the remaining areas of western France may at this stage have submitted to him without further warfare: by 496 at least the frontier of his kingdom lay on the Loire. In 491 Clovis was in action against the Thuringians, whose lands lay between the headwaters of the Elbe and Weser, and "subjected them to his rule" – but not permanently, for the Thuringians were to be a problem for the Franks for nearly two centuries longer. A conquest of the Alamanni in 495 was followed by a campaign further south against the Burgundians of the Rhône valley. Even in Gregory's partisan account these Burgundian wars seem to have led to Frankish defeat, but they brought Clovis' armies to the eastern edge of the Visigothic kingdom.

The fall of Toulouse. For nearly 100 years after the treaty settlement of 418 the Visigoths had enjoyed uninterrupted control of southwestern Gaul. Under Theodoric I (who died in 451 fighting Attila) and his sons, Theodoric II and Euric, the Gothic nobles became a landed aristocracy. The kings appreciated Roman values. Theodoric II is credited with ability to read the poems of Vergil; his brother enacted a series of moderate laws and regulations and fostered the Roman bureaucracy. Both were able, with little interference, to expand their frontiers by the annexation of the adjacent areas of Roman Gaul and Spain. The Gallo-Roman upper classes (whose accounts alone survive) were dismayed. St Sidonius Apollinaris, bishop of Clermont-Ferrand, pictured the result of the supremacy of the Arian Visigoths: abandoned churches with roofs collapsing, choked with thorns and brambles, and cattle grazing in the sanctuaries. In the event the result was milder than expected, and the Gallo-Roman landowners speedily adapted themselves to their new masters.

Writing a century later Gregory pictured the conflict between the Franks and the Visigoths as a crusade by Catholics against Arians, and there are indeed signs of unrest among some of the Catholic bishops. The reaction of the townspeople of Rodez, however, is significant: "If you had your way," they are reported as saying to their bishop, "the Franks would take over our territory," and

The barbarian warrior: a tombstone from Dollendorf near Bonn shows the dead man combing his hair (a symbol of vitality) and holding his sword. Comb, sword and the flask at his feet suggest pagan grave goods; but the stone is Christian: its reverse shows Christ in glory, carrying a spear. 6th or 7th century.

they drove the bishop out of the town. When open war finally came, the Visigothic army was joined by a large body of Gallo-Romans under the command of Apollinaris, none other than the son of Sidonius. Such was the ability of the senatorial classes to survive conquest that the same families whose influence controlled the provincials under Roman and then Visigothic administration rose soon to power under the subsequent Frankish rule: Apollinaris himself was appointed bishop of Clermont by the Frankish king in preference to St Quintianus, who had been expelled from Rodez for his Frankish sympathies.

Clovis was by now a Catholic. His conversion is dated by Gregory to 495/6 and linked with a campaign against the Alamanni. But there are reasonable grounds for suspecting that it was not until 505 or 506 that Clovis accepted baptism. If so, the act would have been a calculated attempt to win over staunch Catholics in the Visigothic kingdom, and perhaps to enlist the support of the empire, for the Franks were the first of the barbarian peoples to embrace the faith of the Romans, and so they alone were able to claim alliance and financial support from Constantinople. During 507 the Emperor Anastasius sent, according to Gregory, "consular tablets" to Clovis, who put on a purple tunic and a diadem and went through the town of Tours distributing gold and silver and being acclaimed "consul or Augustus." Whatever the precise significance of the event, it is clear that Clovis and his policies were now receiving imperial approval; a recent conversion to the true faith seems an appropriate occasion for the recognition.

Meanwhile, with or without divine aid, Clovis had launched his attack on the Visigoths. In 507, together with his cousin the son of the king of Cologne, he advanced from Tours to Poitiers, and near Vouillé met Alaric II and his army of Visigoths and Gallo-Romans. Alaric was killed, his army scattered, and the Franks captured Bordeaux and Toulouse. The third city of the Visigothic kingdom, Narbonne, was seized by the Burgundians, and Alaric's successor, his illegitimate son Gesalic, was forced to fall back into Spain with the remnant of his people. A single battle had decided the fate of the prosperous Visigothic kingdom of Toulouse, but the Franks were not yet able to enjoy the fruits of their victory, for their success threatened the security of the Ostrogothic kingdom of Italy.

Theodoric the Great. The Visigoths and their kinsmen and neighbors outside the empire, the Ostrogoths, had followed different paths in the century since the arrival of the Huns in southern Russia. While Alaric I led his people into Italy, the Ostrogoths disappeared from view among the many tribes who joined the Hunnic nomads. After the death of Attila and the collapse of his kingdom, the Ostrogoths of Pannonia (western Hungary) entered into a treaty with the Eastern Empire: in return for tribute they remained quiet. As part of the agreement the Ostrogothic king in 461 sent his nephew, Theodoric, to Constantinople as a hostage. For nine years this young man was brought up in the heart of the empire. When, at the age of about 19, he succeeded to the throne, his people had crossed the frontiers and were migrating slowly around the Balkans.

The Ostrogoths now posed a considerable threat to communications from east to west, and Theodoric was able to extort favorable terms from the Emperor Zeno – tribute, Macedonia to settle in, and a military rank for himself. For the next 15 years Theodoric proved a useful but troublesome ally, able to hold off barbarian attack but liable to turn on Zeno if it suited him, and in 488 he went so far as to besiege Constantinople. Zeno arranged another treaty: Italy had for 12 years been in the hands of the Skirian mercenary leader Odoacer, nominally with imperial support, but in practice as an independent monarch; now Zeno proposed that Theodoric should depose Odoacer. The emperor was doubtless anxious to rid himself of Theodoric and his army. The Ostrogoths for their part had long been at feud with Odoacer's people, who had in a frontier skirmish killed their king, Theodoric's uncle. In

retaliation Theodoric's father had in 469 killed Odoacer's father Edica, a man who had once been Attila's general. The Ostrogoths invaded Italy in 489 and defeated Odoacer's army; Odoacer's remaining forces, like so many defenders of northern Italy, were shut up in fortified cities and the campaign developed into a series of sieges. After a long naval blockade of his capital, Ravenna, Odoacer finally surrendered in 493, and he, his family and his officers (despite the terms of the capitulation) were promptly murdered.

Theodoric settled his troops in the Po valley and in Tuscany (where their estates are still identified by a few Gothic place-names in -*engo*, for example Gotholengo or Offanengo). Disturbance of the *status quo ante* was slight, for the lands which they occupied were mostly those formerly held by Odoacer's barbarians, and the Ostrogoths found themselves welcomed, not least because of their imperial mandate. The land allocation – the granting to the Goths of one third of estates – was carried out by a Roman official, the prefect Liberius, and the Roman senate gave full support to their new king. With such help Theodoric set up a state in which both Goths and Romans were involved; each people was governed by a separate hierarchy, the Goths by their own *comites* (counts), and the Romans by the traditional governing classes. The emphasis was on continuity, a stability which must have delighted the influential landowners of the senatorial class, among whom, living on a pension in comfortable retirement in southern Italy until his death in 510, was the last western emperor, Romulus Augustulus.

Some contemporary propaganda has come down to us in the writings of Theodoric's chief adviser, the Roman senator Cassiodorus. For Roman consumption Cassiodorus publicized (and invented) a genealogy for Theodoric which traced his line back to the family of Hermanaric, the great Ostrogothic chief of the 4th century whose kingdom had fallen to the Huns. While the respectability of the king was thus emphasized, his attachment to Rome was underlined: Theodoric described the former emperors as "our ancestors," and proclaimed himself "born for the good of the state," for "we rejoice in living under Roman law, which we hope to defend with our arms." The words were, perhaps unconsciously, ironical: Romans themselves were forbidden to bear arms.

In his edicts Theodoric was careful to protect the welfare of his Roman subjects, and stressed *civilitas*, "the observance of laws and the respect of established right and privileges." But it is some measure of contemporary lawlessness that even this conscientious king found it necessary to warn his Gothic troops, as they came to Ravenna to receive their customary donative or retainer, not to plunder the surrounding countryside as they passed; and one may doubt that his followers accepted one remarkable decree, without parallel in the barbarian kingdoms: "To seek gold by war is a crime." In practice

Theodoric's mausoleum, built during his lifetime outside his capital at Ravenna, appears plain since the loss of its colonnade on the second story. The dome, a single huge block of limestone, has been likened, fancifully, to a burial mound or to a Gothic domed tent. Grandiose permanency is a more likely motive.

many of Theodoric's edicts must have been difficult to enforce, but the verdict of the contemporary Byzantine historian Procopius is just: "he was very careful to observe justice, he preserved the laws on a firm basis, he protected the land and kept it safe from the barbarians living round about." Many of these barbarians placed themselves under his protection, and his minister Cassiodorus was to write flowery letters of encouragement to petty German princes hard-pressed by the Franks. The gold he spent on subsidies and on the pay of recruits has left an archaeological trail across Europe from the Alps to Scandinavia.

But as Theodoric was thus consolidating his rule, a new threat, as we have seen, was developing in the north: in the later 490s the Franks began their campaigns against the Alamanni and the Burgundians, and advanced into the Swiss Alps. Theodoric attempted to limit the pressure by dynastic marriages. His wife was a sister of Clovis, his daughters married the Burgundian King Sigismund and

Alaric II, king of the Visigoths, and his sister married the Vandal King Thrasamund. When Clovis, undeterred by these alliances, invaded the Visigothic kingdom and killed Alaric, Theodoric was forced to intervene. In 508 his general Ibbas recaptured Narbonne and a couple of years later relieved the city of Arles from siege. Theodoric made no attempt to drive the Franks out of the Visigothic kingdom; his objective, it seems, was more limited – to check the Frankish advance and, by controlling the Visigothic provinces of southern Gaul, to keep them away from the Mediterranean. In 511, after three years of often desultory warfare, Clovis died at the early age of 45; his kingdom was divided between his four sons, and the immediate danger to the Goths passed.

Alaric II's eldest son Gesalic, who may have resented the growing power of the Ostrogoths in Spain, was soon in conflict with Ibbas. In 511 he was forced out of Spain, fled to Africa, then to Gaul, and after another defeat in Spain was caught and killed in Burgundy. His brother and successor Amalaric was still an infant, and Theodoric, his grandfather, who acted as his regent in Spain, thus made himself overlord of the largest territory in western Europe. Spain was administered separately from Italy,

Amalsuntha, daughter and eventual successor of Theodoric the Great, pictured in an ivory diptych of c. 530. The frame is probably intended to depict part of the palace.

classes, whose loyalties lay with the Catholic Church and ultimately with the emperor in Constantinople. The possibility that imperial favor might be withdrawn from Theodoric as it had been from Odoacer made the future of the Ostrogothic kingdom of Italy uncertain, and the Catholic Franks, however barbarous by comparison with the elegant court of Theodoric, were their obvious rivals.

The succession was a further problem, for the kingdom of Theodoric, to an extent unparalleled among the other barbarian realms, was identified with the person of its monarch, who alone united the separate administrations for Goths and Romans. But by the early 520s Theodoric was over 65 years old, with no son to succeed him: his daughter's son was in his infancy. The western Church, increasingly more vocal under its aristocratic bishops, became hostile, and attempted to coerce to its viewpoint not only its own followers but even the subjects of the Eastern Empire. In response to a western demand for action against heretics – which must mean Arians – the Emperor Anastasius in 517 wrote to the pope: "Your holiness, you can thwart me; you can be offensive; but you cannot give me orders." His successor Justin, less urbane, ended the policy of toleration and in 523 issued a law banning from public service all pagans, Jews and heretics. The law was valid in both east and west and the Gothic states were at once put in jeopardy: persecution of Catholics followed. The philosopher Boethius, an influential royal administrator, was imprisoned and executed for conspiracy with the emperor; Pope John I, for his hostility to Arians, was thrown into prison where he died a martyr. The senatorial classes, whose good Boethius claimed to be considering, identified themselves with the Catholic Church, and when Theodoric died in 526 the kingdom of Italy, which he had built up so skillfully, was breaking apart.

The reconquest of Italy and Spain. Theodoric's daughter Amalsuntha, as regent for her son Athalaric, took over Italy. Spain became once more independent, but friendly; the new ruler of Italy agreed to the ending of Spanish tribute and the return of the Visigothic royal treasure; the frontier was fixed along the Rhône, and Ostrogoths and Visigoths again became quite separate peoples. But a crisis was now growing, provoked by Constantinople. The new emperor Justinian in 532 almost succumbed to a popular revolution. In part to divert internal pressures he undertook a crusade against the heretics. In 533 an expeditionary force under the imperial general Belisarius sailed to Africa to suppress the Vandals, under the pretext of avenging Hilderic, an aged Vandal king whom his subjects had deposed in 530. The result was totally unexpected, at least to the military establishment in Constantinople, for within a month of the Byzantine arrival the Vandal army had been defeated, and Carthage fell. Early in 534 the last Vandal king, Gelimer, surrendered and was taken to Constantinople to be paraded in

under the control of a Roman and an Ostrogothic officer, but the economy of the two realms was more closely linked: the tribute of Spain went directly to Theodoric, who in return undertook the royal responsibility of paying to the Visigoths their annual donative.

In the years of prosperity that followed the deaths of Clovis and Gesalic signs of strain appeared in Italy: the obvious cause was religion, for the Goths were still Arians. Theodoric forbade his own people to attempt conversions, and allowed freedom of worship to the Catholics; but he and his people – whatever his aspirations – were separated by a great gulf from the Italian upper triumph through the city. His people were enslaved or enrolled in the army, and as a nation vanished without trace.

At the time of the conquest of Vandal Africa the Gothic kingdoms were in disorder. The Visigoths, despite appeals, were unable to interfere, for they were once more in conflict with the Franks. The cause of the war was personal: King Amalaric's marriage with Clothild, a daughter of Clovis, had been unhappy. Clothild refused to convert to Arianism and appealed for help to her brothers, the four kings of the Franks. In 531 Childebert, king of Paris, marched into southern Gaul, defeated Amalaric at Narbonne, rescued his sister, who promptly died, and (perhaps the real object of the war) annexed in Aquitaine another fragment of the old Visigothic kingdom. Amalaric, trying to take refuge in Barcelona, was assassinated, probably at the instigation of an Ostrogoth, Theodoric's former general Theudis, who promptly seized the throne, but had to fight off further Frankish attack before establishing control of his Gallic provinces. Meanwhile in 534 Athalaric, the young king of Italy, died without an heir. His mother Amalsuntha, still regent, brought in her cousin Theodat to share her power and regularize her position; within a year the regents had fallen out, and Amalsuntha was locked up and murdered by her cousin.

The consequent weakness of both Gothic kingdoms was Justinian's opportunity. Amalsuntha was represented in eastern sources as a mediator between Roman and Goth, and a loyal follower of the emperor – even as a possible convert to Catholicism. It may be true, and in 534 the Ostrogothic government in Sicily had in fact assisted Belisarius' African expedition, but it smacks of imperial propaganda, for Justinian was thus able, as in Africa, to pose as the avenger of a sovereign wrongfully removed from power. In 536 he sent Belisarius and the African army to invade Italy. Theodat was deposed and eliminated by his own nobles, who replaced him by a capable general, Witigis, but the south of Italy and the city of Rome fell swiftly to the invaders.

Northern Italy, where Theodoric had established his army, proved a different matter, for Justinian's generals seriously underestimated Gothic strength, and the war dragged on for year after year. The fragile symbiosis between Goths and Romans was broken: hostages were taken by the Goths to ensure the loyalty of the senatorial class. But the Romans found it equally difficult to identify themselves with the imperial armies, whose composition was no less barbarian than that of the Ostrogoths, and whose ravages in Italy were worse. In the reconquered territories the Roman administrators were replaced by trustworthy Byzantines. In the Gothic realm Romans withdrew from public life – even Cassiodorus retired, to live on for 40 years in a monastery he had founded on his estate at Vivarium in southern Italy.

Witigis surrendered in 540, offering (apparently with the approval of the Ostrogoths) his support to Belisarius only if the latter took Witigis' place as king of the Goths. Belisarius agreed, and took over the principal Gothic stronghold, the fortress city of Ravenna. To the Goths' surprise he then remained loyal to Justinian, and, the war apparently over, sailed back to Constantinople. The Ostrogoths, who had surrendered to the imperial general, not to Justinian, elected new leaders – relatives, significantly, of Theudis, the Ostrogothic king of the Visigoths; but still no help came from Spain.

At this moment, far to the east, Khusro I, shah of Persia, broke his treaty with Constantinople, the "Eternal Peace" of 532, and swept through Syria, capturing and pillaging Antioch, the second city of the empire. Justinian, who had during the western wars been economizing on the defenses of the eastern frontier, recalled troops from Italy, refused reinforcements and devoted all his resources to resisting the Persian threat. The Ostrogoths under their new king Totila immediately took the offensive and began capturing towns in southern Italy. Even in 544, when Belisarius, who had been campaigning against Persia, was sent back to Ravenna with a fresh army, little was achieved. The armies in Italy had not been paid for several years and were in revolt, and Belisarius himself barely escaped capture in 546 when the Goths took Rome. It was only Totila's invasion of Sicily in 550 that roused Justinian to act. Persia was by now quieter, and the breathing space allowed Constantinople to collect a huge army. Recruits were assembled from every side, and the army which in 552 finally broke the strength of the Goths at the foot of Mount Vesuvius included captured Persians as well as a contingent from the kingdom of the barbarous Lombards.

This victory, however costly, and some further slackening in the war against Persia allowed Justinian to turn his attention to Spain. Theudis had been assassinated in 548; his successor Theudigisel in 549. Gregory of Tours, who disliked Goths, was contemptuous: "The Goths had adopted the reprehensible habit of killing out of hand any king who displeased them." Others too were displeased, for the new King Agila found himself confronted by a rebellion among the citizens of the Roman town of Cordoba. The Cordobans, somewhat unexpectedly, cut the royal army to pieces, and Agila was soon threatened by a second revolt, this time led by a Visigothic nobleman, Athanagild, who seems to have had either too sanguine an opinion of his own popularity or an exaggerated view of the losses Agila had suffered at Cordoba. Athanagild, hard-pressed and fearing defeat, made the mistake of appealing for help to Constantinople. Neither revolt is likely to have been engineered by Justinian, for his resources were at that very time stretched in Italy and Persia, and the final Italian expedition was almost ready to sail. But even if he had not planned it, Justinian was ready to accept yet another favorable chance of barbarian disunity, and in 552 sent out to Spain a small army which joined forces with Athanagild just in time to save him from Agila.

After three years of destructive civil war the Visigoths

A Visigothic eagle brooch of gilded bronze and garnet, belonging to the 6th century and believed to come from Calatayud near Saragossa, Spain. Similar brooches, attributed to the Ostrogoths, have been found in Italy.

Byzantine province which survived the campaigns of successive Visigothic kings, until its disintegration in the 620s, at a time when years of Persian pressure against the eastern frontiers were causing the gradual withering-away of all the Byzantine territories in the west.

After the destruction of the Ostrogoths the last of the imperial commanders in Italy, the courtier Narses, remained in Italy and began a reconstruction. Italy had suffered as never before: the city of Milan (which had declared, injudiciously, for the imperial cause) had been razed by the Goths, who had attempted to demolish the walls of all the cities that fell to them in the final campaigns, to avoid their use against them. Rome, besieged three times, was almost deserted. By 547 its population (once over a million) is said to have numbered only 500. The famine caused by the ravages of both armies was followed by pestilence, for bubonic plague, which had raged in Constantinople in 543, spread to the armies and the countryside, before passing westwards as far as north Wales (where it put an end to the unsavory career of one of those tyrants abused by Gildas, Maelgwn of Gwynedd, the "dragon of the island"). In Italy it was still recurring as late as 571, and the country was exhausted. Pope Pelagius wrote in 556, "It is only from the the islands and places overseas that the Roman Church receives some little revenue . . ." Even the senatorial aristocracy, which had survived and ensured continuity in culture and administration through so many changes of overlord, was now broken. But the restoration of Italy might have been possible, and during the 15 years of Narses' rule there are signs of some improvement. All plans were frustrated by a fresh wave of barbarians from the north.

The Lombard invasion. The new migrants, the Langobardi or Lombards, had traveled by the end of the 5th century from the south shore of the Baltic into Austria. During the 6th century they and other barbarians formed a kingdom in Hungary from which they raided the empire, fought against their neighbors the Gepidae of Pannonia, and formed uneasy alliances with the empire and with the Avars, recent nomadic arrivals from the Asiatic steppes. In the course of the wars in Italy Witigis the Ostrogoth appealed to them for aid, but they remained neutral until Justinian agreed to pay subsidies. In the final Italian campaign of 552 some thousands of Lombardic soldiers under the command of their own dukes joined Narses against the Goths and saw for themselves the weakness of Italy, and perhaps something of its potential. By 567 the close presence of their Avar allies in the plains of Hungary was proving an embarrassment, and the Lombard King Alboin decided to move. Pannonia he left to the Avars and, with a motley army which included Bulgars, Gepids and even Saxons, in 568 he invaded Italy.

The downfall of the north was swift: the eastern city of Aquileia fell within a month, and Alboin took over the Po valley; at the end of the next season he captured Milan.

had had enough. Constantinople may now have shown its real intention, and there are some hints that at this time a second and larger expeditionary force was sent to conquer Spain outright. In 555 Agila's followers brought the civil war to a sudden end by murdering their king and electing his rival Athanagild in his place. Both sides then combined against Justinian's troops, but Athanagild found it easier to call in imperial help than to drive it out, for the invaders had by now consolidated their hold on the Mediterranean coast of Spain. There they set up a

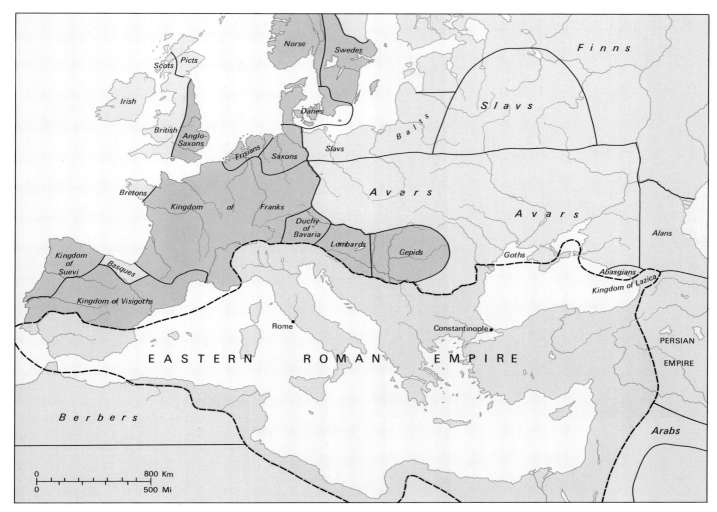

The Frankish kingdoms c. 562 A D. By the end of Justinian's reign the Eastern Empire had conquered Vandal Africa, Ostrogothic Italy and the islands, and part of Visigothic Spain, and the Franks had expanded southwards. But Asiatic nomads, the Avars, now occupied central Europe.

Pavia, still a strong city, took far longer – from 569 to 572 – and during the siege some Lombard war bands crossed the Apennines and spread into Tuscany (to the north of Rome) and passed southwards, perhaps in 571, to found the Lombard dukedoms of Spoleto and Benevento in southern Italy. Alboin himself did not live to enjoy his new kingdom. He was assassinated in 572, apparently at the instigation of his wife, from the skull of whose father, formerly king of the Gepids, he was accustomed to drink wine. His successor reigned only 18 months, and after his murder the chief nobles of the Lombards (36 *duces* or dukes) divided the royal power between them. In warfare this made little difference: a Byzantine army sent in 575 to reconquer Italy was soon driven out. But the lack of a single authority influenced the pattern of settlement. When in 584 another king was finally elected, the Lombards formed not a kingdom but a loose-knit confederacy of dukedoms; each warlord was established

in his fortified city, many of them hostile to their neighbors, and some from time to time even sympathetic to approaches from Constantinople.

Apart from these shifting alliances and despite the blood and treasure spent, the empire now held only the territories around Rome, Ravenna, Naples, Genoa and a handful of smaller cities, under the control of military governors and expensive garrisons. Northern Italy was gradually shaped into a Lombard kingdom based on Pavia and incorporating the dukedoms of the northern cities; the southern dukedoms remained much more independent, and until the 11th century continued to spread around them what the French historian L. Musset has described as "unbelievable disorder." An exodus began, for the battered remnant of the landed aristocracy in growing numbers left their estates and retreated into the protected enclaves of the Byzantine coastal towns, transforming fishing villages into cities but turning their backs on the Italian countryside. There the Lombard armies settled down in kinship groups, supported by, but segregated from, the Romans who still remained working the land. As the civil powers collapsed, the importance of the Church increased.

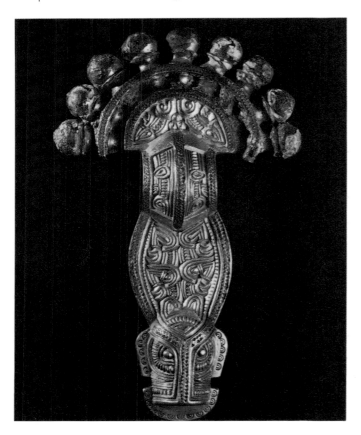

Above: bow-brooch with oval foot and radiate head, one of a distinctive group of brooches found in southern Germany and Italy. From Cividale on the borders of northern Italy; late 6th century, probably Lombardic.

Below: a plate from the helmet of Agilulf, king of the Lombards (590–615). Despite its barbarity the winged victories with banners who flank the king and his guards are not far removed from their Roman originals. North Italian, early 7th century.

The papacy. Service in the Church had for long been a recognized culmination of an official career, and episcopal thrones were commonly filled by aristocratic men whose experience in administration and command was gained not in the priesthood but in the imperial bureaucracy. In an age of increasing asceticism the desire for efficiency might well be at odds with the need for humility and piety. Pope Gregory reflected the conflict when he wrote, sadly, "The man who takes off his secular clothes in order to scramble into ecclesiastical office wants to change his world, not to leave it." But such men were, as we have seen, the natural inheritors of the leadership of their communities, and to a remarkable extent the stability of urban life during the centuries of migration was due to their influence and that of their subordinates.

Monasticism, a life not of administration but of mortification, contemplation and worship, which had its origin before the time of the migrations among the hermits of the eastern deserts, during the disasters of the 5th and 6th centuries grew in its appeal even for the aristocracy. Despite their wish for solitude, ascetics by their reputed sanctity attracted numerous followers anxious to imitate and to contribute to the cause. Vows and gifts to the Roman Church no less than to the monasteries multiplied during the Gothic and Lombardic wars, and the papal see, under Byzantine protection, survived when the Italian monasteries were dispersed by the Lombards. The popes were more than spiritual leaders. They controlled the "Patrimony of St Peter," vast estates, built up by years of pious donations – estates which by the end of the 6th century have been estimated at more than a million acres. The profits were used to feed the multitudes whom the wars had left destitute, for the defense of Rome against the Lombards and for missionary work among the barbarians.

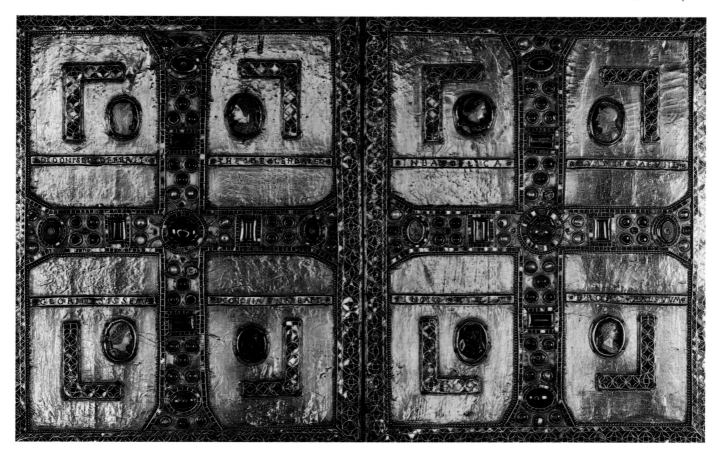

Among the gifts made by Theudelinda to the cathedral she built at Monza is a golden gospel book cover, inscribed with a dedication by the queen to the church, and decorated with enamel, antique cameos, pearls, sapphires and emeralds. Early 7th century.

One pope towers above all in these dark centuries, Gregory the Great, not least because of the survival of many of his writings and a vast amount of correspondence, over 800 letters. Like so many before him, Gregory had been an important secular figure, apparently Prefect of Rome (president of the senate and administrator of the city's food supplies) until in 575 at the height of the Lombard invasions he retired to be a simple monk in one of the seven monasteries which he himself had founded. Although unwilling to take up any office, he was persuaded to act as papal nuncio in Constantinople and finally in 590 on the death of Pope Pelagius was, in the words of his contemporary, Gregory of Tours, "dragged to the Basilica of St Peter and, after consecration, presented to the city as Pope." It is some measure of the burdens of his position that Pope Gregory later wrote: "In the name of 'bishop' I am really brought back to secular life . . . in no part of my worldly career can I remember equal slavery."

His correspondence confirms his words. Many letters deal with the details of landownership. To his officer in Sicily, for example, he wrote: "All those herds of horses . . . are to be disposed of, and only 400 young mares are to be kept for breeding . . . one to be sent to the tenant of each farm . . ." At the same time he was organizing the churches in Africa and Sardinia, giving advice to bishops in Gaul and Spain, preparing for the conversion of Anglo-Saxon England and pragmatically attempting to reconcile the Lombards and the Byzantine generals. The mantle of the imperial government was falling on the shoulders of the bishop of Rome.

The Lombards were perhaps mostly pagan, their chiefs nominally Arians, but in the 590s the Arian Visigoths of Spain were beginning to follow their King Reccared into the Catholic communion, and with care the Lombards might be persuaded to take the same road. Gregory's ally in the task was Theudelinda, a Bavarian Catholic princess who was the queen of the Lombardic King Authari and of his successor Agilulf. Both kings were energetic and on the whole successful campaigners against their barbarian neighbors, against their own dukes and against the Byzantine commanders, and in their time the Lombard kingdom of northern Italy became stable and prosperous. Their queen remained a pious Catholic who founded several religious houses and encouraged St Columbanus' Irish monastery at Bobbio, all within Lombard territory. Gregory sent to her gifts, some of which still survive in the treasury of her cathedral of Monza, including 16 silver flasks made to contain oil from the lamps used in the tombs of martyrs, venerated as a prophylactic against disease. Similar flasks, apparently copies, were found in the crypt of St Columbanus' church at Bobbio, and were presumably gifts from Theudelinda to the new monastery. In 603, shortly before Gregory's death, the queen even had her eldest son baptized a Catholic. Agilulf probably remained Arian, but was clearly tolerant: a letter of St Columbanus, indeed, credits him with the desire to foster the Catholic Church.

To end the endemic state of war was essential, and, despite the considerable reluctance of the emperor, who expressed disquiet about the growing independence of the papacy, Gregory managed to bring Agilulf and the Byzantine commander together. In 599, when Avars were threatening the Danube frontier and distracting the attention of the empire, a treaty was signed, which (though for only two years in the first instance) marked the belated imperial recognition of the presence in Italy of an established Lombard kingdom.

The Frankish kingdoms. While Arian Spain and Italy were suffering from the attentions of the Eastern Empire, the kingdom established by Clovis had been evolving towards the pattern which for centuries determined political frontiers in western Europe. At Clovis' death his realm was divided between his four sons. However repugnant the notion was to Gallo-Romans like Gregory of Tours, such partition was normal behavior, and (as in the case of many societies practicing partible inheritance) each part of the father's possessions was divided between his heirs – each of whom received his share of the ancestral lands in northern Gaul and of the newly conquered lands to the south and west. The division between kings had little effect on administration, which continued to be local, based on the individual cities. But it raised the likelihood of civil wars between kindred who now had the resources to turn family feuds into large-scale devastation.

The partition was not permanent, and Clovis' youngest son, Chlotar or Lothar I, king of Soissons for nearly 50 years, outlived his elder brothers and their heirs to become for a short time (558–61) sole king of the Franks; but at his death the kingdom was once more divided among the four sons who survived him. Civil war, assassination and intrigue, and complex partitions are the details of Frankish history during the 6th and 7th centuries, involving what the historian of Italy Thomas Hodgkin once called "a wearisome succession of Chilperics and Childeberts and Theodorics, [who] scarcely exhibit even a vice which can help us to distinguish them from one another." During these turbulent years the regions within the kingdom of Clovis, lands to which the name "Francia" was being given by the end of the 6th century, began to grow apart. The old Frankish lands of the Rhine and northern Gaul, to which a series of wars added parts of Bavaria, Alamannia, Thuringia and Saxony, formed the Germanic kingdom of Austrasia ("East Lands"); the conquered lands of the west,

still comparatively Romanized and with a smaller Germanic element in the population, were called Neustria ("New Lands"); the kingdom of the Burgundians, absorbed by the Franks in 534 at the start of the Gothic wars, formed a separate unit, as did from time to time Aquitania, a substantial part of the former Visigothic kingdom of southwestern Gaul now made into a march-land between Francia and Spain.

The sons of Clovis continued his aggressive policy towards their neighbors. Childebert of Paris in 531 invaded the Visigothic kingdom and crushed King Amalaric; Chlodomer of Orléans was killed in 524 during an attack on the Burgundians, and the subsequent murder of his sons by his brothers, and the partition of his inheritance, were a longstanding cause of dispute; Theuderic I of Austrasia and Chlotar I of Soissons made successful inroads upon the Saxons and Thuringians. Despite Frankish alliance with the empire, Theuderic's son Theudebert in 539 allowed an army of his recently conquered subjects the Burgundians to join the Ostrogoths against Belisarius, and soon himself invaded Italy to ravage Goths and Romans alike.

The arrival in Italy of Frankish armies in search of plunder was a frequent event in the long years of invasion. The spur was almost certainly economic: as long as the Frankish kingdoms continued to grow the kings were able to support their followers and reward their nobles with the fruits of conquest. When expansion ceased the royal position had to be maintained by disbursement of the king's own accumulated resources. The Merovingians had taken over the former imperial estates in Gaul, and augmented them by confiscations, but land had constantly to be alienated and the royal patrimony could not in safety be allowed to waste away in donations and grants. The Roman land tax and the poll tax on non-Franks continued to bring in revenue, but the free Franks themselves were exempt from personal taxation, and the granting (from favor, for services or to ensure loyalty) of immunity to persons, religious establishments or even to cities (like Tours) deprived the crown of much-needed finance.

Attempts to introduce new schemes or to reform the abuses of old taxes met with determined resistance. When Theudebert died in 548, his minister, the Gallo-Roman patrician Parthenius, (as some measure of his success in taxation) was stoned to death by a mob. In 584 the Frankish count Audo escaped a similar fate only by his flight to sanctuary in the cathedral of Paris. The Church, whose huge estates made its bishops among the largest landowners in the kingdom, opposed the tax gatherers no less stoutly than did the free Franks, and Gregory of Tours tells several improving stories about remission of taxes and destruction of tax lists, without appreciation that the decline in the ability of the Merovingians to reward loyalty would soon disturb the stability of their kingdoms. But the king as a successful war leader could gain reputation and treasure by annual campaigns against his neighbors, and during the later 6th century the attacks on

Italy could also be represented as the bringing of aid to the imperial armies beleaguered by the Lombards. In this way in 584 a huge Byzantine subsidy persuaded the regents of young Childebert II of Austrasia to occupy the Po valley. Shortly afterwards a substantial bribe from the Lombards persuaded them to return home, much to the fury of the emperor, who demanded long and in vain the repayment of his gold.

Financial objectives, however, were not the only motives behind Frankish aggression. Success brought personal prestige, and a feeling of superiority over other barbarians. Theudebert, grandson of that Clovis who in 507 had been hailed as "Augustus," and himself soon to become a figure in Germanic epic, began minting coins modeled on those of Constantinople, but with his own name and image in place of that of the emperor. About 539 he described his kingdom in a proud letter to Justinian: "By the grace of God we have conquered the Thuringians, acquired their lands and destroyed their royal family. The Swabians [Alamanni] are now subject to our majesty. The Saxons and the Eucii have placed themselves voluntarily in our hands, and our domain stretches as far as the Danube, the borders of Pannonia and the Ocean."

The barbarian cultures. Where so much is known from detailed and contemporary accounts the part played by archaeology in our knowledge of specifically political, legal or military events in these kingdoms must needs be small. The archaeological evidence itself is of limited quality: with only a very few exceptions no rural settlements have been found comparable to the great series of the Dutch and north German coastlines, and outside northern Europe the excavation of post-Roman urban sites is still in its infancy. The bulk of our material comes from cemeteries. Here the total number of graves is enormous, probably in excess of 50,000, but the spread of investigation is uneven: concentrated work in eastern Francia and Alamannia has produced hundreds of separate cemeteries; exploration in central Spain, the heartland of the Visigothic kingdom, has uncovered a number of medium-sized and small cemeteries and one, near Segovia, with at least 8,000 burials. Elsewhere, significant distributions are hard to find: in northern Italy a few Lombardic cemeteries, in western Francia burials of Gothic or mixed Gothic and Frankish origin. In most cases the excavations are old, and the techniques of digging and recording inadequate.

The burial rite in almost every case was at least influenced by Christianity, and the cemeteries thus are preponderantly of inhumations. This affects the sorts of material available for study, for the distinctive types of pagan cremation urns which, as we have seen, reveal much of the regional patterns within the Anglo-Saxon kingdoms, are here absent, and studies of the somewhat repetitive vessels that do occur have not yet added greatly to knowledge. In the place of pottery as the principal grave goods we find dress ornament – buckles, brooches, and other jewelry – such as would be destroyed or distorted in pagan funeral pyres, and the "warrior's portion" – arms, shield and helmet – the interment of which (though ecclesiastically improper) was too deeply ingrained in barbarian feeling to be eradicated until the 8th century.

Broad regional distinctions can be made between the southwest of Europe and the Frankish north. The most

widespread form of bow-brooch has a semicircular head, from which protruding knobs radiate, and an oval or lozenge-shaped foot. The simplest and earliest examples of this shape, with plain or only slightly decorated surfaces, occur in southern Russia and Hungary, are paralleled by scattered finds in France and Italy and occur in some quantity in central Spain. The type is therefore frequently termed "Visigothic." In northern Gaul and Germany the same bow-brooch types are found, but the distinctive version has a straight-sided foot and the favorite decoration is in "chip-carving," a combination of ridges and hollows which produces a series of highlights and shadows across the surface of the metalwork. Brooches imitating the shapes of creatures – generally birds or fishes – are found in all areas. In Spain and Italy, however, these are usually large "eagle" brooches; in Francia and neighboring lands we find the smaller "falcon" brooches; in the upper Rhine a more localized group of S-shaped "serpent" brooches distinguishes a subculture. Round brooches, either chip-carved or multicolored, are rare in Spain but common elsewhere, especially in northern Gaul and in Saxony.

The use of semiprecious stones in jewelry is general in migration-period art, but here too distinctions can be made. In the earliest polychrome work of this sort, from

6th- and 7th-century pottery from Herpes-en-Charente (1, 4, 6, 7), Auvergne (2), and St Loup on the Marne (3, 5), showing roulette patterning, horizontal rilling from the potter's wheel, and the high quality of the surface finish. As with the glassware, the Frankish potteries continue Roman traditions.

Hungary and further east, the stones are studs, widely spaced and protruding from the surface of the metalwork. The western links of this technique are with Spain. In Francia a more sophisticated treatment is normal, for the stones are cut into flat sheets and their edges are shaped into minute steps and curves; the goldwork is then built up around them in thin strips, and the piece presents a flat multicolored surface of gold and, usually, red garnets. This technique spreads in the 6th century to Spain, but the more barbaric "studding" of jewelry is here never totally abandoned.

These local fashions in metalwork thus correspond only in a very broad sense to the political units of the historical kingdoms. More revealing, indeed, is the way in which styles ignore frontiers: the brooches with semicircular heads, radiating knobs and long rectangular feet have the center of their distribution on the Rhine with outliers near Soissons, and are thus clearly "Frankish." But the same brooches are found in the cemeteries of Alamannia,

Bavaria and even Thuringia, and in these areas "Gothic" types too are not unknown. Other designs such as the S-shaped brooches of the upper Rhine or the iron buckles inlaid with silver of Switzerland seem from their distribution to be of local manufacture under Frankish artistic influence. While a few examples of these "Frankish" or "Alamannic" styles occur in northern Italy, and even in Pannonia on the Danube, within Francia itself the type is confined almost entirely to the eastern region, Austrasia.

In those few cemeteries excavated in the west the jewelry, radiate brooches whose feet are oval or lozenge-shaped, shows Gothic influence, but the styles can be very mixed. At the cemetery of Herpes near Angoulême, for example, the material culture was identified in the 19th century as "Visigothic." More recent study has shown that many of the objects belong to the 6th century, after the Frankish conquest of the region, and Frankish contacts are obvious, especially in the pottery styles and the inlaid buckles; but another of the buckles has its best parallels in Spain, and among the brooches are two clearly Visigothic examples. Much more remarkable are two groups of ornate square-headed and saucer-shaped brooches, whose nearest parallels are among the Anglo-Saxons in southern England. The quality of the excavation at this important site was unfortunately insufficiently good to make it certain whether this complex blend of cultures was the result of widespread trade contacts or of mixed settlements. It serves, nevertheless, as a warning against the assumption that barbarian groups were uniform.

Perhaps the most provoking part of the study of barbarian metalwork is the difficulty which besets attempts to trace the styles found in the kingdoms of western Europe back to their origins in the historically known homelands of the various peoples concerned in the migrations. The fashion for polychrome jewelry, for example, has been traced back to the studded brooches of the 4th-century Greco-Pontine cultures of the Black Sea,

Radiate brooches from the cemetery at Herpes-en-Charente, SW France. The lozenge-foot brooch (*left*) was fashionable in Spain and Italy; that with straight-sided foot (*right*) in eastern France and Germany. They are thus often distinguished as "Visigothic" and "Frankish" types. British Museum, 6th century.

The distribution of brooches with radiate heads and straight-sided feet, clustering thickly in the Frankish homelands near the Rhine. These brooches, of silver or bronze, varying considerably in the style of decoration and number of knobs, belong in the main to the 6th century. After N. Åberg and H. Kühn.

and studded pieces similar to these archetypes are found from Hungary through northern Gaul, and in Spain continued to be manufactured until the 6th century. The skillful polychrome technique using flat and interlocking garnets, however, appears suddenly at Tournai in 481, and in identical form, perhaps a little later, on a sword pommel from Lavoye near Metz. For neither have convincing antecedents been found, and the technique, so suddenly evolved, continues with surprising conservatism into the 7th century.

It is equally difficult to identify "Frankish" cultures in Germany before the 5th-century settlements within the empire or to trace the origins of north German animal ornament before its flowering in the course of the same century. In view of the continued use by the Franks of the late Roman pottery and glassware industries of the Rhine, one may, in fact, wonder to what extent these examples of barbarian metalwork are truly barbarian, for the techniques employed – chip-carving, precise stone-cutting and accomplished bronze-casting – belong to the craftsmen of the late Roman factories, men who, it seems, were now providing for their new masters exuberant jewelry in styles which they had not previously enjoyed. The survival and eventual modification of Roman institutions, traditions and language during the migrations are a recurrent theme of the documentary sources; it is by no means inappropriate that the study of the exuberant "barbarian" metalwork styles should lead to the same conclusion.

The Victory of the Church

The missionaries, Italian, Frankish or Anglo-Saxon, who were sent out to convert the heathen to Christianity were confronted by a paganism which was strongly held. Their predecessors, the priests who preached the new imperial religion to early 4th-century rustics, encountered the adherents of a Roman pantheon which, through time and tolerant philosophy, had lost much of its early teeth, and the followers of deities who, though still with recognizable Celtic attributes, had become Romanized, and civilized. Dark forces were seen to be still at work in the forests of northern Europe, evil totems, impious graves and sacrifices. The reality of the threat gave force to the catechism in which St Boniface's German converts were required to renounce their heathen beliefs: "I forsake all the devil's works and words, Thunor and Woden and Saxnote, and all the fiends that are their companions." The alien religion of Christianity, readily adopted by the conquered because it had proved strongest in battle, during the struggles of the free Germans against the Catholic Franks was a symbol of foreign oppression. The victory of the Church, partially military, partially through persuasion and teaching, is marked by the still-surviving church buildings, a spread of architectural relics that by the year 1000 had extended across Europe to the south coast of Greenland.

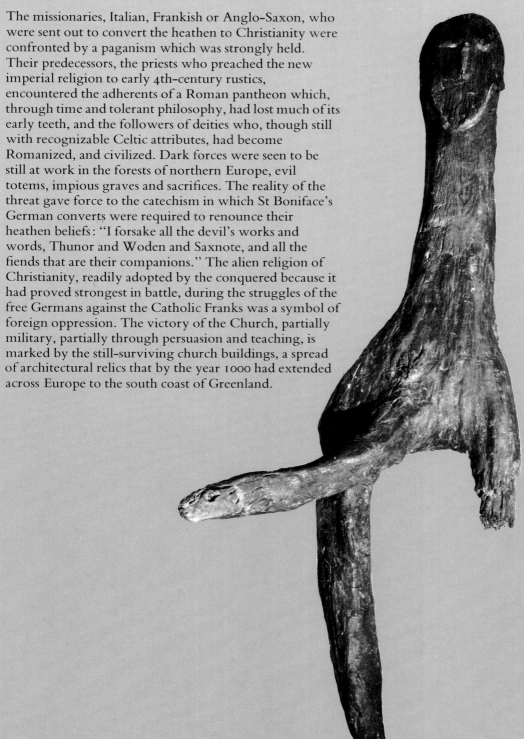

The official adoption of Christianity as the imperial religion (marked by the first general Church Council at Nicaea in 325) changed the role of buildings intended for worship. The churches of the early Christians were private and small. The state religion demanded urban churches sufficiently large to accommodate huge congregations. Buildings of this sort were already available in the great halls, their roofs often supported on rows of columns, used in the marketplaces of the cities of the empire as commercial exchanges and judgment halls. These *basilicae* (literally "royal porticoes") provided the model for the first urban churches of the 4th century, and in these new churches the officers, bishops and priests, celebrated a liturgy which borrowed much of its flavor from the imperial court. The bishop's garments and throne were those of a magistrate; his entry to the basilica and solemn procession led to a high altar that stood below a colonnaded pediment (like that below which the emperor showed himself to the people) and might be placed within an apse (a semicircular or rectangular recess) like that within which a magistrate would sit enthroned.

Opposite: the serenity of an established religion: the wooden statue of the Virgin from the church at Giske, Sunnmøre, Norway. Historisk Museum, Bergen, Norway.

Previous page: wooden idol from a peat bog. Broddenbjerg, Viborg, Denmark. First half of 1st millennium A D. National Museum, Copenhagen.

Below: the basilica of S. Paolo fuori le mura, on the Ostian Way outside Rome. Built in 385 above the shrine of St Paul, the total width of the church was 240 feet and its length over 300 feet. At the end of the nave stood a broad, continuous transept, in which the altar was placed, and the vista was closed by a huge apse. The basilica, seen here in the 18th-century engraving by Piranesi, was razed by fire in 1823 and subsequently totally rebuilt.

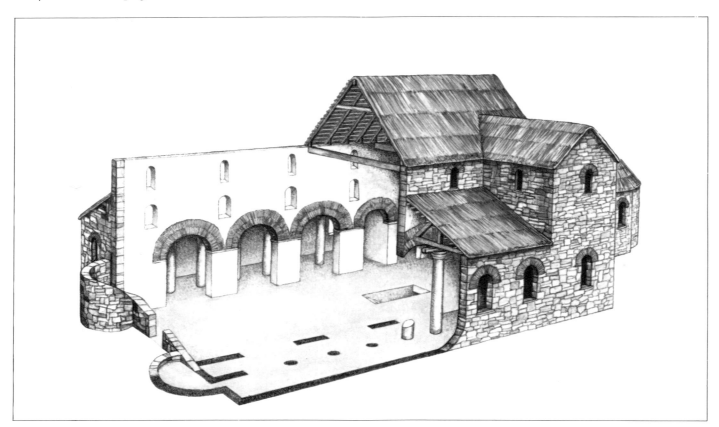

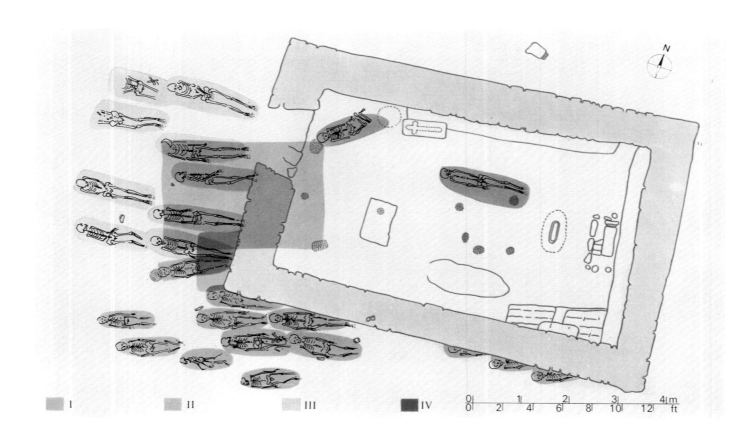

I   II   III   IV

Below: the development of the monastic church of St Augustine, Canterbury, Kent. The first church of c. 605 consisted of a nave and (?) apsidal chancel flanked by lateral chapels. A smaller chapel of c. 620 stood to the east. About 750 a further chapel was added to the north, and in the 10th century the church was extended by a new west porch; later a detached chapel and belfry tower were added to the west. Finally the detached churches were linked by a great octagon, modeled on continental designs, which was demolished before its completion, during the replacement of the Saxon complex by a Romanesque church (1070–87).

In the countryside there was little need for buildings like the great basilicas of the Roman cities. Few churches within the newly converted Anglo-Saxon kingdoms matched those of the Mediterranean world. Typical of the small Saxon churches is Escombe, Durham (*above*), a tall, narrow church of simple plan (a plain nave and square chancel) built perhaps in the 8th century.

Opposite above: a monumental basilica was built in the 670s, originally as a monastic church, at Hexham, then a rural area in Northumberland. Its site (empty of buildings until the unfortunate erection in 1910 of the present nave of Hexham parish church) was trenched in 1908–10, and the foundations then recorded indicate that the church was a four-aisled building about 100 feet long and 65 wide, with a transept at its eastern end and stair turrets on its west front, leading to galleries and an upper chamber. Steps in the nave led to the still-surviving crypt below the altar, and a detached chapel stood beyond its east end. As William of Malmesbury noted in the 12th century, "Those who have visited Italy say that at Hexham they see the glories of Rome repeated." Its founder, the ambitious Wilfrid, bishop of York, had himself stayed in Rome. After plans by H. M. and J. Taylor.

Opposite below: Ardwall Isle, Kirkcudbright, Scotland. The development of a small religious site: (I) a small shrine of the 5th or 6th century; (II) timber mortuary chapel of the 6th century; (III) stone chapel of the 7th or 8th century; (IV) graves of c. 1000 A D. After C. Thomas.

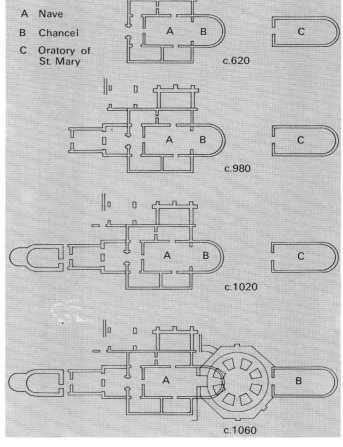

A Nave
B Chancel
C Oratory of St. Mary

c.620

c.980

c.1020

c.1060

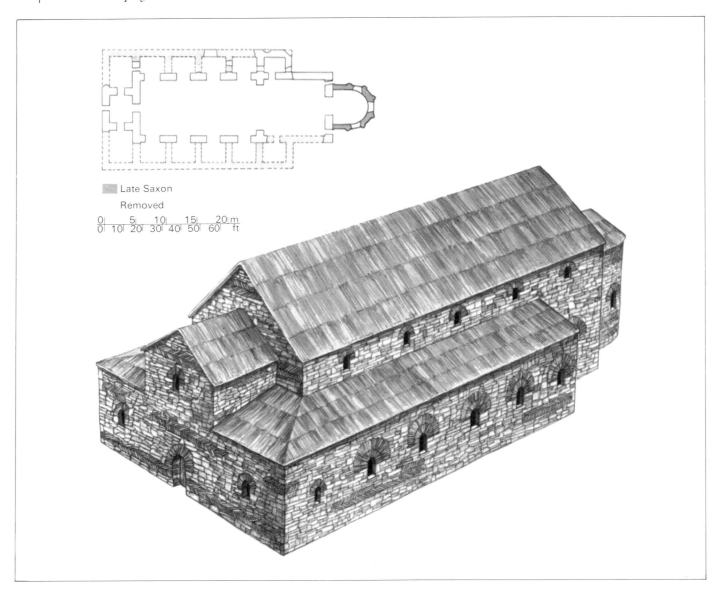

Above: Brixworth, Northamptonshire (described by the architectural historian A. W. Clapham as "perhaps the most imposing architectural memorial of the 7th century yet surviving north of the Alps"), poses several problems. The date of c. 670 sometimes cited rests on no good authority, and despite its preservation the 7th-century ascription is no more certain. The church has now lost its lateral chapels, its apsidal sanctuary has been rebuilt, and its low western porch has been heightened to form a belfry tower with a protruding staircase turret; but the elements of the reconstruction are tolerably clear. In an Anglo-Saxon context it was a major building, probably erected under the influence of the thriving Kentish Church. After plans by H. M. and J. Taylor.

Opposite: the west front of Corvey on the Weser, Germany, a monastery founded in 822 by monks from Corbie in Picardy. The monumental west front, built between 873 and 885, is in the style evolved in the Carolingian renaissance of the late 8th and early 9th centuries. Two lofty towers flank the nave (whose façade was heightened by two stories in the middle of the 12th century). Behind them stood a massive square tower towards the western end of the nave. The spires are not original.

Late Saxon

Removed

0 5 10 15 20 m
0 10 20 30 40 50 60 ft

While the Germanic kings were transforming themselves from barbarian chieftains into national rulers whose existence even the emperor might acknowledge, the life of their subjects continued, so far as one can tell, without interruption in a steady round of subsistence farming. In general, urban life declined: excavations in the Roman cities of northern Gaul and Germany have shown that during the 6th and 7th centuries huge areas of the old towns were unoccupied; where townsmen survived, in fact, they seem to have lived in a series of separate nucleated settlements within the extensive enclosures of the former Roman town walls.

Outside established towns, in the forests and marshlands which dominated the landscape even during the Roman period, the bulk of the population must have lived in hamlets and small villages. One such, at Brebières between Cambrai and Tournai, seems to have been a ribbon development of sunken-floor huts, the largest no more than 15 feet by 12, between a main road and an area of marsh. The earliest part of the settlement, four scattered huts, belongs to the years before 550. By 600 a small hamlet of at least a dozen huts was spread in a line about a quarter of a mile long. During this period are some signs of prosperity, and the rubbish inside the huts includes glassware and bronze tools. In the 7th century the hamlet shrank to perhaps five or six huts, and was abandoned about 700. The village certainly extended beyond the area available for study, for a hut of similar type was uncovered in a small hole some 30 yards to the north of the main group; how far beyond is uncertain, but the occupation in no part of the excavated zone could be described as dense. Contrary to expectations, the diet of the inhabitants of Brebières included almost nothing in the way of game animals – deer, birds or rabbits: what meat they ate was largely pork and a little beef, presumably their own stock.

All the structures found at Brebières were sunken-floor huts. At Gladbach, north of Cologne, the excavation of part of a 7th-century village revealed more than 20 such huts, half a dozen of which were grouped in a ring around a substantial timber house, some 25 by 20 feet in size, which the excavators have reconstructed, with considerable optimism, as an irregularly planned bungalow-like dwelling with five rooms. A little further north, beside the Rhine, excavations in a sand quarry at Wittenhorst uncovered a fragment of a late 7th- or 8th-century Frankish village which contained several sunken-floor huts, one perhaps a weaving shed, and two large wooden houses measuring about 40 by 20 feet. Here trade contacts are evident: the pottery from the village included early examples of the 8th-century products of the revived Rhineland industry. Only one of the sites so far examined in the area, Warendorf, beside the river Ems in Westphalia, shows the same density of occupation and the superimposed phases of building that one finds in the settlements of the *terpen* on the North Sea coast. At Warendorf nearly 200 structures have been uncovered,

belonging to at least four successive villages occupied from about 650 to 800. In the virtual absence of observed stratigraphy the interpretation of the settlement plan is to a degree conjectural. The structures form clusters: at the center of each stands a long rectangular hall, up to 90 feet in length; around it lie one or more smaller rectangular buildings, some perhaps barns, and groups of sunken-floor huts. Other sets of postholes have been seen as the bases for cart sheds and for raised haystacks of types that can still be seen in the Rhineland. The complexity and size of this settlement, by no means all of which has yet been excavated, distinguish it from the known Frankish sites further westwards, and the pottery belongs not to the Rhine but to the North Sea coast. It seems, indeed, that this large village was an outlier of these northern nucleated settlements, and its foundation has been associated with Saxon expansion inland; its abandonment about 800 has plausibly been seen as a result of Charlemagne's conquest of Saxony.

Peasants and nobles in the barbarian kingdoms. However important the investigation of settlements is to our understanding of the manner in which people live, the results of these and similar excavations are too partial, and the sites too scattered, to allow firm conclusions about the social levels of their inhabitants. Clearer evidence about settlement patterns and about the structure of barbarian society comes from the cemeteries, or rather from those comparatively few cemeteries which have been totally excavated and adequately published. The occasional very large cemetery, such as the huge Visigothic burial ground at Castiltierra near Segovia, catered for a local population of perhaps two or three thousand. Whether they lived in small towns or in many scattered villages is generally unknown. But the more normal small cemeteries, typically from 50 to 300 burials in a century, must have belonged to no more than half a dozen extended families or kinship groups. The inhabitants of a single village may indeed have used more than one cemetery at a time, but in those areas where significantly large numbers of cemeteries have been discovered it seems more likely they did not; and it is, of course, possible that the inhabitants of a number of dispersed farms used a single burial ground. In this respect, then, the cemeteries confirm the picture derived from settlement archaeology – one of scattered hamlets.

Skeletal remains in the cremation cemeteries, despite the normal inadequacy of combustion, are rare, and it is from the inhumation burials that we get most of our knowledge of the people themselves. Their expectancy of life was short: the largest age group is commonly from 15 to 30 years, and under a quarter of the population reached their fifties. Brief lives seem to have been the lot even of the nobility: King Clovis himself, as we have seen, died in his forties. His son's wife, Arnegunde, on the evidence of her skeleton, was aged about 45, and an anonymous

Peasants at work: an illumination in an early 11th-century manuscript (dated 1028) of Archbishop Raban Maur's *On the Universe*, a 9th-century encyclopedia drawing its material from both Classical and theological sources. Monte Cassino, Italy.

Frankish princess buried in Cologne cathedral was no more than 30 years old. Even the last of the great Merovingian kings, the heroic Dagobert, when he died in 639, was only 36.

As the various kingdoms stabilized during the 6th and 7th centuries, the Germanic customary laws by which their peoples had been governed were codified and committed to writing. Early law codes (some updated and corrected in the 8th and 9th centuries) survive from the Visigoths – these the earliest, belonging to the 5th century with later alterations – the Franks (the "Salian" laws of the 6th century), the Lombards (640s), the Frisians, the Bavarians, the Alamanni, and from the 6th- and 7th-century kings of Anglo-Saxon Kent and Wessex. Most are written in Latin, and much of their judicial thought derives from the empire and the Church, and owes less than appears to the primitive customs of the barbarians. But these laws tell us something of the structure of society.

It was clearly hierarchical, most obviously to be seen in the varying amounts of money due as recompense to the victim or his kin for personal injury or death and designed to end vendetta after assault or murder. These fines were graded in two ways. In the first place according to the gravity of the offense: the 7th-century legislation of the Lombard King Rothari even distinguishes between the fines to be paid, for example, for the amputation of individual toes and fingers – for a freeman from 2 *solidi* for the little toe to 17 *solidi* for the index finger. Secondly, the fines varied according to the social class of the victim. All codes distinguish between free and unfree, and many preserve a distinction between Roman and German, even to the extent of providing separate legal systems for each people. Not all now state explicitly which precise social grades were recognized; but they all must once have had tables of comparison to allow calculation of individual cases. From the laws of King Aethelbehrt of Kent, for example, we learn that an offense against a *dependant* of a husbandman (a *ceorl*) cost the offender 6 shillings; against the dependant of a nobleman (an *eorl*) 12 shillings; and against a royal dependant 50 shillings. Elsewhere in the Kentish code we find a further subdivision of the dependants of the gentry into classes valued at 12 and 20 shillings. Homicide was more expensive. The blood money varies from that for a slave (generally about 50 shillings), through that for freemen (in classes varying from some 60 to 200 shillings), to the compensation for the death of nobles, from 300 to as much as 1,200 shillings for a *thegn*, or companion of the king, in 7th-century Wessex and Mercia.

These documentary sources give us but little idea of the numbers of the various classes, or of their proportionate size within their societies. Some clues come from the excavated cemeteries, where the quality and numbers of grave goods buried with the dead give indications of status. The Frankish code assesses the cost of a warrior's full military equipment as equivalent to the price of 20 oxen – the plow teams of ten peasant holdings – and in general the possession of a sword seems to be the mark of a man of importance, for this most aristocratic of weapons (one in which the technology of the barbarians reached its most sophisticated level) is found in few graves. At the 6th-century cemetery at Bifrons, Kent, for example, about 150 burials were excavated, but only 63 were wealthy enough to have grave goods. Of these, eight were of richly adorned women, and only five were of men with swords. In a similar but smaller cemetery at Hellmitzheim near Nuremberg in Germany, of 31 burials only two were of men with swords; in the same area the cemetery of Kipfenberg contained some 86 graves: this was a poorer community for in only one was a man buried with a sword. On average one in ten to twenty men was buried with his sword; of the rest a larger number, perhaps one in three to six men, was accompanied by a large single-edged knife, the *sax* or *scramasax*, or by a spear – both much less expensive weapons than swords. In a few cemeteries the proportions are so different that they must be special cases: at Sarre, Kent, a large cemetery of over 250 male and female graves produced no fewer than 26 swords, and eight of the twelve men buried in the small Frankish burial ground of Gnotzheim owned swords. Sarre, at the road bridge between mainland Kent and the island of Thanet, was perhaps the cemetery for a guard post, while the Gnotzheim cemetery lay just outside the ditches of a Roman fort; in both we may be dealing with a warrior society. In the normal cemeteries it is tempting to equate the sword-burials with what would be later termed the "lords of the manor," and the richly garbed women's graves as their female dependants.

A few graves stand out as being so remarkably rich that their occupants are likely to have been figures of national importance. Within the village church at Morken near Cologne rescue excavation in 1956 uncovered an early 7th-century burial of a man with sword, shield, spears and axe, a superb gilt-bronze helmet, glassware, buckles and other grave goods. Some 25 miles to the north, during the steady investigation of a huge cemetery at Krefeld-Gellep, workers in 1962 came upon the grave of a warrior buried about 630 AD with objects comparable to those from Morken but even more lavishly ornamented with gold and garnets, and including a silver spoon imported from the Mediterranean. As in the case of the plain sword-burials of the rural communities the rareness of the discovery gives an indication of status: the Krefeld-Gellep "chieftain" was by far the richest of more than 2,000 interments in this cemetery: he is likely to have been a great landowner, perhaps even the local count.

At the higher end of the social scale such nobles can hardly be distinguished from royal kindred. In southern England an aristocratic burial of about 620, poorly excavated at Taplow, Buckinghamshire, in 1882, contained elaborate gold and garnet jewelry and a Mediterranean bronze bowl: the grave may well have been of one of the local under-kings. More clearly royal are two mid-6th-century graves found in 1959 below Cologne Cathedral: one was that of a woman aged about 30, who

The burial chamber within the Frankish church at Morken near Cologne. The 7th-century warrior in his coffin is surrounded by weapons and grave goods. After K. Böhner.

The helmet from the Morken grave. It is made of riveted iron plates, covered by a framework of decorated and gilded bronze sheets, and has been dented by sword blows. The chain-mail neck guard is a reconstruction. Early 7th century.

Signet ring and cloisonné garnet jewelry of Queen Arnegunde (died c. 570) from her grave in the church of St Denis, Paris.

was wearing a gold headband and quantities of gold and garnet jewelry, and was accompanied by numbers of bronze and glass vessels; the other contained the body of a boy aged about six, who had been buried with warrior's equipment, including a miniature helmet, and, most significantly, a lathe-turned wooden stick which was probably a toy scepter. The contents of these graves and their prestigious location within the cathedral rather than in an open graveyard make it certain that both belonged to members of the royal family of Austrasia. Another Frankish royal burial, excavated in 1958 within the church of St Denis, Paris, can actually be identified by inscription as that of Arnegunde, one of the queens of Chlotar I of Soissons. The burial was comparatively simple, the only grave goods, apart from the queen's jeweled clothing, being a glass bottle and an elaborate belt-set from a man's costume, presumably a grave-gift from Chlotar himself or from one of his royal sons; but Arnegunde's silver, gold and garnet jewelry in style and elaboration compares well with that from the Cologne royal graves.

At the apex of society stood the king. Apart from the now largely lost treasure of Childeric only one chieftain's grave seems rich enough to be that of the king himself, the anonymous ship-burial excavated in 1939 at Sutton Hoo in Suffolk. This burial, dated by its associated Merovingian coins to the years after the early 620s, stands among a group of similar mounds close to Rendlesham, a place described by Bede as a royal township of the kings of East Anglia. The ship was discovered in the last weeks before the outbreak of war by diggers working for the landowner; recording and retrieval of the material were carried out by a hastily assembled team of experts, and study of the objects, largely postponed until after the war, is still in progress. Within the center section of a large sea going ship had been piled a treasure almost as remarkable for its bullion value as for its delicacy of workmanship. In addition to the normal aristocratic war equipment of helmet, richly ornamented sword, shield, axe, scramasax and spears, and the buckets, drinking horns and cauldrons, was a collection of silver bowls and dishes, including a great dish stamped over a century before the burial by the silversmiths of the Byzantine Emperor Anastasius.

The other metalwork shows a variety of cultural influences, chiefly Scandinavian (and probably of Swedish make) and Frankish, but there is little doubt that much of the jewelry, which involves techniques of gold-and-garnet cell formation more sophisticated than the normal Frankish types, is itself of local manufacture. Two objects are taken to be specifically regal, what is apparently a great scepter made of hard stone and a tall iron framework which is plausibly seen as a barbarian imitation of a Roman military standard (similar perhaps to those standards which, according to Bede, were at this time being carried before the Northumbrian King Edwin). Though the

Reconstructions of the helmet (*left*) and scepter (*above*) from the Sutton Hoo ship-burial, Suffolk. The helmet of riveted plates shows scenes of figures paralleled in Sweden, and is considered to be derived from Roman types.

ritual of ship-burial and the lavish deposition of grave goods are entirely pagan, a pair of silver spoons, the one inscribed "Saul" and the other "Paul," must refer to the act of conversion, and are likely to be Christian baptismal gifts. One king best fits the conflicting evidence of religion, Raedwald, who died in 625 as king of the East Angles and Bretwalda (perhaps "High King") of all the English, converted to Christianity by the Kentish mission but a backslider, notorious for his placing of Christ's altar beside (and not instead of) those of his old gods.

From king to peasant too poor for grave goods the ranks within society can be traced by archaeology. During the actual invasions the barbarian groups *may* have been loosely knit bands of warriors distinguished chiefly by their prowess. But once the kingdoms were established, and in all probability long before that time, the societies were hierarchical, dominated by the nobility. As the English historian H. P. R. Finberg has said, "For positive evidence of independent and self-governing rural communities we search in vain." Every man had his lord and his responsibilities, and out of this complex framework of ownership and duty the medieval kingdoms were formed.

The later Merovingian kings. The kingdoms which the descendants of Clovis ruled were subdivided into territories each of which could conveniently be administered by a single aristocratic royal officer. In practice the sizes of these areas varied considerably, in the south of Francia generally corresponding to the ecclesiastical dioceses, and in the Frankish homelands of the northeast being much smaller; and their boundaries were not fixed but were altered to suit the changing needs of the time. Within such an area a count acted as deputy of the king, with wide-ranging powers. He presided over the law courts, informed the local freemen of the king's wishes, collected taxes and tribute, used the revenues to carry out necessary public works, and assembled and led the local troops when summoned to war. His tenure of office was dependent on the continued good will of his king, but the king's support alone was insufficient for him to carry out his duties: for these the count relied on his own retainers. His loyalty was rewarded by an *ex officio* gift of land from among the royal estates within his county, and his income was augmented by the granting of one third of the local taxes and of the fines exacted in his court.

In general the count held office for life, and if he carried out his duties to royal satisfaction he might expect to be succeeded by his son or at least by a member of his family: in consequence a few dozen noble families, whose members filled most of the 200 or so county posts, amassed lands and power. Initially their rise was at the expense of the peasantry on their estates, or on the royal estates which before long could hardly be distinguished from the count's own land, for the peasants, by taxation, rents and services, had to produce the surplus needed to maintain the nobility and their retinues. But the growth in a community of a powerful noble family affected the smaller free landowners too, and during the 7th and the 8th centuries it became common for such men to seek the protection of the local noble, and submit themselves to him as vassals, expecting in return to be defended against enemies, including other nobles, and supported in times of hardship. The nobles gained substantially, not simply in prestige: they could call on their vassals for labor and for service in their retinues, and the inheritance of a vassal's lands depended on the will of the lord. Gradually the difference between a free peasant and a serf was being obscured by the reduction of the freeman's status. A church synod of the late 8th century discussed the problem and complained of the impoverishment "of those so-called freemen who live under the dominion of the mighty."

The growing power of the noble families weakened the position of the king, weak enough after the second half of the 6th century, when a series of civil wars followed by vendettas and assassination did much to undermine the

The king and the peasant: social distinctions in wheeled vehicles from Raban Maur's *On the Universe*. Monte Cassino, Italy, 1028.

Merovingian dynasty. But the crucial weakness was shortage of resources. As generation after generation of Merovingian kings rewarded the loyalty of their followers by grants of immunity from taxation or services, or by the distribution of royal estates, or ensured their own salvation by the permanent alienation of property to religious houses, they and their successors found their income dwindling and their supremacy consequently eroded. In the 630s Dagobert, one of the last strong Merovingian kings, complained that his nobles had robbed him of the best demesnes and lands in his kingdom. The chronicle of Fredegar preserves the landowner's point of view: Dagobert "longed for church property and for the goods of his subjects, and greedily tried to amass fresh treasure." The decline is seen clearly in the gold currency: until the 7th century the coinage was of fine quality; after about 630 it suffered from a rapid debasement in purity of metal. Now that the kingdom no longer expanded by fresh conquests, the wealth of the Merovingians was drying up.

Einhard, friend and biographer of Charlemagne, presents the most vivid picture of these last descendants of Clovis: "The king had nothing left but the enjoyment of his title and the satisfaction of sitting on his throne, with his hair long and his beard trailing, acting the part of a ruler."

Einhard, writing some 80 years after the end of the dynasty, exaggerated: despite their growing weakness the Merovingians survived the loss of their wealth by over a century. But real power lay more and more in the hands of a small group of aristocrats, and the career of an energetic king might well be short: Dagobert II, restored to the throne in 676 after 20 years of exile, survived only three years. A Frankish bishop explained the reasons for his assassination: he was a destroyer of cities who despised the advice of his elders and of the Church, and imposed taxes, "humiliating the peoples by tribute." Such exercise of royal authority could no longer be tolerated, and the king was eliminated by his magnates.

The later 7th century saw the rise of one noble dynasty in particular, the Arnulfings, the descendants of Dagobert I's adviser St Arnulf, bishop of Metz, a family who later (because of the popularity among them of the Christian name Charles) were known as the Carolingians. A few noble families, prospering under royal favor, were becoming preeminent. In the words of Einhard, "The wealth and power of the kingdom were held tight in the hands of certain leading officials of the court, who were called the Mayors of the Palace, and on them supreme authority devolved." These *Maiores Domui*, a title which originally meant "stewards of the household," were great landowners and controlled the administration within the separate kingdoms of Francia, regions which now were slowly growing apart. Disputes arose over the control of the fertile borderlands between Austrasia and Neustria, and for half a century after the death of Dagobert I peace was disturbed by the conflicting claims of the aristocratic families to the estates around Rheims. The Arnulfings were the largest landowners of the eastern kingdom, and in 687, when Pippin of Heristal, Duke of the Austrasians and grandson of St Arnulf, defeated the Mayor of the Neustrian palace in battle, his success confirmed the supremacy of Austrasia over the other kingdoms and established his family as the most powerful in Francia.

The kings continued in office, but more of their functions were lost, for Pippin himself undertook the royal duty of defending the kingdom against its neighbors, the Frisians, Bavarians and Alamanni. Pippin died in 714, and his son Grimoald was almost immediately assassinated. Much to the dismay of the legitimate Arnulfings, Pippin's bastard son Charles (later known as "Martel," the Hammer) managed to win control of Pippin's former partisans, took over his father's lands and soon raised himself to the same position of power as his father had held. As Einhard, protégé of these Carolingians, put it, "He smashed the tyrants who were claiming supremacy." His aims were the same as those of Pippin, to protect Francia, or more precisely the northern parts of Austrasia where his own estates lay, against Frisians, Saxons *and* Neustrians. But a new enemy had now arisen in the south, and the Frankish kingdom was soon to be in conflict with Islam.

The conquest of Spain. The followers of Muhammad, once a merchant of the Arabian town of Mecca, had during the first half of the 7th century set out on a rapid series of conquests: in 630 they gained control of Mecca; by 640 they had seized Antioch and Jerusalem, and had absorbed the huge Persian Empire, and in 642 they took Alexandria. By the end of the century Arab armies stood outside the walls of Constantinople, and looked across the straits of Gibraltar at the Visigothic kingdom of Spain.

That kingdom for nearly 100 years seems to have been enjoying comparative peace. The long dispute between Arians and Catholics was resolved in 589 by the conversion to Catholicism of King Reccared and, except for outbreaks of anti-Jewish feeling, the country was free from religious problems. In the south the last remnant of Justinian's Byzantine province was absorbed in the 620s. Thereafter our surviving sources are scanty, principally the minutes of the regular councils of Toledo, ecclesiastical records alluding only vaguely to the usurpations and rebellions which are a normal feature of Visigothic history and which seem to have been inspired merely by rivalry among the nobility. Frankish interference in the affairs of Spain is attested: in 631 King Dagobert I, bribed, it was said, by a gold dish weighing 500 pounds, led an army to support the usurpation of a Visigothic nobleman; until the middle of the century edicts refer to rebellious émigrés supported by foreign powers. Disturbances increased at the end of the century: King Wamba's army law of 673, which laid down penalties to be imposed on men who shirked their duties of defending the realm, presents a striking picture of decline, for the majority of the army were no longer free peasants but servile conscripts, and a subsequent law of King Egica implies the existence of large bodies of escaped slaves.

The end of the Visigothic kingdom was hastened by its endemic internal rivalry. In 710 after a prosperous reign King Wittiza died, and his throne, according to an 8th-century chronicler, was taken by a usurper called Roderic. During the ensuing dispute the Arab governor of Africa sent across an army which in 711 defeated and killed Roderic. The Spanish cities fell one by one, and by 716 the Arabs were masters of most of Spain and of the Visigothic territories in southern Gaul. The bulk of the population seems to have shown little interest in the conflict: there are, indeed, stories of active support for the Arabs among the Jews and other hard-pressed minority groups. The surviving Visigothic nobility withdrew to the mountains of northern Spain, where they founded the small but independent kingdom of Asturia, and plotted the recovery of their estates.

Charles the Hammer. While Spain was collapsing before the Arab armies, the early years of the rule of Charles Martel were spent in fighting his enemies inside Francia and the Germanic peoples on its eastern borders. Cash remained a problem: the royal estates of the Merovingians

The votive crown of the Visigothic King Recceswinth (653–72), intended to be dedicated as a religious offering. Part of the Guarrazar treasure discovered near Toledo in 1859, perhaps concealed during the Arab conquest.

From Catholic kingdom to Arab emirate: part of the interior of the Great Mosque at Cordoba, Spain. The mosque occupies the site of the Visigothic cathedral. Late 8th century. The Arabs were masters of most of Spain by 716.

had long ago been dissipated and Charles was compelled to maintain his armies by confiscation and acquisition of the lands of others. Some of his campaigns, such as those against the inhabitants of prosperous Burgundy, Aquitaine and Provence, brought in much-needed booty; for the rest, he had no option but to commandeer some of the vast church estates, which at this time may have amounted to as much as one third of the arable land in the kingdom. How much was taken is not precisely recorded, but the confiscations seem to have been extensive. The policy was not at all intended to be anti-clerical, but rather a necessary part of the defense of the Church and kingdom against enemies, and the Church agreed, however reluctantly, to its loss, as Pope Zacharias wrote, "because of the present threats from the Saracens, the Saxons, and the Frisians."

Some compensation was made by reducing taxation, and, by 755 at least, holders of the old church lands were compelled to pay one fifth of their produce to the former owners. But the effect of the redistribution was considerable, for the confiscated estates were handed over to the Frankish vassals on condition that they served in the army. The creation of this elite, endowed with lands in order to enable it to fight effectively, accentuated the already growing division between noble landowners and peasants. The result may have been even more significant, for it is a popular view among historians that Charles Martel's reforms created in Europe the beginnings of the feudal system, that relationship in tenure and society between king, lord and vassal which dominated the Middle Ages.

The American historian of technology Lynn White has even connected this change with the invention of new fighting tactics: the stirrup was being introduced into Europe in the early 8th century, and now for the first time it was possible for mounted warriors with their lances at rest to use their full weight in a charge without being unhorsed. The importance of cavalry in battle was greatly increased, but horses were expensive and new developments in arms and armor magnified the cost of equipping a knight to a price which the peasant-warriors of the old system could not afford. Hence the necessity for Charles Martel's confiscations, to create a new arm in the Frankish army. But the extent to which the notion of a peasant army, in any of the barbarian kingdoms, was ever realistic is doubtful, and this striking theory remains unproved, for the date of introduction of the stirrup is by no means certain.

Changes, which certainly took place, seem rather to be gradual, and the Franks still had an infantry army in the 730s, a little after the beginning of the confiscations. Arab horsemen, seen by some as the catalyst for the new tactics, seem not to have been more than mounted infantry until after their wars with Charles Martel; the later Arab cavalry, indeed, may have been imitated from Frankish practice. At all events, the strategic developments in the armies of Charles Martel's successors, including the use of knights, were made possible by the existence of a class of military landowners made wealthy by his land grants, even if the grants themselves were intended for nothing more subtle than to reward loyal followers for whom the treasury had insufficient cash. In the words attributed to Charlemagne by Notker the Stammerer, "With this estate . . . I can make as good a vassal out of some faithful retainer as any of my counts or bishops."

The first recorded confiscations took place on the lands

Carolingian cavalry, some in armor, using stirrups and lances. in a 9th-century Psalter from the monastery of St Gall, Switzerland.

of the bishop of Orléans in 732. During the next campaigning season Charles Martel encountered and destroyed a large Arab raiding party on the outskirts of Poitiers: far off in Northumbria Bede inserted into the final chapter of his History a note that the unbelievers had suffered their just deserts. The battle marked the end of Arab expansion in western Europe, and at least since Gibbon (in the 18th century) it has been viewed as a turning-point in European history. It did, indeed, confirm the military reputation of Charles Martel, but the final withdrawal of Arab forces beyond the Pyrenees was in large part due to internal crises in Spain, and their failure subsequently to advance into Francia was the result of changes at the heart of their empire. For far to the east the Persian upper classes in a new, Arabic, guise were rising to dominate the Arab world, and the expansionist leaders of the Bedouin shock troops etablished by Muhammad fell from power. The Arab Empire under the Persian Abbasid dynasty (with its center in the new city of Baghdad and its interests in trade with India and China) turned its back on the Mediterranean. Within a few years Arab movement into Europe ceased, and Arab Spain became a backwater, in which the Christian population, known as the *Mozarabs* (the "Arabized"), with their own laws and counts, enjoyed considerable tolerance from their Arab emirs.

The Carolingian succession. In 737 Theodoric IV, monarch in name of the whole kingdom, after a reign of

some 17 years in which he played no detectable part, died without an heir, and for nearly seven years the throne remained vacant. Charles continued to govern without opposition and when he died in 741 he divided the lands he ruled, in the customary fashion, between his sons: Carloman took the east, Austrasia and Alamannia, and Pippin ("the Short") the west, Neustria and Burgundy. Both had to deal with immediate revolt in the Frankish dependencies, and the disturbances may have induced them to pacify royalists by bringing out from obscurity another Merovingian, Childeric III, the son of Chilperic II, a monk who himself had been removed from his cloister over 20 years before to enjoy the throne for a few months. After six years of rule in Austrasia Carloman, "fired," according to Einhard, "by love of the contemplative life," abdicated and retired eventually to St Benedict's monastery of Monte Cassino, now refounded after its destruction by the Lombards.

Pippin was thus sole ruler of Francia, and soon brought to an end the constitutional pretense. In 750 he sent messengers to Pope Zacharias to ask "whether or not it was good that those called kings should have no power to rule." The pope, perennially anxious about Lombard expansion and now involved in a bitter religious dispute with Constantinople, needed powerful allies and could not afford to displease the Arnulfings. He replied that the title should belong to the one in power, a response entirely in accord with doctrine; as St Augustine had said, "A king [*rex*] is so called because he rules [*a regendo*]." Childeric, the last royal descendant of Clovis, was deposed, tonsured, and with his son confined to a monastery. In his place, in November 751, Pippin (as the most suitable candidate for office) was chosen king, according to the old and somewhat disused Frankish custom, and was anointed by bishops with sacred oil – a novelty which may have been intended to recall the kings of the Old Testament, and whose purpose was probably to rid him of the sin of oath-breaking; for Pippin's assumption of the throne was a clear breach of his fealty to the Merovingians.

The help of the new king was soon needed. The Lombards captured Ravenna and the neighboring Byzantine territories, and prepared to march on the papal state itself. In the winter of 753/4 Pope Stephen left Rome and traveled across Francia, "worn out," he said, "by frost and snow," to meet Pippin in his royal villa on the Marne. In a ceremony in the Merovingians' abbey church of St Denis in Paris Pippin and his sons were anointed, this time by the pope himself, and in the next two years the Frankish king led invasions into northern Italy in support of the pope. In 756 Aistulf king of the Lombards, besieged in Pavia and with no hope of relief, surrendered one third of his treasure, swearing never to rebel against the Franks, and handed over to the pope a series of border cities and strongholds.

The intervention in Italy benefited both allies. The papal state was freed for a time from the Lombard threat, and the Franks returned with enough booty to reconcile the most reluctant nobles (some of whom had openly threatened to desert) to their king's new international role. In thus defending the pope, Pippin was undertaking a responsibility hitherto discharged by Byzantine armies, and the changed position of his nation was acknowledged in mass-books, where prayers on behalf of the king of the Franks and the Frankish state replaced the customary intercession for the emperor and empire. In the words of the English historian Donald Bullough, "The God of the Old Testament and of the New had acquired a new Chosen People."

The activities of Pippin's last years were more in accord with Frankish tradition: with the aid of the surviving Visigothic population in the later 750s he drove the remaining Arab settlers out of southwestern France, and recaptured Narbonne. During the 760s almost annual campaigns were fought to break the stubborn independence of Aquitania, whose duke had been alarmed by Pippin's conquest of the neighboring lands. In 768, in the final stages of the Aquitanian war, Pippin died, a few days after dividing his kingdom, as his father Charles had done, between his two sons, the younger Carloman and that Charles who was distinguished by later generations as Carolus Magnus, "Charles the Great," Charlemagne.

War without end. The two brothers were soon at loggerheads, and in 769 Charles was compelled to settle another Aquitanian revolt without Carloman's assistance. But in 771, before serious conflict could arise, Carloman died at the age of only 21 – "of some disease," says Charlemagne's friend Einhard, vaguely enough – and his family fled to take refuge at the Lombard court. Charlemagne, ignoring his infant nephews, took over the whole kingdom, and soon afterwards began the first of those campaigns against the Saxons, the Saracens and the Lombards which were to occupy him for almost the whole of the 43 years of his sole rule.

The wars started propitiously: in 772 Charles' army captured the Saxon fortress at Eresburg and destroyed the sanctuary of the *Irminsul*, the totem of the sacred tree which held up the heavens; the Saxons surrendered hostages. Meanwhile the Lombards were again threatening the papal states, and in 773 the Frankish army was brought by Charlemagne, with some reluctance, into Italy. The Lombard King Desiderius, until recently Charles' father-in-law, was for nine months besieged in Pavia. During the siege many Lombard magnates transferred their allegiance, and when the city fell in July 774 Charles took over the royal treasury and adopted the title "King of the Franks and the Lombards and [a title given to him and his father by Pope Stephen 20 years before] Patrician of the Romans." Desiderius and his son, like the Merovingians, were consigned to a monastery, and Charlemagne left his new kingdom with a mass of booty

The Tassilo Chalice, dedicated by Tassilo III, Duke of Bavaria (748–88). The figure drawing and interlace seem English, and the chalice may be a product of Northumbria. Kremsmünster Convent, Austria.

and a number of bishops and magnates as hostage for the obedience of the Lombard nobility.

The Saxons, in the absence of the king and his army, had revolted, and on his return to Francia Charles sent over raiding parties in retaliation. In the next year, 775, he led an army which established garrisons in two of the captured Saxon strongpoints; but while he was in Saxony a rebellion broke out in Italy, and at the end of the year Charles was again forced to march south. He returned in 776, laden with booty and fresh hostages, only to put down another Saxon revolt, a serious uprising which he countered by the construction of further fortresses and (less successfully) by the enforced baptism of the heathens.

In the midst of his preparations Charles was approached by Suleiman, governor of Barcelona, and asked to intervene in Arab dynastic struggles. Suleiman's enemy, the emir of Cordoba, ruler of Spain, belonged to the old Umayyad dynasty, supplanted elsewhere in the Arab Empire by the Persian Abbassids, and Charles was told that Arab enemies from Africa and sympathizers within Spain would join in the attacks on the emir. Inspired perhaps chiefly by the anticipation of booty, in 778 the Frankish armies marched across the Pyrenees. There they found few allies: the Christian Spaniards were uncooperative, the African armies arrived but quarreled with Suleiman and stayed inactive, and the cities proved too strong to take without sieges for which Charles was unprepared. The Franks withdrew to the Pyrenees with as much booty as they could take, and in a pass, traditionally that of Roncevalles, to crown the disastrous campaign the army was ambushed by Basque guerrillas. The Frankish rearguard was cut to pieces; among the dead commanders was Roland, duke of the Breton marches.

The official annals suppressed this debacle in the Pyrenees, but later writers were less tactful, and the story, magnified almost beyond recognition by oral transmission, survives as the great *Chanson de Roland*, noblest of medieval heroic poems. Contemporaries too were hardly unaware of the setback, and Charles' prestige suffered: the Saxons were soon again in revolt; the pope appealed for help against fresh pressure by the Lombards of southern Italy; and the Franks, suffering from a failure of the harvest, aggravated perhaps by the long absence of so many men in Spain, were so restless that in 779 Charles had to prohibit the raising of private armies. Even after ten years of predominantly successful effort Charles' position was not yet secure.

The pattern of annual campaigns and almost ceaseless movement thus established in the first decade of Charlemagne's reign continued throughout the whole of his long life – more than 50 important campaigns in 47 years, some 30 led by the king himself; towards the end of his life he left the direction in the field to others, generally his sons. The relationship between the papacy and the Lombard dukedoms of the south (the survivors of the Lombard kingdom) was always liable to cause trouble, and Saracen pressure on the Spanish marches from time to time called for redress, especially in the 790s during the holy war incited by the new emir of Cordoba, son of Charles' old adversary. But the overriding problems were those of the east, where Frankish victories over the Bavarians brought them face to face with the nomadic Avars, and where the pagan Saxons threatened the prosperous estates along the Rhine, the heartland of Charles' kingdom. In 33 years at least 18 major Saxon campaigns were fought, and Charles' countermeasures were made ever more severe, from forced baptism to the execution of thousands of prisoners and the deportation of thousands more. In Einhard's words, "No war ever undertaken by the Franks was more prolonged, fuller of atrocities, or needed more effort."

Unlike the Lombards, the Saxons had no unified state whose fate could be decided by the fortunes of its king. Saxony was controlled by independent tribes, ready to fight guerrilla campaigns among the forests and marshes which had so hindered the Roman legions of the empire. As the war and the reprisals continued, something very like national feeling arose, anti-Christian and anti-Frank. The Saxon leader, a nobleman called Widukind, survived a series of reverses by withdrawing from Saxony into Jutland when Frankish armies looked too dangerous to withstand. After Charles' hosts had been disbanded at the end of each fighting season, Widukind returned to plague the garrisons of the Frankish strongholds and to burn the monasteries. In this war of ambushes Frankish setbacks were so serious that in 784 Charles found it necessary to keep his army together (a considerable feat of persuasion and organization of supplies) and spent the winter of 784/5 in Saxony, in the fortress of Eresburg.

Widukind, in safety in Denmark, presumably saw that resistance was useless as long as the main Frankish army remained in Saxony, in charge of the growing crops. In the spring of 785 he was persuaded to return and surrender himself to Charles. Widukind was received with consideration, and baptized amid considerable publicity – Pope Leo decreed three days of thanksgiving in the whole of the Christian west – with Charlemagne as his godfather. Among the treasures of the State Museum in Berlin is a reliquary from the monastery of Enger, a casket of gold and silver gilt, traditionally one of Charles' christening gifts to the Saxon leader. Celebrations were premature, for the Saxons were again in revolt in 793. But by now the tribes were divided, and many had followed Widukind in accepting the new religion and Frankish control. By mass deportation of Saxons into Francia and by the establishment of colonies of Franks in Saxony Charles achieved final settlement of the area at the end of the 790s.

The Church in the east. Behind the Frankish armies, and with royal encouragement and assistance, came Frankish bishops and priests, to convert the conquered territories into peaceful, Christian realms. These Carolingian ecclesiastics were the successors of a series of missionaries who had for over a century worked in lands still hostile, and whose activities brought together the continental Church and the Church in Anglo-Saxon England.

Those pagan English kingdoms which, as we have seen, towards the end of the 6th century took over the territories of the British princes did not remain heathen for long. In 597 Pope Gregory the Great, who had often entertained the notion of himself converting the English, sent the abbot of the monastery of St Andrew at Rome, St Augustine, to the kingdom of Kent. Aethelberht of Kent had been prepared for the new religion by his wife Bertha, Catholic daughter of the Merovingian King Charibert, and the mission prospered. Northumbria, then approaching the zenith of its power, was converted in 626 by Augustine's successor Paulinus, and even the midland kingdom of Mercia, fiercely pagan under its vigorous King Penda, succumbed to Irish missionaries in the middle of the 7th century. By 700 only pockets of heathenism survived in the English territories, and despite the incessant warfare between the kingdoms, the Church itself was united under the supervision of the archbishop of Canterbury.

The Celtic Church, once preeminent in the north, had in

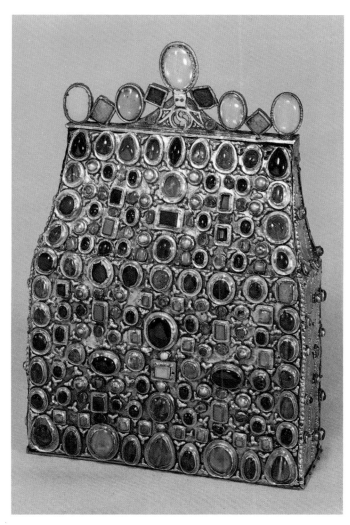

The reliquary made to contain earth soaked in the blood of St Stephen. Gold and silver gilt on a wooden core, studded with pearls and semiprecious stones set *en cabachon*. Early 9th century, Carolingian school (?).

tery at Ripon, Yorkshire, was sent out to carry on the conversion. He arrived shortly after the Arnulfing Pippin of Heristal had seized part of Frisia, and with Pippin's powerful support began his work. Thanks to St Augustine's mission the English Church was linked to the papacy in a way quite different from the Frankish Church, independent under the Merovingians; and Willibrord's journeys to Rome, in 690 to seek the pope's blessing and in 695 at Pippin's behest to be consecrated archbishop of the Frisians, for the first time brought together the pope and a ruler of the Carolingian dynasty in that alliance which was maintained by Pippin's descendants.

Willibrord was given for the site of his cathedral the Roman fortress of Utrecht, like the other Rhine *castra* a royal demesne, and through Utrecht passed a stream of English monks bringing Christianity to the Frisians and Saxons. Within areas controlled by the Franks were signs of progress. Outside the borders of the kingdom work was difficult and dangerous. Two of Willibrord's first missionaries were martyred by the Saxons, and his friend and successor, the Englishman St Boniface, with all his followers, was killed in 754 by a band of robbers, at the end of nearly 40 years of work in Frisia. The place of his martyrdom, commemorated by a turf mound and memorial chapel, has been excavated in the market square of the town of Dokkum near the Frisian coast, in an area by then nominally under Frankish control. Despite years of effort progress was slow, and the successful conversion of Saxony was not achieved until Charlemagne's conquests opened up the country to more peaceful missons. But the Anglo-Saxon evangelists, however partial their successes among the pagans, had a lasting effect on the state of the Frankish Church.

The Carolingian renaissance. The scholarship and learning of the Classical world, still alive in the 6th-century Gaul of Gregory of Tours, declined markedly during the course of the next 200 years. Few laymen were now literate, and even priests showed remarkable ignorance. A sermon of this period, preserved in manuscripts in the British Museum and Zurich, attacks heathen practices in the barbarized Latin of the Merovingian kingdom; much of it is derived from earlier writers, but the author makes a contribution of his own: he attacks Venus in terms which show that he believed this goddess to be a god. Ignorance undermined the stability of the Church, and opened the door to those superstititions which were seldom wholly abandoned by the recently converted. Catholic doctrine, in which exact observance of established forms was fundamental, and in which the distinction between orthodoxy and heresy was often finely drawn, could easily be corrupted by inaccurate or perverse teaching. Even the learned might go astray: the results of the conversion of the Goths to the heresy of Arianism was a warning to the heads of the Church, who might themselves be sometimes in doubt precisely what con-

664 been abandoned in favor of Roman observance, and a multitude of English pilgrims (including four kings) during the 7th and 8th centuries trekked across Europe to Rome, to seek relics, books and spiritual sustenance at the shrine of St Peter. The practice, in excess, was censured: St Benedict had frowned on monks who were "always wandering and never stayed put." In the 8th century St Boniface wished to forbid the pilgrimages of English women to Rome: most fell from virtue during their journey. But the traffic attracted the attention of the English churchmen to the state of their kindred living as heathens in the ancestral homelands of Saxony and Frisia.

In 678 the fiery Northumbrian bishop Wilfrid, on his way to plead his case before the pope, preached the Gospel to the Frisians. The result was transitory, but a new area had been opened up for missionaries, and 12 years later Willibrord, a Northumbrian trained in Wilfrid's monas-

Top: the untidy script of the Merovingian kingdom. A page from an early 8th-century manuscript of Gregory of Tours' *History of the Franks*.

Bottom: the clear script evolved in the court school of Charlemagne. A page from the Acts of the Council of Ephesus, with annotations in Alcuin's handwriting. Late 8th century.

stituted a heresy. When an 8th-century Bavarian priest garbled the baptismal formula (substituting for "Father and Son" the Latin words for "Fatherland" and "Daughter") St Boniface ordered rebaptism, but the pope disagreed: the priest was not heretical, only ignorant.

Even the proper teaching of the clergy was in itself insufficient. They needed accurate and, above all, standardized texts to refresh their memories. Since the late-medieval invention of printing and the consequent widespread dissemination of information it is hard for us to envisage a world in which bibles and sacramentaries were so rare that copies might be specially sought in Rome, and be brought across Europe to the monasteries of Northumbria, and in which the dispatch of a requested volume might be delayed because "in this wintry cold the scribe's hand is slow." Difficulties were increased by scribal error, the misreading or omission of words which might sometimes alter the meaning of a passage or cause obscurity.

During the period of decline in the literacy of the Frankish Church, in Anglo-Saxon England there arose a series of notable schools, helped by the close links with Rome: in the 680s, Canterbury, under the influence of an archbishop from the east, Theodore of Tarsus; in the early 8th century, Northumbrian Lindisfarne, and Jarrow, the home of Bede; in the later 8th century, York, staffed by Bede's pupils. Quantities of English books were sent to the Anglo-Saxon missionaries in Frisia, and volumes of Italian or Irish origin were copied, under English influence, in the monasteries of Francia.

This revival of learning was enthusiastically supported by Charlemagne, partly no doubt for its own sake: in the biographies and in contemporary letters are scenes from the royal court of learned debate, and of playful punning and Latin versification. Of wider importance was the education of the clergy. In an admonition sent around his kingdom Charles commanded observance of the "right faith" and the correction of blemishes in sacred books "for men often wish to address God, but do so badly because the works are incorrect." At his court Charles gathered some of the foremost scholars in Europe, the Northumbrian teacher Alcuin, once master of the school of York and now in charge of the school of the Frankish palace, the Visigothic theologian Theodulf, and the Italians Peter of Pisa, Paulinus, later patriarch of Aquileia, and Paul the Deacon, a Lombard educated at the court of Pavia, and later to be the historian of the Lombardic kingdom. Their role was not only the education of the clergy. The sons of noblemen were to be taught so that when they rose to positions of responsibility they would not need the

The philosophers debate while a scribe with an inkhorn makes notes. From *On the Universe* by Raban Maur, himself a prominent figure in the court circle. Monte Cassino, 1028.

presence of a churchman to spell out for them royal decrees or instructions or to interpret charters and law codes in their comital or ducal courts.

The renewal of the Roman Empire. Under the influence of the court circle Frankish attitudes to their kingdom were changing during the last decade of the 8th century. *Imperium*, the word used in the west to refer to the Roman Empire, had often been used as a synonym for "kingdom" to describe the successor kingdoms of England or of Gaul, at a time when, outside Byzantium, there was no larger political unit to be distinguished as an "empire." In the letters written by Alcuin in the later 790s Charles' expanding dominion begins to be called "Imperium Christianum," the secular arm of Holy Church, and is referred to as an "imperial realm." To an Englishman like Alcuin the notion was familiar: Charlemagne's realm was wider than a single kingdom, and he had as his under-kings his sons Louis of Aquitaine and Pippin of Italy; both Saxon and Irish custom

recognized such an overlord as a high king, superior to monarchs who ruled only their own people.

So far the empire was merely a matter of terminology. Discord in the papacy gave the imperial idea political substance. In the autumn of 800 Charles traveled to Rome to preside over an assembly called to inquire into serious allegations of misbehavior against Pope Leo. The accusers, daunted it seems by the dignity of the proceedings, refused to present evidence of what are likely to have been mischievous charges, and the pope (to avoid being judged by laymen) was allowed to clear himself by oath. Two days later, on Christmas Day 800, while Charles was praying at St Peter's shrine, the pope came up to him and placed a diadem on his head; while Leo made obseisance, the well-rehearsed bystanders proclaimed Charles "Augustus" and "Emperor."

The motives of the participants are obscure: the pope, who had so recently escaped deposition, and had been restored by the Frankish king, was now perhaps reasserting his authority by making that king into an emperor. According to the "Donation of Constantine," a papal document forged perhaps in the 750s, Constantine, the first Christian Roman emperor, had resigned his crown and power to the bishop of Rome, Pope Sylvester I, in return for being cured of leprosy. Pope Leo was now restoring the diadem to Charlemagne. Charles is said to have accepted the imperial dignity on the day before, but Einhard tells us that he now received it with reluctance. It may have been conventional modesty, or perhaps an objection only to the proposed role of Leo in the ceremony, for Charles might well expect to place the imperial crown on his own head, and not receive it as a gift from the pope in a ceremony in some respects similar to that of the surrender and restoration of lands which made a Frank into the vassal of a lord. Charles was the pope's

Right: Roman revival: a drawing of one side of a now lost wooden reliquary, plated with silver, in the form of a Roman triumphal arch, once at Maastricht Abbey. The inscription, in a debased Classical frame, records that Charlemagne's biographer Einhard was the donor. Early 9th century.

Below: the detached gatehouse in the outer court of Lorsch Abbey near Worms. It echoes the design of free-standing Roman triumphal arches, but its immediate ancestor was perhaps the three-arched gateway of old St Peter's in Rome, a combination of Classical and Catholic ideas mirrored in the literature of the Carolingian court. Probably c. 805.

Charlemagne's empire at his death in 814, showing the additions made by his conquests.

support, but he was now also the pope's man.

The court of Constantinople, more traditional in its attitudes to empire, was outraged, and branded Charles as a usurper. But the Byzantines were in a weak position, for the Empress Irene, until 797 the regent for her son, had had him murdered and now ruled in her own right; she was unrecognized by the westerners, who chose to regard the imperial throne as vacant when taken by Charlemagne. This fiction could not be maintained after Irene's deposition in 802, but Charles, who continued to use the name of "Emperor," who was now putting on his seals the legend "Renewal of the Roman Empire," and who clearly valued his title more than do those modern historians who regard the whole business as an elaborate charade, was prepared to spend time and money in negotiation. After 12 years of diplomacy the Eastern Emperor Michael I agreed to recognize Charles' right to be called "Emperor," in return for the abandoning of Frankish claims to Venetia and Dalmatia, at the head of the Adriatic, and on the understanding that Charles' empire was a western, not an eastern realm.

The imperial coronation made no great difference to the administration, or indeed to the stability of the new empire, which still lacked a civil service, a standing army, or even a unified system of law. But it is clear that the Frankish court took the matter seriously and fostered the imperial ideal: the empire already possessed a capital city, Aachen, in the Frankish homelands, where Charlemagne since 789 had been building the greatest palace complex to be seen north of the Alps since the end of the Roman Empire. The model on which Aachen was based was almost certainly the old imperial capital of Ravenna, and in the minor works of art being produced in the Frankish realm we can see the same attempts to mirror the surviving fragments of the old empire. But the Carolingian renaissance, understood today in terms of its material products – illuminated manuscripts written in a newly evolved and beautiful hand, works of art, and architecture – was only part of the intended rebirth of Frankish society, a regeneration to be achieved by stricter adherence to ecclesiastical and secular law, and by firmer control of the jurisdiction of the counts through the supervision of special royal commissioners.

In his last years Charlemagne increasingly spent his time in his new palace at Aachen, hunting, enjoying the hot

Charles the Bald, youngest son of Louis the Pious, in a mid-9th-century manuscript. The hand of God emphasizes his divine right.

spring waters, reforming and publishing the various law codes of his subject nations, and issuing quantities of administrative edicts. Here in January 814 he died, and was buried in his palace chapel, commemorated by a simple inscription: "Beneath this tomb lies the body of Charles, the great and orthodox emperor, who nobly extended the kingdom of the Franks, and reigned prosperously for 47 years. He died in his seventies in the year 814 . . ."

The legacy of Charlemagne. The myth-making which was to transform Charles the Great into the Charlemagne of the 11th-century *Chanson de Roland*, the vice-regent of God whose vigor was unimpaired by his age, "two hundred years and more," was already well developed by the end of the 9th century, given force by the contrast between inflated memories of the august and glorious age of Charlemagne and the visible collapse of the power of his successors. The legend does scant justice to Charlemagne's heirs, for the pressures to which they succumbed were already visible in Charles' time – the beginning of barbarian movements against the frontiers, the steadily growing power of a nobility whose forebears had been aggrandized by the early Carolingians, and the fragmentation of an empire into regions some of whose boundaries were older even than the Frankish kingdom.

For nearly 70 years, from 771 to 840, the Frankish world was in the hands of only two rulers. But this was solely the result of the chance of survival, for the division of his kingdom between his male heirs was as natural to Charlemagne as it had been to his ancestors and to the Merovingians before them. The partitions and consequent civil wars of the 9th century which wrecked the empire of Charlemagne, and laid the states of Europe open to the attacks of fresh barbarians, would have been familiar to Gregory of Tours.

The disintegration of the Carolingian empire. Charlemagne's competent eldest sons, his deputy Charles and Pippin, king of Italy, died before their father. Their deaths forestalled the customary division of his realm that Charlemagne had planned; when his health failed in 813 he summoned his surviving son Louis from the sub-kingdom of Aquitaine, and crowned him as sole successor both to the kingdom and to the empire. Louis, who had lived most of his life in Aquitaine, was out of sympathy with many of his father's advisers. The court of Aachen was purged, and the reformers who became for a while his councillors fostered the ideal of an empire that was both universal and Christian. Soon after his accession he abandoned the ancient titles "King of the Franks and King of the Lombards"; henceforth he was to be "Emperor" and "Augustus." It shows, perhaps, a failure to appreciate the realities of power, for Louis, no less than his father, was emperor because he was king of the Franks; he too relied on the support of his Frankish magnates and followers, and he needed land to reward them. He had already shown an incautious generosity in Aquitaine. Now his estates were whittled down by extensive grants to the Church, while, ironically, his indulgence of the papacy encouraged a series of popes to evolve their own independent policies: for good reason was Louis called "the Pious."

A crisis which was to undermine the kingdom soon arose over the succession. In 817 Louis made his eldest son Lothar co-emperor, and gave Aquitaine and Bavaria to his sons Pippin and Louis ("the German"). Italy was entrusted to Bernard, son of Charlemagne's son Pippin. The arrangement broke down immediately: Bernard, for some reason dissatisfied, rebelled, was blinded as a punishment, and in 818 died of his injuries. Not long afterwards Louis remarried and, spurred on by his new wife and her supporters, he spent nearly 20 years in attempts to revoke his settlement of 817 in favor of his new son, Charles. The 820s in consequence were years of growing disturbance: the developing rift between Louis the Pious and his elder sons added to the troubles caused by poor harvests and failures on the frontiers and complaints about the oppression of the magnates. Feeling ran so high that in 829 Louis banished Lothar to Italy and gave part of Alamannia to his infant son Charles.

Events moved swiftly: in 830 the elder sons banded against their father and compelled him to restore Lothar.

The Husterknupp, a fortified manor in the Rhineland, built in the 9th century. Excavations have shown how this simple enclosure grew during the next 200 years with the increasing independence of its owners to become a powerful feudal castle. After A. Herrnbrodt.

In the course of the next winter Louis held Frankish assemblies which reversed the position, and when his sons rebelled he declared Charles king of Aquitaine in Pippin's place; since he was unable to enforce his decision he merely divided the loyalty of the Aquitainians. In 833, faced with a united army led by all three elder sons, and supported by the pope, Louis surrendered, and was kept confined for a year. The union of the brothers was short-lived, and the emperor came to terms with his sons Pippin and Louis the German, but his continued efforts to give Charles a share in the empire led in 838 to fresh fighting with Louis the German, and Pippin's death in the same year caused a split between the Aquitainian vassals who supported Charles and those who favored Pippin's son, Pippin II.

Shortly before his own death in 840 Louis made one more attempt at partition: Charles' share was to be Aquitaine and western Francia, Louis the German's Bavaria and the east, and Lothar's Italy and a broad belt of land in eastern France. The animosity of many years was not so easily forgotten, and after their father's death the brothers turned on each other. The only result of three further years of civil war was a stalemate, and an agreed settlement was made at Verdun in 843, on the basis of the territory each actually held when fighting stopped. Lothar retained Italy, and a corridor running from the Alps to his lands around Aachen, a corridor which divided Louis' realm in Germany from Charles' kingdom in the west, and which soon became known as "Lothar's kingdom," *Lotharingia*, now Lorraine. The division confirmed the growing separation of east and west Francia, which had been visible even under the Merovingians. The two regions by now had evolved distinct languages of their own, a situation recognized by the bilingual texts of the treaty of 842 between Charles and his brother Louis. In the next century the king of Germany

and the duke of the western Franks had to communicate through an interpreter.

Lothar, though nominally still emperor, had no suzerainty over his brothers, and his three sons, who divided his lands between themselves in 855, had little opportunity to establish authority: the younger sons, Lothar II of Lotharingia and Charles of Provence, were a prey to the ambitions of their uncles; Lothar I's eldest son, the Emperor Louis II, was no more than king of Italy, and spent his energies defending his kingdom against Saracens. When his brothers died he found himself unable to prevent his uncles from annexing Provence (863) and Lotharingia (868), and when he himself died without issue in 875 his uncle Charles (who by now deserved his soubriquet "the Bald") took his throne and the imperial title. Encouraged perhaps by this success, when his brother Louis the German died in 876, Charles attempted to take over the eastern kingdom, but was thwarted by Louis' sons, Louis the Young, Carloman of Bavaria, and Charles the Fat, who divided their father's kingdom between themselves. Charles the Bald's own kingdom passed in 877 to his short-lived son Louis the Stammerer, whose chief act was to surrender Italy, which he could not control, to Carloman of Bavaria in exchange for Lotharingia, which he thought he could. His territory in 879 was partitioned between his sons, Louis III and Carloman of France. By 885 both were dead, and their kingdoms had been taken by their father's cousin, Charles the Fat, the last surviving son of Louis the German, and the sole Carolingian now on the throne.

For two troubled years Charles the Fat was nominal ruler of the whole of Charlemagne's empire, but the position for which he and his relatives had fought for half a century was now almost without power. Duke Guy of Spoleto was supreme in southern Italy; Duke Boso of Provence, who for a time had usurped the throne of Aquitaine, was still master of the central Rhône and in 887 was succeeded by his son Louis, king of Provence; Brittany and its marches had been surrendered to the Bretons; Hugh the Great, duke of the Franks, was his vassal, but in practice controlled the lands between the Loire and the Seine; Paris itself preferred to take instructions from its own Count Odo, and, as we shall hear, bands of pirates were ravaging the coasts almost without opposition. Charles' impotence to exert his authority provoked a coup, and at the end of 887 he was deposed by his vassals.

Disintegration continued: the western throne was given by the dominant faction to Count Odo of Paris; the kingdom of the east was seized by Arnulf, an illegitimate grandson of Louis the German; Guy of Spoleto successfully claimed the throne of Italy, but had to contend with the opposition of his former ally King Arnulf, and, for a while, with the hostility of the papacy. The imperial title was bestowed in turn on Guy (891–93) and Arnulf (894–99), without making any appreciable difference to their positions; nor was either recognized by the other Frankish kings. Arnulf's son, Louis the Child, succeeded his father in 899 at the age of six; when he died at 18 in 911 the eastern Frankish kingdom had split into virtually independent duchies, Bavaria, Suebia, Franconia, Saxony and Lorraine, all but the last corresponding to the various territories annexed by the early Arnulfings. Only one Carolingian was now a king, Charles the Simple, king of western Francia, the youngest son of Louis the Stammerer, grandson of Charles the Bald, and great-great-grandson of Charlemagne, a man who because of his youth had been passed by in the 880s at the death of his brothers Carloman and Louis III, and had recently been chosen by the legitimist factions to succeed Odo of Paris. Charles himself, after many vicissitudes, was imprisoned by Radulf, duke of Burgundy, who usurped his power in 923 and his throne when Charles died in 929, but he established a royal line which survived in central France through three increasingly powerless generations until the death of Louis V in 987.

Meanwhile, in Germany, Henry I ("the Fowler"), descended on his mother's side from the Emperor Arnulf, from 919 to 936 was establishing a strong Saxon dynasty. His son Otto I ("the Great"), who could, we are told, speak Slavic and French, but normally spoke his native Saxon dialect, expanded his realm eastwards into Slavic territories, intervened in the politics of Lorraine and Burgundy, and in the right of his wife (the widow of a former king of Italy) conquered much of Lombardy. Otto's power continued to grow: in 962 he was crowned emperor in Rome, and shortly before his death he persuaded Constantinople to recognize his position, and to send a Byzantine princess to be his son's wife. Otto was the first non-Carolingian to establish an imperial dynasty, and when he died in 973 he passed his title and a strong kingdom to his son and grandson.

The empire of Charlemagne by 962 had long dissolved into its separate parts, and the last royal Carolingians, Lothar and his son Louis V, were to rule for little more than two decades longer in an atmosphere of intrigue. Hugh Capet, duke of the Franks, was the most powerful of the western magnates, and held a position in the shrunken western kingdom analogous to that of the Arnulfing dukes under the last Merovingians. In 985 the courtier Gerbert, later archbishop of Rheims, wrote what could have been said of the ancestors of Charlemagne: "Lothar is king of France in name alone; Hugh, it is true, is not king in name, but he is king in deed and fact." But Hugh, unlike the Arnulfings, had no vast estates which he could bring to swell the royal demesnes and encourage loyalty when he succeeded the childless Louis V. He and his descendants the Capetians, who were for centuries to rule the fragment of Francia which was the medieval kingdom of France, were kings of a small enclave around the city of Paris, surrounded by mighty duchies which may have been nominally part of the kingdom but in practice were nevertheless independent and frequently hostile.

Imperialists and nobles. Concentration on the imperial ideal of Charlemagne's circle or the universal Christian empire of Louis the Pious exaggerates the enormity of the collapse. Charlemagne's empire was personal. It seems, indeed, that as late as 806 he had had no intention of passing the title on to his sons, or perhaps that he believed that unlike the kingdom the title of emperor was to be earned, not given. The lands he ruled, however, were to be divided among his children in the time-honored Frankish way, and the eventual succession of Louis the Pious as sole emperor was an accident of mortality. Louis inherited little but name and lands, and could expect none of the awe for the venerable Charlemagne felt by a people whose average lifespan was half his. The kingdom had already reached the limits of easy expansion, and without either the booty from new lands or the confiscation of the estates of the Church (always unpopular and for Louis unthinkable) he and his descendants, like the Merovingians, had no alternative but to augment the wealth of their vassals to their own cost, by alienating the royal demesnes. Furthermore, though the Carolingians were swift to unite against others – Duke Boso's usurpation of Aquitaine brought down on him the combined forces of all Louis' sons – they used up their resources in internal rivalry. Their divisions increased the separatist feelings of the component parts of the empire, obscured, not eliminated, during Charlemagne's lifetime, and multiplied the power of the royal vassals, dukes and counts, whose continued loyalty was essential for royal survival, but who now were strong enough to withdraw their services from one Carolingian in order to follow another.

The Saracens, Slavs and Magyars. The decline of the empire and the break-up of the traditional patterns of loyalty to central Carolingian authority were a provocation to the barbarians outside the empire, and their pressure caused further collapse. In the south the strong Spanish March effectively controlled the Sarraceni of Umayyad Spain, but the coastline of southern France and Italy was vulnerable to Arab pirates. Based on the secure coastal stronghold of St Tropez, between Marseilles and Nice, these raiders interfered with trade and travelers by land and sea until late in the 10th century. The central Mediterranean fell prey to expeditions from the Emirate of Tunisia. In the 820s Tunisian landings in western Sicily began a series of bitter campaigns which lasted until the fall in 902 of Taormina, the final Byzantine toe-hold in the island. Southern Italy lay open to invasion and from the 840s was ravaged by Saracen fleets. Rome itself was pillaged in 846, and a second attempt in 849 was beaten off with difficulty.

During these grim years Louis II, son, deputy and eventual successor of the Emperor Lothar, tried to

The Holy Roman Emperor at worship. Ivory diptych showing the kneeling figures of Otto II and the Byzantine princess Theophanu with their son, the future Emperor Otto III, flanked by St Maurice and St Mary. c. 980.

central Danube plains. In a series of campaigns between 791 and 796 Charlemagne and his son Pippin annexed the western half of the Avar land, and for much of the next century the kings of eastern Francia fought wars with the ill-defined principalities of the Slavs, border raids which advanced Frankish frontiers and changed the terminology of subservience: the Latin slave (*servus*) had long since become confused in western speech with the peasant bondsman, and both were serfs. The Slav captives of the eastern frontier were numerous enough to introduce to Europe a new term for the old concept, the slave. Pressure from the east grew towards the end of the 9th century, as fresh nomad hordes followed the path of the Huns and the Avars into Europe. The newcomers, the Magyars (probably, like their predecessors, a confederation of Asiatic nomads from many tribes), had for more than a century lived at the edge of Europe between the Volga and the Dnieper, until the expansion of Turkish tribes from the Caspian Sea pushed them westwards. By the beginning of the 10th century the Magyars had settled in Hungary, blending with the remnants of the earlier nomads, Avars and Huns. Made all the more fearsome by the parallels with the Huns of Attila, the "scourge of God," which they recalled to the minds of contemporary ecclesiastics, they resisted for two generations all attempts to stop their raids into Germany, Italy, and Francia.

The eastern Frankish kings found it necessary to set up strong marcher lordships to whom the defense of the borders could be entrusted. One of these, the duchy of eastern Saxony, grew to rival the power of the king himself, and, as we have seen, its duke, Henry the Fowler, in 919 established his dynasty as the successors of the Carolingians in Germany. In the face of the Magyar threat Henry and his son, the future Emperor Otto I, resorted to an expedient which shows the straits to which the kingdom had come: the construction of a remarkable series of hillforts, defensive refuges into which the local population could retire when the Magyar raiders approached. After half a century of warfare Otto's army crushed the Magyar power in 955 at the battle of the Lechfeld, and restored a measure of stability to the eastern kingdoms of Europe. The victory brought a hitherto comparatively insignificant Saxon family to the forefront of Europe, and to Rome. At his coronation in St Peter's in 962 Otto wore a crown whose arch was sufficiently high for him to wear a miter beneath, to symbolize power in church and state in a Christian empire. The Saxon dynasty regarded itself as heir of the old empire, and by the end of the century Otto's grandson, Otto III, had made Rome his capital and his motto that of Charlemagne, *Renovatio Imperii Romanorum*, "the renewal of the [Holy] Roman Empire."

reconcile the conflicts between the holders of the old Lombard dukedoms, and their feuds with the surviving Byzantine authorities, and to unite all against the Saracens. He succeeded in recapturing Beneventum, and the Neapolitan cities joined in a strong defensive alliance, but the Saracen base in the coastal fortress of Bari held out for another 20 years until 871. Before his death in 875 Emperor Louis II had reestablished Frankish control over southern Italy, but his preoccupations with the south, which prevented him from playing any effective role in Francia, still further separated the imperial title from the government of the kingdoms of Francia and Germany.

The southeastern borders of Austrasia marched with the lands of the Avars, the Asiatic nomads who during the later 6th century had taken the place of the Lombards in the

The Royal Palaces

The German chieftains who led their men across Europe in the course of the 5th century found themselves in lands where specialization in the function of houses was normal. They would have been familiar with the distinctions between rich and poor. But they may well have found the great administrative blocks (which had grown up during the later empire to house the governors and their staff) more difficult to appreciate. In some cases the first generations of kings adapted the structures to a new use: excavations at Cologne have suggested that the official governor's residence was by a series of alterations being transformed into a Frankish palace.

Theodoric the Great, brought up in Constantinople, entered into the spirit of the court ritual. In his mosaics at Ravenna he depicted his great classical palace and originally portrayed himself and his court arranged in Byzantine style against its facade. A succeeding, intolerant generation damned his memory and expunged his image from the composition. At Toulouse the Visigothic court of southeastern Gaul dazzled even Gallo-Romans, but of their palaces we know nothing.

The tribal chieftain before the migrations may have

occupied no more than a single hall on his small estate. When these chieftains became the monarchs of the successor kingdoms we find them to be the owners of a series of demesnes, and on many of these stood the substantial farmhouses or *villae* of former officials. Not until the end of the Middle Ages did rulers abandon the custom of visiting their domains in the course of a regular progress, and the scattered royal possessions – no less than the guesthouses of the monasteries – were useful in billeting the royal party. To distinguish between a palace and royal rustic estate can be misleading: a king on the march took his court, and his "palace," with him.

But two forms of royal residence develop in the migration period. The first, the common rural mansion, might differ little from the comparative unsophistication of the houses of the nobility. The second, the established center for urban and royal administration, was rarer, and when it occurred in the barbarian kingdoms it seems likely that it reflected contemporary Byzantine practice.

Top: throughout the migration period rural mansions continued to be built in traditional styles. The reconstructed palace at Lojstra, Gotland, Sweden, probably of the later 10th century, in its construction resembles the farmsteads of the Roman Iron Age at nearby Vallhagar: a three-aisled building about 90 feet long and 35 feet broad, whose roof rests on low stone walls; its appearance may originally have been brightened by carving and painting. Perhaps like the great timber hall Heorot in the epic poem *Beowulf,* "the rich banqueting hall glittered with plated gold."

Above: the clearest example of an early chieftain's house comes from the excavations at the Roman Iron Age site of Fochteloo, Drenthe, Holland. Here a longhouse of normal aisled plan lay within its own fenced courtyard, a short distance from a contemporary cluster of three smaller farmsteads which were associated with small huts and granaries. It is difficult to interpret the isolated longhouse as anything other than the home of a noble and the small group of farmsteads as the dwellings of his followers. The reconstruction (after A. E. van Giffen) shows the main house in its enclosure, with associated sheds and pens.

Left: the story of Theudelinda, queen of the Lombardic King Agilulf, portrayed by the brothers Zavattari (1444) in the cathedral at Monza. Each age tends to reconstruct the surroundings in its own image, and palaces (like the one shown here) are normally made up-to-date.

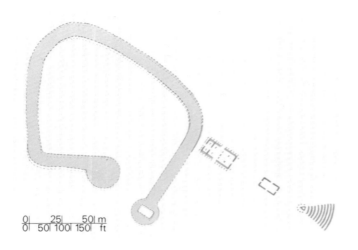

0 25 50 m
0 50 100 150 ft

An aerial photograph at Yeavering, Northumberland, taken by Dr St. Joseph in 1949 (*below*) revealed the outlines of what Bede called the *villa regalis ad Gefrin*, the royal house of the Northumbrian kings. Excavations between 1953 and 1957 revealed a complex series of buildings, some of which are shown on the plan (*left*, after B. Hope-Taylor): outside a large timber fort of the later 6th century stood a massive rectangular hall (rebuilt six times), a structure identified as a timber grandstand (*bottom right*), and (not visible on the aerial photograph) a group of subsidiary buildings, perhaps retainers' halls. After a life of some three generations, the site was abandoned c. 685. Mobility was a hallmark of barbarian kings.

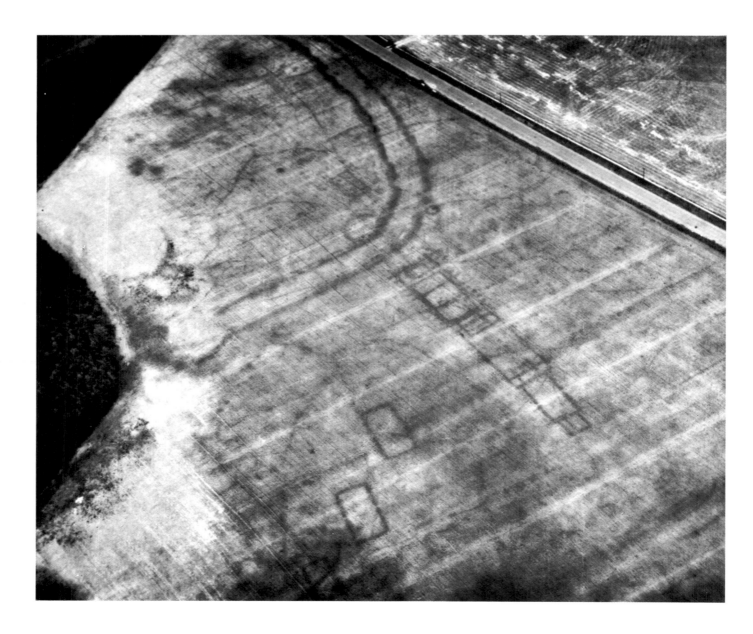

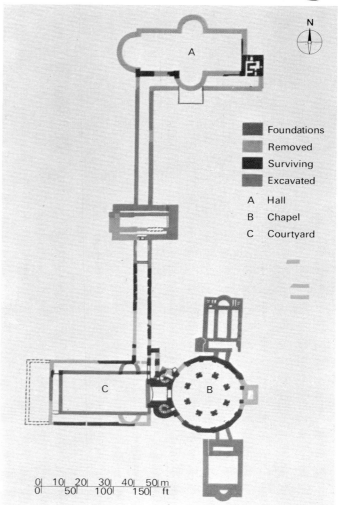

Foundations
Removed
Surviving
Excavated

A Hall
B Chapel
C Courtyard

| 0 | 10 | 20 | 30 | 40 | 50 m |
| 0 | 50 | 100 | 150 | ft |

Few monarchs traveled as much as Charlemagne, with his annual campaigns and progresses around Francia, but the notion of a fixed royal residence, a novelty north of the Alps, came first, it seems, to him. Beside the thermal bath at Aachen in the early 790s Charlemagne began to build a great palace. *Above right* (after F. Kreusch): at the north of the site stands the much-restored great hall (A), a massive stone building with apsidal throneroom on its upper story and residential accommodation below. At the south stands the chapel (B). The original small square chancel has been replaced by a vast Gothic choir, but the squat octagon and the imposing west front are largely intact (*below right*). To the north and south of the octagon stood annexes partially traced by excavation. The hall and chapel were linked by an elaborate two-story corridor, across which stood a gateway with an upper-floor hall. The second story of the corridor led to the upper part of the *Westwerk* of the chapel, where Charlemagne's throne stood, looking across the octagon to the altar (*above left*). Outside the *Westwerk* lay a courtyard (C) where Charlemagne's subjects could stand and glimpse their king. The ceremony was akin to court ritual in Constantinople and the architecture of Aachen echoes imperial planning. The model for the chapel was the 6th-century Byzantine church of S. Vitale, Ravenna, and from Theodoric's palace at Ravenna came the marble columns used in the octagon. Their capitals, despite their purely classical Corinthian style, are of local stone. To emphasize his position, in 801 the new emperor brought back from Ravenna an equestrian statue be believed to be of Theodoric the Great, and set it up outside his palace. The ambitious and costly building program was intended to underline a political point.

Above: after the plan by P. A. Rahtz. The great stone palace of Aachen remained unique outside Italy, and the kings of the 9th and 10th centuries spent much of their time in traditional timber halls. Excavations at Cheddar, Somerset, revealed one

·such rural mansion, the *palatio regis* of King Alfred's successors, kings of Wessex and England. The earliest period (9th century) was a simple cluster of timber buildings – a hall, which may have been two-storied, and three small structures (one of which may have been a private chamber) within a small enclosure.
Below: the royal palace of Tilleda, E Germany, was part of the demesnes of the Saxon emperors of the 10th and 11th centuries. Excavations have shown that the citadel c. 1000 contained a church attached to a small fortified tower, presumably the king's private quarters (A). Across the courtyard stood a timber great hall (B) for ceremonial occasions. Other buildings on the citadel were probably those of royal servants. In the lower enclosure a long entrance passage (C) led past rows of sunken-floor huts. Occupation was dense in all areas sampled.
Right: the "church" of Sta Maria de Naranco, near Oviedo, northern Spain, was built as a ceremonial great hall in the 840s. The photograph shows the western end of the building. Its vaulted basement contained a chapel, dedicated in 848 by Ramiro I, king of Asturia; its upper story, a lofty vaulted room lit by broad openings and decorated with carvings, formed the hall itself. With the exception of a fragment of the original chapel royal, the other buildings of the palace have now disappeared.

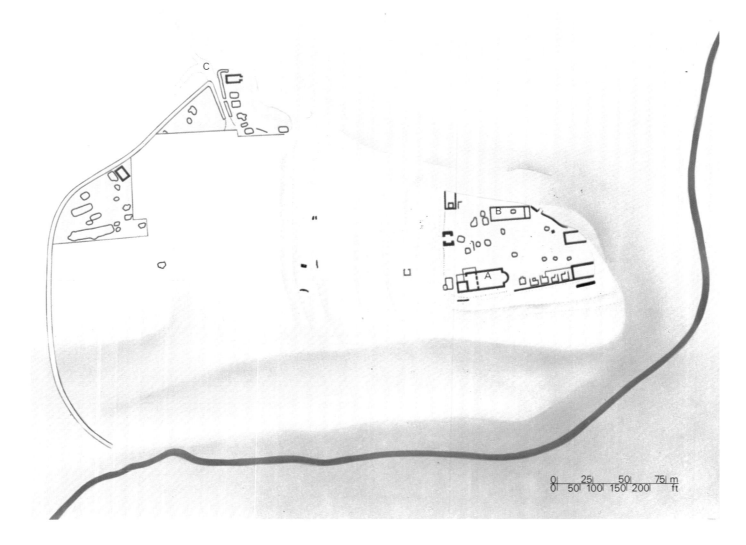

| 0 | 25 | 50 | 75 | m |
| 0 | 50 | 100 | 150 | 200 | ft |

6. The Vikings
and After

In the year 789, when Charlemagne's reign still had 25 years to run, and the most powerful of the English monarchs, Offa the Great, had been king of Mercia for 32 years, three ships from Norway came to Wessex and landed at Portland on the south coast near Dorchester, Dorset. A reeve of King Beorhtric of Wessex, hearing of their arrival, rode up with a few men and told the Norwegians to go, presumably for questioning, to the king's vill. The official had mistaken the newcomers for merchants, "for he did not know what they were; and then they slew him." The rest of the story is omitted both by our main source for the period, the *Anglo-Saxon Chronicle*, and in the account of the 10th-century nobleman Aethelweard, but both agree that the incident marked the "first coming of the Northmen to England."

In 793 a raiding party, preceded, it was said, by high winds, lightning and fiery dragons in the sky, fell on Holy Island, off the Northumbrian coast, and "destroyed" the monastery of Lindisfarne. The news of the monks' fate shocked their fellow countryman Alcuin, then about to leave Charlemagne's court to become abbot of St Martin's at Tours. "For nearly 350 years," he wrote, "we and our fathers have lived in this lovely land, and never before has such a terror appeared in Britain as we have now suffered from a pagan people, nor was it thought that such an attack from the sea was possible." Further raids followed: an attempt on a Northumbrian monastery, probably Jarrow, was thwarted in 794, and in the next year raids are recorded in the western sea, at Iona and on an island off the Irish coast. By the end of the 790s Norwegian sea-borne raiders were ravaging the coast of Aquitaine. The Vikings (a name of obscure origin, but clear significance – "pirates") had suddenly thrust themselves into the world of the civilized states of Europe.

The unexpectedness of the attacks was due to ignorance. The scholars and ecclesiastics of the western kingdoms, concerned with biblical studies or the history of their own nations, had paid scant attention to the activities of the peoples around the Baltic, and if the vagueness of the incidental references (to wars between Danes and Norwegians or tribal conflict in Sweden) is any guide, there had been little recent contact between the courts of the Christian world and the pagan tribes of the north, whose very location was in doubt. Even after a century of Viking raids King Alfred of Wessex thought it worthwhile to record quite elementary details of the geography of the Baltic, taken down from conversation with two shipmasters who had sailed in the area. The story of Scandinavia before the 9th century is consequently for us part of prehistory, and is intelligible, if at all, only from the results of archaeological investigation.

Opposite: Viking craftsmanship in wood. The "Academician" headpost from the ship-burial at Oseberg near Oslo, originally perhaps part of a chair. Late 9th century.

Scandinavia before the Vikings. The Germanic peoples, Goths, Vandals, Burgundians, Lombards and others, whose traditions placed their ancestral homelands in the "island" of Scandza, had by the 5th century left the shores of the Baltic far behind and were evolving strong and centralized kingdoms in central and southern Europe. The tribes who remained in the north, split up by mountains and inlets of the sea, continued for centuries in disunity. Their material cultures show contacts with the workshops of Germany: the cruciform brooches of Angeln, north Germany and England are common in Norway, and new styles in Scandinavian pottery – down-curving linear ornament ("swags") and stamping – seem to have a similar southern origin. Distinctive bronze cauldrons of angular profile with triangular lugs projecting above their rims, attributed to Rhineland Frankish factories, were exported to Switzerland, England and Norway. The glassware from northern France or the Rhineland continued to find its way north, as it had done in Roman times. Quantities have been uncovered in Norway.

The north was clearly thriving in the 5th century during the years in which the hard-pressed Western Roman Empire collapsed. From the middle of the century a stream of late Roman and Byzantine gold coins was reaching the Baltic islands – Gotland, Öland and Bornholm. The greatest numbers of eastern coins belong to the 460s; by the end of the century western issues are common. The ultimate source may have been the huge bribes paid to barbarian kings – like the 432,000 gold *solidi* paid to Attila by Theodosius II in 443 – and the changing pattern corresponds with the movements of the Ostrogoths, from 454 to 487 in the pay of Constantinople, and afterwards, under Theodoric the Great, masters of Italy. The major trade routes, from Pannonia in central Europe (for long the Ostrogothic homeland) to the Baltic via the Oder and the Vistula, are the likely directions in which the imperial gold flowed. Why it came to Scandinavia is less certain. In the 6th century some may have been sent to pay for mercenaries or to subsidize princelings; but trade, perhaps in furs, is the most probable agency, for the coins are found almost exclusively on the Baltic islands. Öland especially seems to have acted as a distributing center or market for the suppliers and purchasers of goods, and the coins may have circulated on these islands as currency.

If the islands grew rich on trade, there is little doubt where the ultimate beneficiaries of the exchanges lived. The neighboring mainland of Sweden is at this time almost devoid of coins: its wealth is measured in objects presumably manufactured from the imported gold coinage, gold arm-rings, neck-rings and collars, amulets and pendants, and simple bars of solid gold. Their distribution spreads across southern Sweden and Norway, but one important center of power seems to have lain in Uppland, on the coastal plain to the north of modern Stockholm, the territory dominated by the tribe of the Svear, who have given the whole country its modern name. At Old

Gold collar decorated with twisted gold wire (filigree) formed into back-turned and couchant animals, from Alleberg, Västergötland. One of a series of great collars from central and southern Sweden.

Uppsala, in a large grave-field of small mounds and unmarked cremations, stand four huge barrows, the largest nearly 40 feet high, the burial places of 5th- and 6th-century kings of central Sweden. Excavation here has proved disappointing: in comparison with the richly adorned burials of the later Viking age the furnishing of the graves was plain and uninformative. Simplicity indeed seems to have been a general custom, for cremation was the normal burial practice, and though some burned remains were interred in expensive bronze cauldrons many were simply placed in shallow pits. Richer grave goods may have been lost: the migration-period graves of Valsgärde, near Uppsala, were robbed in antiquity. The motive here and elsewhere in Sweden and Norway may have been merely treasure-hunting, but it may have had a grimmer origin: Professor A. W. Brøgger, formerly director of the Viking Ship Museum in Oslo, has shown how those who broke into the rich ship-burial at Oseberg intended only to steal the body of the dead queen and destroy her bier. The purpose, echoed in mythology, was to make the grave uninhabitable, and was directed against the mighty dead, whose influence was as great in death as in life.

In consequence of the burial practice and the plundering, the finds of gold and silver come almost entirely from hoards, whose burial and the subsequent failure of the owners to reclaim them are clear signs of danger and disturbance. The bullion hoards can be ascribed only in vague terms to the 5th, 6th or 7th centuries. More precision in dating comes from the coin hoards of the islands. On Öland the coin types in most cases predate 491; the majority of the hoards contain issues of Leo I, only a few continuing to the time of Anastasius. The hoards of

Bornholm run on a little later, ending with issues of Anastasius. The island of Gotland shows still later burial, in groups belonging to the first half of the 6th century, and including coins of Justinian. The hoards generally contain from 20 to 30 gold *solidi* (cash sufficient, perhaps, to purchase a year's corn and the plow teams for two or three peasant holdings), and in each case the reason for burial is likely to have been the safeguarding of a family's accumulated wealth during a pirate raid.

Confirmation of such disturbances comes from the study of settlements. Huge numbers of ruined houses built with low stone walls are still visible as surface features in the islands – in Öland an estimated 900; in Gotland as many as 1,400. Fewer than one in 30 so far have been excavated, but all these belong to the migration period, and most show clear signs of destruction and abandonment approximately datable to the time when the hoards were being buried. Investigations on Bornholm, furthermore, showed that two hillforts had been occupied (and may have been constructed) during the disturbances. The situation on Gotland is still unclear, but on Öland some of the circular stone forts belong to the migration period, and many must have served as temporary refuges when the unfortified hamlets near the coast were pillaged. The troubles extended to the mainland too, for a wide belt of these forts, assumed to be innovations of the migration period, stretches across central Sweden and southern Norway.

The most thoroughly investigated of these structures, the fortress of Eketorp on Öland, appears indeed to have been continuously occupied from about 450 to the early 8th century, and was reoccupied during the late Viking period, but few of the population can have lived in such defensive groups: the typical settlement pattern is of clusters of three to five buildings enclosed by walled fields for arable farming and in-field cattle, and surrounded by open pastures. The largest excavated site, the hamlet of Vallhagar on Gotland, contained in all 24 aisled houses, dwellings whose roofs were supported internally on two rows of posts and rested on thick, low, stone walls. Four contained clear evidence of cattle-stalling at one end of the building, and the hamlet was divided into six separate farm units (house, barn, storehouse) which the excavator, Mårten Stenberger, has suggested belonged to an extended kinship group under the control of a patriarch, in a system similar to that practiced in Gotland through the Middle Ages. The hamlet was founded in the 2nd century AD and grew to its greatest size in the 6th century, shortly before its abandonment during the period when the Gotland hoards were being buried.

Elsewhere isolated farms are more common, the farmhouses, like some of those at Vallhagar, of "house-and-byre" construction, with one or two subsidiary buildings, within enclosures which vary from two to 25 acres. Structures of different design have been found in only two areas, both in Norway, in Rogaland in the southwest and in Nordland towards the Arctic Circle. In both regions are settlements consisting of clusters of houses arranged radially around an open space, with timber gable ends facing the center and their other walls of stone. Their roofs were supported in the normal way on two rows of posts, but they were not byre-houses, nor do they seem to have had attached field-systems. In plan they resemble the layout of the interior buildings of a ring-fort like Eketorp, and they may have been intended to be at least partially defensive refuges, probably of the migration period; their inhabitants have little apparent connection with agriculture, and it is tempting to see them as merchants, dealing perhaps in furs and walrus ivory, and moving in groups, for safety, between the hunting grounds in the Arctic and the trading zone around Stavanger Fjord.

The coin hoards show that the late 5th and the 6th centuries were periods of insecurity, but the disparity in the dates of these burials shows that we are not dealing with only one horizon of destruction such as might be the result of a single wave of invasion, but with a series of devastations, in Öland in the 480s and 490s, in Bornholm soon after 500, in Gotland at several points in the first half of the 6th century. In the years that followed, the Baltic countries grew more remote from Europe. The causes of the change are uncertain. The successors of Theodoric in Italy presumably failed to maintain connections with the north and any remaining links were perhaps severed by the Lombard annexation of northern Italy. By now those Scandinavians who joined in the colonization of England had established their hold over their new lands, and, with the possible exception of the East Angles, they were becoming insular Anglo-Saxons. The piracy indicated by the hoards was presumably inspired by an increase in trade; it may have been a symptom of a general collapse of the authority of an established aristocracy, or, indeed, the response of returned mercenaries whose services were not required in their homelands. At all events, it must have made distant contacts hard to maintain. For whatever reasons, from the 6th century onwards the language of the Scandinavians developed rapidly away from the Germanic speech of the southern Germans. Within Scandinavia itself until the 11th or 12th centuries a common tongue was recognized, *vox danica*, Danish, which despite regional differences was understood throughout the area and was scarcely intelligible to continental Germans. The art styles, with motifs and techniques at first borrowed from a common tradition of metalworking, begin to develop along purely Scandinavian lines, changing geometric and stylized animal ornament into sinuous, interlaced patterns.

During this period in which the local regions of Scandinavia were evolving their own independent cultures, the Svear lords of Uppland remained wealthy. Their importance is underlined by two rich cemeteries a few miles north of Uppsala, Vendel (which has given its name to the pre-Viking culture of Sweden) and Valsgärde. Both

The helmet from grave I at Vendel, Sweden. The technique of its manufacture and its decoration resemble the helmet of the Sutton Hoo burial in Suffolk. 7th century.

were in use from the 7th century until the 10th or 11th, and seem to have been the burial places of two chieftain families. The graves contain lavishly decorated swords, scabbards and helmets, as well as imported glass and the bones of sacrificed animals. Most significantly, in 26 of these graves the body of the warrior was laid in the stern of a medium-sized boat (some 30 feet in length) with his grave goods piled amidships. Boat burial is known from a few cremations and inhumations in 6th-century Norway. But as a regular custom these Vendel-period burials are a novelty, and their obvious emphasis on seafaring may explain the continued prosperity of the Uppland nobility during the Baltic disturbances: they may indeed have been causing some of the trouble themselves.

Swedish influence spread beyond Scandinavia in the Vendel period, for the sword and shield, buried about 625 or a little later, in the great ship at Sutton Hoo in East Anglia are perhaps of Swedish manufacture, and the Sutton Hoo helmet shows quite remarkable similarity to one from Vendel. The connection is reasonably seen as dynastic, a marriage or the inheritance of an English throne, and Anglo-Saxon interest in the area, not later than the 8th century, is clear from the Swedish setting of

Picture stone from Lillbjars, Gotland, probably intended to show the shrouded dead making their last journey in a ferry. 8th century.

the Old English epic poem *Beowulf.* The hero of the poem, however, is not a Svear but a Geat, from the southern Swedish tribes of Gotland, and the East Anglian royal genealogies preserve names similar to those of the royal family of the Geats. The Vendel-style metalwork at Sutton Hoo need not establish a link with Uppland, for too little is known of the royal burials of southern Sweden, and the Vendel style has a distribution that ranges beyond the political territory of the Svear.

The Viking ships. The chieftains of Uppland were not the only Scandinavians to be interested in ships. In the 9th century Ermoldus Nigellus considered that the Danes "live in the sea," and Danish involvement with the sea even after death has been shown in the excavations of the large cemetery at Lindholm Høje, beside Aalborg in northern Jutland. Here the graves of the 5th and 6th centuries are simple cremations in pits, some marked by upright stones. By the 8th century oval stone-settings enclosing cremation patches were being succeeded by grave types found also in southern Sweden – settings of stones in the form of a ship, with taller stones at either end to represent the head and stern posts. Such symbolic ships attest the growing maritime connection of Scandinavians.

Our understanding of the ships themselves is based partly on the Viking-period carved stones (most from southern Sweden), which show detail of rigging and sails, and partly on the discovery of ship remains in burial mounds and harbors.

Technical improvements are clear: the earliest of the migration-period vessels, belonging to the 4th or 5th centuries, comes from the bog deposit at Nydam near Schleswig. It was clinker-built, each plank being the full length of the boat and overlapping the one below, the edges securely fixed with iron rivets. Despite its size (a length of nearly 80 feet) the ship had no keel, merely a broad bottom plank, and no provision for a mast. Without a keel, attempts to sail such a boat in anything but a following wind would be hampered by lateral movement from current or wind – the vessel would be blown sideways – and the Nydam ship is rightly seen as an enormous rowing boat. The same defect is found in the Sutton Hoo ship, an even larger vessel (about 89 feet long) of about 600 AD. Construction had improved – the planks were made up of several jointed timbers and the lines of the ship were smoother – but motive power was still in the hands of 38 oarsmen. Such a vessel would be capable of sea voyages, for smaller rowing boats, utilizing currents, have crossed the Atlantic, but it would be most suitable for coastal journeys.

Quite distinct designs are visible in the ships of the Viking period. The 9th-century craft discovered in the burial mounds at Gokstad and Oseberg were sophisticated sailing vessels with full keels and massive seatings for the mast, and the fixing of the lower planking to the strakes was so arranged with lashings that in heavy seas the ships were flexible. Ocean worthiness was put to the test: in 1893 a replica of the Gokstad ship sailed from Bergen to Newfoundland in under a month. Its captain reported that thanks to the elasticity of the hull and its fine lines speeds of up to 11 knots were achieved under sail.

This development of fast oceangoing ships can plausibly be seen as one factor which made possible the Viking attacks on Europe from the end of the 8th century. But there is a danger, not always avoided, in supposing that the improvements in some sense caused the raiding. Significant here is a ship from a bog at Kvalsund, Norway, which seems to belong to an intervening stage in the evolution of sailing longboats. The Kvalsund boat was about 59 feet long, somewhat shorter than the Oseberg and Gokstad ships, and was, like the examples from Nydam and Sutton Hoo, designed for oar propulsion, but its bottom plank was cut to form a rudimentary keel. This vessel, however, was not found in association with datable objects and its general ascription to the 7th century is based on its typological place halfway between the Nydam and Gokstad ships.

It is indeed risky to assume that the vessels so far discovered fall into a single evolutionary pattern, and that that pattern can itself be dated (partly by its own typ-

The Oseberg ship, reconstructed in Oslo. The Gokstad ship is of similar construction, though less ornately carved.

ology) with sufficient precision to show at what point the Vikings invented ships capable of making ocean voyages. To concentrate on the coastal rowing boats and prestigious yachts thought suitable for ceremonial burial may be to ignore the existence of less spectacular craft, for a notable absentee in the typology of ships from Nydam to Gokstad is the sail-propelled cargo vessel, which must at all times have been the most common type in use. No chronology of these merchant ships can yet be traced, for only two examples have so far been discovered, part of a group of five ships of the late 10th or early 11th century, which were filled with boulders and sunk to block the fairways of Roskilde Fjord in the island of Sjaelland, Denmark. The Roskilde finds include several otherwise unexampled ship types. One was a Viking longship, the true oceangoing warship, which was developed during the 10th century. Little remained of this vessel – but enough to show that it was longer and narrower than the

Oseberg and Gokstad ships. The two best-preserved wrecks were a stocky vessel 55 feet long and 15 feet broad (a heavy cargo ship) and a lighter merchant ship 45 feet long and only 11 feet in beam, with about a third of the carrying capacity of the cargo ship. Both could be rowed with a few oars, presumably for harbors and narrow rivers, but were primarily sailing vessels. The lighter ship was perhaps intended for Baltic and river navigation. The cargo ship is our only example of the famous type called a *Knarr*, and must be a descendant of the deep-draught ships in which the Scandinavian settlers of the 9th and 10th centuries had made the Atlantic crossing to the Faroes, Iceland, Greenland and America, and which presumably resembled the *Kogg* used for centuries by the Frisian traders, a type of craft of which little is known beyond the name.

The role of these sturdy vessels in the Viking expansion has perhaps been underemphasized. Scandinavians themselves had a less sanguine view of the seaworthiness of their warships than the success of modern experiments now justifies. In the words attributed to Earl Haakon in the

Part of the excavations of the great trading center at Dorestad, showing stumps of posts preserved in the damp sand.

Faereyinga Saga, "The seas around the Faroes are dangerous, with much surf, and longships cannot reach there." The first Viking raiders very probably arrived in ships much less specialized than those warships (the familiar image of Viking ships) designed by the royal navy-builders of the late Viking period. Beaduheard the reeve, after all, could hardly have mistaken the Norwegians at Portland for merchants had they landed in dragon ships. The Vikings, it is frequently noted, followed established trading routes: it is difficult to see how a successful pirate could do otherwise. But the difference between a Viking and a trader might be small – pirates at will, and merchants at their pleasure – and many voyages must have begun with the collection of booty abroad and ended at home with its peaceable and profitable distribution.

Towns and trade. Viking expansion followed a fundamental change in the basis of the regional economy in northwest Europe, and the raiding must be seen against a background of revived trading and newly founded towns. The urban decline during the 6th and 7th centuries within the successor kingdoms depopulated the Roman cities of the northwest. At Cologne, once the administrative center of the lower Rhine, with a walled area of 240 acres, the Merovingian royal palace was surrounded by a small settlement and pastures. At Bonn and at Xanten hamlets ignored the Roman sites and clustered around religious establishments founded on Roman extramural graveyards. Only in Spain, Italy and southern France is continuity of site, defenses and city life recognizable. Elsewhere the focal points of the countryside became the estates and manors of the king and his nobility. Many of these were away from the old Roman centers – St Denis outside Paris, or the rural sites at Ingelheim in Germany, or Yeavering and Rendlesham in England. Others were built, like the palace of Cologne, within the walls of former towns whose population had all but disappeared. Together with the newly established bishops' sees and monasteries these manors served as a focus of urban regrowth. Excavations in the city of Winchester, Hampshire, have shown how this once-important regional capital was partially reoccupied by the kings of Wessex, and how the medieval town grew up around the royal palace and the nearby minster. At Trier on the Rhine the center of the new town, growing up within the former Roman city of 450 acres, was the *Immunitas*, the cathedral precinct; Frankish manors were established at a distance, on the edge of the Roman built-up area, and were linked by a road network which ignored the grid pattern of Roman streets. At Bonn and at Xanten the cathedral immunities developed into small urban centers.

The origin of this urban growth was the commerce attracted by the wealth and security of the manors and monasteries. At Bonn a street of single-room houses straggled up to the minster; at Cologne and at Mainz a merchant quarter grew up in the lower part of the old towns beside the Rhine; at Winchester a street market formed, within the old walls, at the edge of the palace and minster precincts, to be rearranged late in the Saxon period as a regularly planned town. Great open-air fairs served to bring merchants together. In 634 Dagobert I granted licence for such an annual event to the monastery of St Denis, and Saxon and Frisian traders soon joined Franks in buying and selling at this fair outside Paris. The importation of Frankish metalwork into Kent was followed in the first half of the 7th century by the introduction of Frankish currency, and of Anglo-Saxon versions of the coins. Digging at the former Roman forts of Reculver and Richborough, Kent, which produced coins of this date, has revealed what may have been open market sites similar to that of St Denis. At Southampton, Hampshire, however, recent excavations have uncovered part of a mercantile town, perhaps the port for royal Winchester. The total occupied area of this settlement, Hamwih, is estimated at some 75 acres, and the results suggest that the town was laid out towards the end of the 7th century on a regular grid plan. This was the *mercimonium* of Hamwih, the "marketplace" from which in 720 Willibald, kinsman and biographer of St Boniface, and later bishop of Eichstätt, took passage to the *mercimonium* of Rouen on the Seine. In the same decade Bede was able to describe London as an "emporium of many people coming by land and sea," and from London in 716 St Boniface sailed to the most important of the continental trading towns, Dorestad, near the mouth of the Rhine, now the small Dutch town of Wijk bij Duurstede.

The Dutch State Archaeological Service's investigations at Dorestad, by now perhaps the most extensive excavations ever carried out on a single site, have been in progress in advance of urban redevelopment since 1967. Preliminary reports of the work (which by 1969 had exposed nearly 50 acres) record rectangular and bow-sided

Rough infertile country where communications are best by sea. A view of Sognfjord, Norway.

timber houses, some of them perhaps farmsteads, probable warehouses, and shipyards, and great quantities of imported pottery, much of it from the Rhineland and almost all of the 8th and early 9th centuries.

From Dorestad Frisian traders worked their way across to the Baltic, where market centers were growing in importance. On the former island of Helgö in Lake Mälar, that great arm of the sea which runs past modern Stockholm to Uppsala and the heart of Svealand, excavations have revealed a settlement which consisted of a series of rectangular houses along the shore and on terraces cut into the hillside. Founded in the 5th century, the settlement expanded rapidly during the 7th and early 8th centuries. The site was rich in finds – pottery, glass and metalwork imported from Germany and the southern Baltic; and quantities of mold fragments, slag and waste-material showed the development of industry beside the marketplace, in small sheds attached to some of the houses.

The Scandinavian expansion. Despite the shortcomings in the evidence it seems clear that 8th-century Scandinavia was prosperous, with a major center at Helgö supplying the rich Svear chieftains, and doubtless with such sites in other areas still to be identified. There are some signs of internal colonization of the countryside: in Denmark in particular attempts have been made to distinguish settlements (whose names originally ended in -*ing*, -*heimr* or -*leif*) from later colonizing sites with -*by* or -*thorp* suffixes, such as Aaby, Kjaerby, Volstrup or Ajstrup. Expansion into more marginal lands and consequent overpopulation may be suspected, but cannot yet be demonstrated. Similarly difficult to prove are the claims of the later Scandinavian migrants that their movements were the result of political grievances, the consequence of the growing power of the kings and the nobility. Historians, assuming that huge numbers of warriors took part in the Viking invasions of Europe, have long regarded as inadequate these explanations in terms merely of population pressure and politics, but the provocative work of the English historian Peter Sawyer has clarified some issues. Sawyer has emphasized the way in which our sources, anxious to magnify the Viking threat, exaggerated the size of the pirate fleets, and has pointed out that *here*, the word normally used of the Viking forces in England, and customarily translated as "army" or "host," gives a misleading impression of numbers; for, according to the early 8th-century laws of King Ine of Wessex, any band of men more than 35 strong (a single shipload) is to be described as a *here*. Thus *micel here* should not be seen as "The Great Army" to be counted in thousands, but as a larger *here* than normal, a few hundred men. The effect of such a warrior band might well be great: the Viking "army" which in 866 ravaged northern France, and defeated a Frankish "host" led by a marquis and three counts, numbered only 400 men. Not all would agree with Sawyer in detail, particularly in his estimates of the very limited scale of Scandinavian immigration into the British Isles, but even his most conservative calculations make the Viking movements seem less extraordinary. They should be seen, in his words, simply as "an extension of normal Dark Age activity made possible and profitable by special circumstances."

The origin of the profit we have already seen: the steady growth of trade across the North Sea and the Baltic must have increased the opportunities for piracy. The circumstances that made piracy now possible are less definite. The Viking ships at the end of the 8th century may indeed have been better suited than before to long voyages, but the evidence for this is, as we have seen, too uncertain. A more realistic immediate cause for the Viking outbreak is the Carolingian conquest of Frisia and Saxony, for by 800 the sea power of Denmark's neighbors had been suppressed and the Franks made little attempt to supplant them. When the Danish pirates of the 830s sailed southwards and westwards, at sea they moved without opposition against kingdoms whose stability was already uncertain, and whose internal rivalries were an invitation to barbarian inroads. They were not the first to sail westwards, though most of them perhaps did not know it. A generation or more earlier, land-hungry Norwegians had begun to settle in the Northern Isles.

The Norwegian settlements. After the first Norwegian raids on England and the continental coasts at the end of the 8th century, our sources all but ignore the Northmen for nearly 40 years. The apparent lack of activity is misleading, for there are signs of movement outside the confines of literate Europe, in the islands of northern and western Scotland, an early colonization which has left little trace even in the Scandinavians' own sagas. Dates in the second half of the 8th century have been suggested, on no very good grounds, for the earliest archaeological finds in the Northern Isles, and it is possible that the early raids on Northumbrian Lindisfarne or on Ireland were merely activities at the edge of a wave of Norwegian settlement in north Britain.

Opposite: a drawing (after J. R. C. Hamilton) of the 9th-century settlement of Jarlshof. The photograph shows (*foreground*) the Iron Age village and tower eroded by the sea and partially overlain by a medieval house; (*right*) foundations of Bronze Age houses; (*inland*) the Viking-period buildings.

Viking-period houses and graves have been excavated in the Orkneys, Shetlands and Hebrides. They range in scale from Birsay, Orkney, an extensive complex of major buildings which included the palace of the earls of Orkney and their cathedral, to the customary huddle of stone-walled buildings found in the farmsteads of Scandinavia. The nature of these early agricultural settlements is seen most clearly at the thoroughly excavated farmstead of Jarlshof, Shetland. The first farmhouse, tentatively ascribed to the early 9th century, was an aisled building containing a kitchen and a long living room, with associated outbuildings, identified as a detached byre or barn, a smithy, a bath-house and a serfs' hall. Animal bones – sheep, ox, some pig and domestic fowls – indicate a range of farming, and hunting and fishing were shown by bones of deer, seals, whales and cod. The settlement survived until perhaps the 14th century: the houses were repaired, rebuilt or resited as the settlement grew, probably in response to the needs of an expanding kinship group; the finds suggest an increasing isolation and a greater reliance on fishing.

From the Scottish islands the Norwegians sailed to Ireland, where the Irish annals record the fortification in 841 of a base for their ships at Ath Cliath, later known as the Black Pool, *Dubh Linn*, on the River Liffey. A large cemetery of 9th-century date was discovered on the outskirts of Dublin during 19th-century development, but the earliest part of the town itself has so far eluded investigations. The settlements had been preceded by raiding, reviewed by the *Annals of Ulster* under the year 820: "The Ocean spewed out torrents of foreigners over Erin, and no harbour or landing, fort or stronghold was free of fleets of Scandinavians and pirates." Irish resistance was at first strong, and the Danish Vikings who arrived in 850 joined in attacks on the Norwegians. In 853, however, the Scandinavians were united by a new arrival, a Norwegian prince, who, as King Olaf of Dublin, founded a realm that included much of the Irish coast, but very little of the interior of the country.

The Danish Vikings. The Danish colonists in Ireland were part of a great wave of Danish pirates who during the decades after 830 swept westwards to England and to Francia. By the beginning of the 9th century, when the frontier of Charlemagne's empire lay along the Elbe, hostilities between the Franks and their Danish neighbors were inevitable. Gottfrid, first of the Danish kings to figure in Frankish records, about 800 built a bank and ditch across the root of the Jutland peninsula, and in 810 led to Frisia a fleet which crushed the Frankish coastal

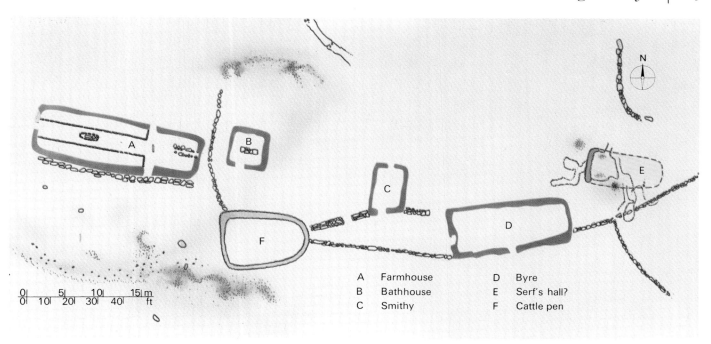

A	Farmhouse	D	Byre
B	Bathhouse	E	Serf's hall?
C	Smithy	F	Cattle pen

Hilt of a sword from Dybeck, Skane, richly decorated with silver gilt and gold wire in the late Viking style. Perhaps south Swedish, influenced by English designs. Late 10th century.

defenses. The crisis passed, for Gottfrid was soon assassinated and Charlemagne was by now too infirm to contemplate direct attack on Denmark. After 814 his son Louis the Pious contented himself with maintaining the coast guardships to such good effect that Viking attacks are recorded only in 820, on the coast of Flanders and at the mouth of the Seine, and in each case the raiders were driven off. The respite lasted as long as the Frankish monarchy remained steady.

As soon as Louis' sons rebelled against their father, the Vikings seized their opportunity: in 834, after Louis' surrender to Lothar and his subsequent imprisonment, a fleet of Danish ships sailed up the Rhine and sacked the great trading center at Dorestad. For the next 40 years Frisia was under Viking control, and Dorestad, pillaged four times and greatly depopulated, for ever lost its trading preeminence. From Frisia the Danes advanced to the coast of England: in 835 "the heathens" devastated Sheppey on the north coast of Kent. The southern English kingdoms had recently passed into the hands of Egbert, king of Wessex, whose realm stretched from Cornwall to Kent, and whose supremacy was recognized by the Mercians (weak under the rival successors of Offa the Great) and even by the distant Northumbrians. For a few years Egbert and his shire leaders (*ealdormen*) fought with success against raiders on the south coast of England, and Viking attacks were diverted to more promising targets on the continent.

In Francia raiding and plunder multiplied during the civil war between Louis' sons, increased perhaps by the use of Scandinavian mercenaries on both sides. In 841 a fleet entered the Seine and sacked Rouen; another in 842 "so ravaged the port of Quentavic [on the French coast near Boulogne, and by then the chief surviving town trading with England] that they left nothing in it except the buildings which were ransomed." A third fleet in 843 attacked the town of Nantes on the Loire. Some of these raids may have been the work of privateers; some, however, were large-scale expeditions mounted with the aid, and perhaps under the instructions, of Danish kings. In 845 a fleet said to number 600 ships was sent by King Horek to burn Hamburg. Early in the same year a fleet (of 120 ships, it was said) sailed into the Seine under the command of one Ragnar, who was perhaps a relative of the Frisian chiefs and of the Danish royal family; he may indeed have been the original of the half-legendary Ragnar Loðbrok ("Shaggy-breeks") whose Viking career, with its courageous ending in a snake pit in York, and the revenge of his sons, was a favorite Scandinavian story during the Middle Ages. His raid along the Seine, at any rate, was memorable enough: the ships rowed past Rouen, taking captives and pillaging the monasteries and towns on either bank; despite the efforts of Charles the Bald, on Easter Day 845 the Vikings sacked Paris and then repaired their ships with timbers hacked from the church of St Germain-des-Prés. When they retired they took not only their booty, but the first of the Danegelds, a payment of 7,000 pounds of silver from Charles, to persuade them to go away.

The raiding was serious enough, but the raiders seldom stayed for long. A more ominous development was the establishment of permanent fortified bases from which the Vikings could terrorize the coasts. The first recorded was on Noirmoutier, the large island at the mouth of the Loire, on which, in 843, the raiders of Nantes settled, as the Frankish annalist notes, "as if they meant to stay for ever." In England the *Chronicle* records the same phenomenon: in 850 "the heathen men for the first time remained over winter, in Thanet." This force was ultimately destroyed by the army of Wessex, but others took its place: in 855 "the heathen" wintered nearer London, in the isle of Sheppey. In the 860s a dismal picture was painted by Ermentarius, a native of the Loire: "The number of ships grows. The endless stream of Vikings never ceases to increase . . ." The annalists of the time, each concerned with his own region almost to the exclusion of others, present a truly chaotic picture of the attacks.

Comparison of the dates of the arrival and departure of the raiding parties arouses the suspicion that in many cases a single army has transferred the scene of its activities from one region to another, according to the likely quantity of plunder or the strength of the opposition. A party which in 860 landed unexpectedly and sacked the city of Winchester may even have been that Viking band then under contract to Charles the Bald but still waiting for its pay. By that time some of the pirate companies were looking for richer prizes than remained in the southeast of England and on the coasts of France. In 859 a powerful force of 62 ships (perhaps as many as 2,000 men) sailed from the Loire and harried the Spanish coast. After some reverses there, and uncertain success in a subsequent attack on the North African coast, they wintered on the Rhône, and ravaged the country as far as Arles. From there they sailed along the shores of Italy, and may have entered the eastern Mediterranean. The fleets of the Saracens, at that time engaged with the Franks in Italy, seem to have proved unexpectedly strong, and when the Viking fleet returned in 861 to the Loire it had been reduced to 22 ships.

The resistance of the Saracens may have dissuaded imitation of the exploit, and the Mediterranean remained an Arabic sea. The Vikings turned their attention elsewhere, and their pressure on England now increased. The sober account in the *Anglo-Saxon Chronicle*, even in outline, is a remarkable picture of the collapse of kingdoms. In 865 a large body of warriors, the "Great Army," occupied East Anglia, apparently peacefully: the East Anglians presumably paid blackmail. Reinforced in the next year, it seems, by the Vikings from the Seine valley, the raiders, now on horseback, advanced northwards and entered York. The levies of Northumbria tried to drive them out, but the Vikings with a single battle destroyed the power of the kingdom; the survivors paid Danegeld. In 867 the Vikings moved south into Mercia, and in their fortification at Nottingham held off the combined levies of Mercia and Wessex, who seem to have been unwilling, after the experience of the Northumbrians, to try to storm the ramparts. The peace which the Mercians then made was presumably sealed by another Danegeld, and the army retired again to York. In 869 the Danes returned to East Anglia, but the Angles this time attempted to resist them: their king, Edmund, became a saint, and the kingdom was ravaged.

After a winter in the ruins of East Anglia the Vikings advanced into Wessex, where the Saxon levies resisted long enough to persuade them to retire to London with another Danegeld, described in a contemporary charter as "the immense tribute to the barbarians." Wessex had proved too strong for easy taking, and the army turned its attention to the conquest of Mercia. Part of the force now partitioned the lands of the Northumbrians and settled down to farm. The rest moved in 875 to Cambridge, and in 876 launched a surprise attack on Wessex, in con-

junction with Vikings from Ireland. The new king of Wessex, Alfred the Great, outflanked the army (which seems to have been on horseback) and finally bottled up the Vikings in Exeter; under truce they retired back to Mercia in 877, waited until winter, and then overran Wessex. Alfred escaped from the debacle, and from his fortified base in the Somerset marshes he assembled his levies, defeated the Danes in battle, and imposed a treaty by which his kingdom for a while was made secure.

The defeated Vikings retired to East Anglia and in 879 shared out the land. Another force, based near London since 878, and perhaps attracted by the likely pickings in Wessex, was warned off by the West Saxon recovery and retired to the continent, where for eight years it ravaged Flanders. In 885 part of this army crossed again to England and besieged the Kentish town of Rochester, but Alfred's advance drove them back to their friends on the continent. The attempt on Rochester seems to have been a trial of strength, and the failure in England concentrated Viking attention on Francia. The Franks were unable to stop them as they moved from Amiens to the Seine and besieged Paris. The long and ultimately successful defense of this city increased the reputation of its governor, Odo count of Paris. The prestige of Charles the Fat, who found himself unable to raise the siege except by the payment of Danegeld, declined still further, not least because of its consequence: the Viking army moved into the interior and began a career of pillage which lasted until its defeat in 891 by the Emperor Arnulf, son of Louis the German.

In a way by now familiar, the army, short of supplies, retired to Boulogne in 892 and sailed across to try its luck in England. King Alfred's attempts to separate this new army from that now settled in East Anglia were frustrated, but he and his lieutenants won a series of victories in battles in the southeast and in Mercia, and the expected booty was not forthcoming. In 896 the Danish army broke up: some settled down in East Anglia and Northumbria "and those that were without booty got themselves ships and went south oversea to the Seine." The Seine Vikings, who seem to have been established there since 876, were to prove a nuisance for another generation at least. Many seem to have settled on the lower Seine, interfering with river communications and launching raids into Francia. By 911 Charles the Simple was prepared to recognize the control which they had won over part of his domain. By the treaty of St Clair-sur-Epte the Viking leader Rollo (first mentioned 35 years before) accepted the grant of the land he already effectively ruled. By later grants in 924 and 933 the whole of the metropolitan province of Rouen was ceded to the Vikings, and became during the course of the 10th century the duchy of Normandy, governed, sometimes with difficulty, by the descendants of Rollo.

Raiders and defenses. The very success of these and other smaller Viking raids has surprised generations of historians, many of whom have looked for explanations in terms of huge fleets – by accepting the annalists' figures of 200 or 300 vessels carrying perhaps 5,000 or 10,000 men, though ignoring the blatantly inflated estimates of 40,000 or so – or in the excellence of their equipment, or their barbarian ferocity. The results of such considerations make the problems even more perplexing, for these armies were kept in being for year after year (a feat of supply and command that, if true, had not been seen in the west since the end of the Roman Empire), and yet, from time to time, they unaccountably allowed themselves to be shut up in their fortresses by local levies of no great size. The Viking tactics make sense only if their numbers were comparatively small. One may doubt, too, that with the exception of the half-mad "berserkers," whom even hardened Vikings shunned, the raiders were noticeably more ferocious than their contemporaries. They seem, indeed, to have taken a thoroughly professional attitude to their fighting, balancing likely profit against probable loss, sounding out the readiness of the defenses by exploratory raids, and glad to accept tribute rather than pressing their advantage. The terror they inspired was felt most strongly by the Church, for the Vikings were pagan, and they directed their attention (to an extent unparalleled outside the Irish civil wars of the 8th century) to robbing churches and monasteries of their accumulated wealth. Lay-folk seem to have taken a more pragmatic attitude, sometimes using the raiders, as did the Emperor Lothar and his brothers, when it was convenient, and sometimes paying blackmail to be rid of them.

That such small armies of professional freebooters should have proved a threat to the Frankish Empire, whose soldiers had recently conquered much of western Europe, is itself not surprising. Unlike almost all the previous opponents of both Franks and English, the Vikings came from the sea without the advance warning inevitable in movement by land. By the time that the local levies had assembled, the pirates had normally retired or were secure behind fortifications. Against such mobility only localized defense was possible, and the increasing reliance of Francia upon the resources of the local counts diminished royal authority and accelerated the fragmentation of the empire. In England, by contrast, the kings of Wessex established a network of local defenses that was under their own control. During the last few years of the 9th century King Alfred began to build the *burhs*, small fortified settlements at strategic points some 20 miles apart, which served to protect local interests and threatened the progress of raiding parties. By 918 over 30 such sites had been developed. They were significantly different from the 10th-century fortresses which Henry the Fowler was to build against the Magyars in Germany, for they were envisaged not simply as refuges but as planned nuclear settlements with their own populations and economic life, their upkeep centrally ordered but locally provided, as part of the duties of landholding. Many, such as Oxford, Wallingford, Buckingham or Warwick, were to become prosperous towns, and their existence was part of the success of 10th-century Wessex.

A greater contrast could hardly be found than that between the Viking devastations of 9th-century England and the submission of the descendants of the men of the great army to Alfred's successors. By 920 Alfred's son Edward the Elder was master of England as far as the Humber and was nominal overlord of the Danish and English kings of the lands as far as central Scotland. The change almost certainly owed its origin to the settlement of the Danes in the Midlands and northern England. The aim of many, perhaps the majority, of the Vikings was to acquire sufficient treasure to settle down in comfort on their own estates, and this, as we have seen, was the choice of parts of the armies of the 870s and the 890s. But, once settled with a stake in the country and an interest in farming in peace, the Danes were as vulnerable to attack as their former victims, and, as recent studies of the early medieval taxation units of midland England have shown, the Viking settlement was spread too thinly for easy concentration in the face of a threat.

Pressure from a different source may have persuaded the inhabitants of what was soon to be called the Danelaw, the lands now controlled by the former Vikings, to submit to the West Saxons. In the late 9th century Norwegian Vikings in the Irish Sea had become rarer; the colonization of Iceland, as we shall see, was at this time distracting the interest of the more adventurous. By the 910s Iceland was filling up with settlers, and the Norse returned in strength to Ireland, to reestablish their kingdom in Dublin, and to begin their settlement of the west coast of the British mainland. By about 920 Norwegian Vikings were raiding Cumbria, and in that year an army from Dublin was stopped in Cheshire. The established Danish settlers had no reason to welcome the attentions of the Norwegians, and seem to have thrown in their lot with whichever side seemed stronger.

The Norse objective was Yorkshire, and a succession of kings of Norwegian origin set out from Ireland to claim the throne of York. For nearly 40 years the West Saxon kings accepted some and ejected others, according to the necessities of the moment. After a series of successes gained by Alfred's son and grandsons, Alfred's grandson Eadred was strong enough in 954 to expel the last of the kings of York, the archetypal Viking Eirik Bloodaxe, who was the son of King Harald Finehair, and who for a brief and violent period had himself been king of Norway. The kingdom of York was given to the earl of Northumbria, and thereafter remained part of the English kingdom. Norwegian conquest had failed, but pirate bands remained until, at least in legend, the high king Brian Boru destroyed the power of the kingdom of Dublin in 1014. It is a mark of the times that when Eadred died at the height of his authority in 955 he left in his will a large sum of money to be used if it should ever prove necessary to buy off a heathen army.

The migration to the west. By the end of the 9th century the first wave of Viking raids was over. The kingdoms of western Europe were, it seems, no longer an easy prey for pirates, and in the Atlantic a new land for settlement had been discovered: Iceland, hitherto occupied by a tiny handful of Irish hermits, lay no more than 250 miles beyond the Faroes, and from about 870 a steadily growing stream of migrants sailed in *Knarrs* from Norway, the Northern Islands and from Ireland. The western adventure involved considerable numbers – by 930, according to the 13th-century History of Iceland, the *Landnámabók*, some 400 named leaders, representing perhaps as many as 3,000 families – and it is no coincidence that during these years Norwegian pressure on Ireland declined: by 902 indeed the Irish had retaken Dublin.

The migration may have been inspired by dissatisfaction with the growth in Norway of a strong monarchy under King Harald Finehair, and the migrants clearly reacted against royal autocracy: by 930 they had devised what was perhaps the first republican constitution in modern Europe. The settlement pattern, too, demonstrates the sturdy independence of the new Icelanders, a scatter of stone and turf farmstead complexes, their farm buildings, like those of the Hebrides, huddled together for protection against the weather. The first settler, Ingólf Arnarson, in 874 built his farm (according to saga) amid the hot springs of Reykjavik, where scanty traces of occupation of 9th- or 10th-century date have been uncovered in the heart of the modern city. The likely appearance of such a farm is best seen in the valley of Thjórsárdale in central Iceland, where 20 farmsteads were buried in volcanic ash about 1104. The best preserved, the farm at Stöng, consisted of a long rectangular building divided into a vestibule (probably containing the owner's box-bed) and a main hall with a central fireplace, and earth and timber benches along its wainscoted walls. Further rooms, in attached outshots, were probably a more secluded living room, a dairy and a meat store. Outside lay a detached byre and a smithy. The complexity of the layout of the main house at Stöng is perhaps an evolution from the earlier types, with few or no outshots, found in the Scottish islands.

From Iceland to the coast of Greenland is less than 300 miles and accidental landfalls were made soon after the colonization of Iceland. The first visitors found the east coast too inhospitable, and a thorough exploration was not made until the 980s. The explorer, Eirík the Red, in exile from Iceland, found the west coast fertile, and named the country Greenland, because, as he said, "men would be the readier to go there if it had a pleasant name." From an Iceland that was already overpopulated he led a fleet of 25 ships (only 14 survived the journey) to establish two settlements on the east coast. Eirík himself settled down at Brattahlíð on the south corner of the island, where excavations have exposed the turf and stone walls of his farmstead, four barns and byres for 28 head of cattle, and the foundations of a tiny turf church, built by Eirík's wife shortly after the year 1000.

The colony in America. In 985 or 986 Bjarni Herjólfsson, an Icelander on his way to join his father in the Greenland settlements, was blown off course and sighted

The Icelandic farmhouse at Stöng, abandoned c. 1104. Designed for a harsh climate, the domestic outbuildings are linked to the main structure. A further outhouse or smithy and a byre stood to the east of the farmhouse. After Stenberger.

A	Living room	D	Dairy
B	Hall	E	Stores
C	Hearth	F	Box bed

land nine days' sailing time to the west of Greenland. His story excited the Greenland settlers, and Eirík's son, Leif the Lucky, about 990 set off in Bjarni's old ship to retrace the journey. Coasting past Helluland and Markland (probably Baffin Island and Labrador) the expedition finally came to a country full of grass, salmon and wild grapes: Leif called it Vínland, "Wineland," and built some houses – the Norse equivalent of raising the flag – before returning to Greenland. From about 1011 to 1014 a colonizing expedition under an Icelandic merchant, Thorfinn Karlsefni, took a lease on Leif's houses (Leif refused to sell) and established itself in Vínland, but was driven out by hostile Indians. Thereafter detailed information is lacking, though the memory of Vínland was never lost, and Greenlanders and even Icelanders may well have made regular voyages to the American coast for timber and game.

The location of Vínland itself still provokes controversy, fed recently by the publication of a supposedly 15th-century map of the then known world, including Iceland, Greenland, and at a distance to the southwest the "Island" of Vínland. The map tells us nothing new, and is very likely not genuine; Leif's Vínland itself probably lay to the south, perhaps in New England, but the area is so far unconfirmed by archaeological discovery. From the coast of Vínland, trappers and explorers may have advanced further into the continent of America; if so, they have left no record, and none of the objects for which a Viking origin has been claimed has an unquestioned pedigree. Other, presumably much more regular, contacts were made further north, and from 1960 to 1968 the excavations at L'Anse aux Meadows in north Newfoundland have revealed a complex of eight houses of normal Norse type, whose date had been shown by radiocarbon determinations to lie at some point between the 8th and the 12th centuries. Vínland, Newfoundland and other Norse landfalls disappear from view in the Middle Ages – the last recorded visit to Labrador was in 1347 – and, as the climate deteriorated during the 14th century, Greenland itself became depopulated. Before the middle of the 15th century all contact between Iceland and Greenland had been broken. The last Icelandic ship to call left in 1408, and the end may have come soon afterwards: Eskimo stories tell how the last survivors of the once-thriving colony were burned to death by Eskimos in the small 11th-century church whose ruins still stand at the extreme south of the island, on the seashore at Hvalsey.

The Swedish connection. The Vikings in the west came almost entirely from Norway and Denmark. Swedish expansion lay eastwards, across the Baltic to the great rivers of Russia. By the middle of the 9th century we hear from Arab sources of Europeans bringing beaver-skins, black fox fur and swords into the Black Sea and the Caspian, and traveling overland to the markets of Baghdad. The quantity of trade is confirmed by the tens of thousands of Arabic coins which have been discovered in hoards buried along the trade routes and in Sweden.

Trade from the east and plunder from the west greatly increased the commerce in the Baltic, and the market centers expanded rapidly. Foremost among them was the Danish town of Hederby, founded by King Gottfrid in 808 at the head of the Schlei estuary opposite Schleswig. This town, about 60 acres inside its ramparts, has been excavated intermittently for some 70 years. The densely settled town center was surrounded by extensive empty spaces within the late 9th-century walls, areas which are plausibly seen as huge open-air markets. Some of the goods for sale were locally made, for signs of iron- and bronze-working have been found, and pottery was also produced in the town. The results of the investigations suggest that Gottfrid's town was built beside an 8th-century Frisian settlement, that the peak of the town's prosperity was in the late 9th and 10th centuries, and that the town was in decline before its destruction about 1050 by Harald Hardraði.

Local market towns must have flourished along the Scandinavian coasts. One, an unfortified site at Kaupang ("Market") near Gokstad, was a straggling line of buildings around an open market space. The finds, which include Rhineland glass and pottery and Anglo-Saxon artifacts, suggest that the settlement was flourishing during the 9th and early 10th centuries. In central Sweden the market at Helgö was replaced by a fortified town of about 30 acres, Birka on the island of Björkö. Little is known of the town itself: it was commanded by a fort like that at Hederby, and traces remain of wharves and of an artificial harbor. The graveyard, extensively excavated in the 19th century, seems to have been established about 800 and the latest graves belong to the years after 950. On the opposite side of the Baltic, at Staraja Ladoga near Leningrad, excavations inside a fortified site of nearly 160 acres have revealed 9th-century Swedish material, within a settlement of closely packed wooden buildings, a town which was probably a transit point on the routes from the Baltic southwards via the Dnieper and the Volga.

One town on the Dnieper was probably established by the early 9th century, Kiev, inhabited by Swedes known to the Byzantines as Rhos (hence "Russia"), and the center of a network of trade – westwards overland through Cracow and Prague to the Rhine, and along the rivers northwards to the Baltic and south to the Black Sea. Objects of Scandinavian origin come from the gravefield of old Kiev, but the Rhos are seen by Russian archaeologists as only an insignificant fraction of the town's Slavic population. The same view is taken, less plausibly, of the old town at Smolensk on the upper Dnieper, whose enormous cemetery of 250 acres has produced plentiful evidence of Swedish presence. Between Smolensk and the Gulf of Finland, the city of Novgorod was founded about 860, according to the *Russian Chronicle*, by a Scandinavian prince. The recent excavations have concentrated on the

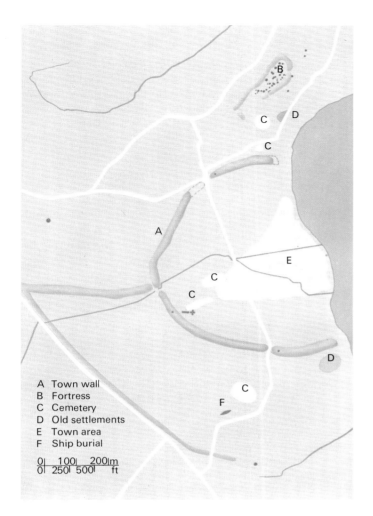

A Town wall
B Fortress
C Cemetery
D Old settlements
E Town area
F Ship burial

0   100   200 m
0 250 500   ft

great medieval city, and the site of the 9th-century settlement has not yet been investigated. Significantly, it lies in the area of the later market center, for the city's importance was based on trade. The Byzantine emperor Constantine Porphyrogenitus noted that "the ships which come to Constantinople from further Russia are from Novgorod where Prince Sviatoslav Igorsson of the Rus has his seat."

The apparent contrast between the fierce Vikings of the west and the town-building Swedish merchant-princes of Russia is unreal. The methods of one prince are illustrated in the *Russian Chronicle*'s account of the Rhos dynasty of Kiev: in 883 Prince Oleg conquered the Drevlians and taxed them at the rate of one black marten per head. In 884 he conquered and taxed the Severians. In 885 he sent envoys to the Radimichians to ask to whom they paid tribute. They replied, "To the Khazars [the Turks of the north Caucasus]." Oleg said, "You shall not pay tribute to the Khazars but to me." And they gave Oleg a shilling each, the same as they paid to the Khazars. The exaction of tribute and tolls was the normal behavior for any state, Arab, Greek or Scandinavian, which controlled a trade route or could force its neighbors to pay. Occasionally, too, we hear of Viking raids. One, on the city of Constantinople itself, was indeed led by Prince Igor of Novgorod, father of Sviatoslav. Furthermore, the de-

Hederby near Schleswig during the 9th and 10th centuries was a huge fortified marketplace at the edge of the Baltic, which inherited much of the trade formerly controlled by Dorestad. The town itself covered only a third of the defended area; the rest was probably used for open-air markets (plan, *left*, after H. Jankuhn). The photograph (*below*) shows the remains of buildings under excavation near the center of the old town.

Above: Frankish jug from the lower Rhine found in the excavations of the market center at Birka, Sweden, decorated by tinfoil diamonds and strips glued into the clay. Early 9th century.

The Viking trade routes eastwards to Russia, the Eastern Empire and Islam and westwards across the Atlantic. The distribution of Arabic coins shows the success of eastern trade.

structiveness of the western Vikings is easily over-emphasized. We have seen how the Norwegian settlers colonized the Atlantic islands. Their kindred in Ireland set up a kingdom in which, as the recent excavations in Dublin show, trade flourished, encouraged, not checked, by overseas adventures. The profit, of course, enriched the merchants, and ultimately the princes. If the feelings of the Slavic neighbors of Kiev or Novgorod had been recorded, they would very probably have echoed the reiterated Irish complaints of oppression and taxation.

Commerce, in fact, no less than adventure or dissatisfaction at home, seems to underlie the Scandinavian movements. The Franks noted, not without surprise, that Viking communities settled in Frisia and northern France found no difficulty in developing highly lucrative trade, and the archaeology of the Danelaw of 10th-century England indicates rapid growth in town life and industry. Purely Scandinavian objects here are remarkably rare, perhaps through the influence of Christian burial practice in churchyards: apart from scattered burials only one entirely Scandinavian cemetery is known, that at Ingleby near Derby. But it can be no coincidence that the fundamental change in English pottery styles (from the traditional Anglo-Saxon vessels made by hand or on a primitive slow wheel to sophisticated fast wheel-thrown pottery with the first glazes to be seen in England since the Roman period) occurs in the late 9th or early 10th century, and that the new pottery is largely confined in its distribution to the Danelaw. The clays show that manu-

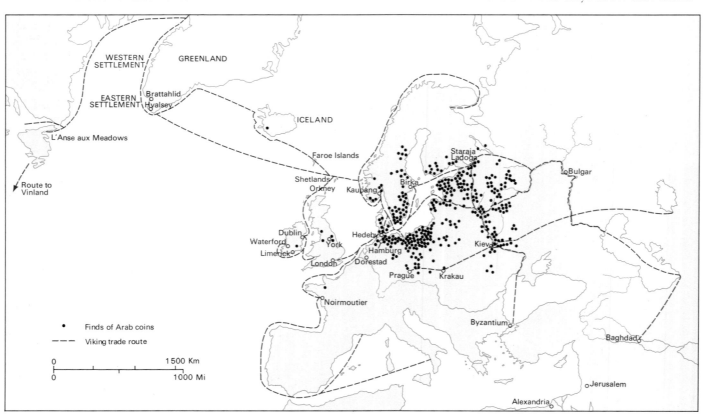

facture was local, but the influences which led to the change were foreign, perhaps from the Rhineland potteries or Constantinople, or even from further afield, from Islam, for Arabic coins imported into Scandinavia reach a peak in the late 9th century, and came, in the course of trade, to join the coins of Wessex and York in English and Irish hoards.

The Danish empire. After the successes of Alfred's grandsons England enjoyed a generation of relative peace. The second wave of Viking attacks began in 980, and were directed principally at England. Their cause was perhaps partly financial, for the stream of Arabic silver which for two centuries had poured into Europe was dwindling by 930, and by 970 had all but disappeared from the west. As a result Vikings who had been plundering Baltic merchants turned their attention back to the west. Ultimately more important, perhaps, was the emergence in Denmark of a strong monarchy. In 980 King Harald Bluetooth ordered a great stone to be carved, as its runic inscription declares, "In memory of his father Gorm and of his mother Thyri: Harald who won the whole of Denmark for himself, and Norway, and made the Danes Christian." About 986 Harald's son Svein Forkbeard succeeded his father, after a revolution he may have engineered, and devoted his considerable resources to the creation of a mercenary army. To his reign belongs a series of novel fortifications, the great Danish camps at Trelleborg, Fyrkat, Aggersborg and Odense, the most striking monuments of the Viking period.

In each camp the massive bank and ditch form a perfect circle broken by four symmetrically placed entrances. Roads divided the interior into quadrants in each of which stood regularly orientated squares of bow-sided buildings. At the most fully excavated camp, Trelleborg, a further line of buildings, their alignment concentric with the main rampart, stood behind their own outer bank. The planning was precisely measured in units of $11\frac{1}{2}$ inches, only one eighth of an inch shorter than the normal Roman foot. At Fyrkat each house was 96 units long, at Aggersbord 110 units, and at Trelleborg 100 units. Most remarkably, the internal diameter of the Trelleborg enclosure (234 units) was exactly the same as the distance from the center of the enclosure to the nearer gable end of the outer buildings. The symmetry of the design distinguishes these camps from all other barbarian fortifications, and, like their distant ancestors the Roman *castra*, they are certainly the bases of a professional army such as occupied Jomsborg on the Baltic coast in the 12th-century Icelandic *Jómsvikinga Saga* – a memory of a warrior society which shared all booty equally, fought in the summer, and in the winter lived under severe discipline in Jomsborg, allowing no women to enter the camp, and granting its members no more than three days' leave at a time. The camps appear to be contemporary, and are ill sited to defend Denmark. They are, therefore, reasonably seen as the barracks of

Svein's army, built with the royal share of the takings from the initial plundering raids of the late 10th century: by 1012 the Danegelds paid to the Danish Vikings amounted to no less than 146,000 pounds of gold and silver, a staggeringly large sum apparently raised in part by the sale of English land to Danes. The capacity of the camps is estimated at 5,500 men, a force sufficiently large to threaten the security of any kingdom in the west.

The success of the initial raids, and the feebleness of English resistance under King Aethelred II, nicknamed "the Ill-Advised" (*Unraed*), encouraged further intervention and the feud was made more bitter in 1002 by Aethelred's hasty massacre of English Danes, including Svein's own sister. In 1003 Svein himself brought over a host which until 1006 harried Wessex and East Anglia. Svein returned in 1009 with a larger army, which ignored the fleet Aethelred had been building, and for 16 months ravaged the south and east before withdrawing with a Danegeld of 48,000 pounds. By 1013 Svein had clearly decided that Aethelred's kingdom was weak enough to conquer; he led his fleet northwards to the Trent, in the heart of the Danelaw, and he accepted the submission of the northern leaders before marching south and taking over Wessex. Aethelred fled to Normandy where he took refuge with the duke, whose sister he had married.

But the situation in England remained confused, for Svein died in Lincolnshire almost immediately after entering his new kingdom, and his younger son Knut (Canute), threatened by Aethelred's supporters, retired across the North Sea, leaving Aethelred king once more. Loyalties of the English magnates were wavering, and Knut (with the assistance of his elder brother, now the king of Denmark) in 1015 brought yet another fleet to harry Wessex. The levies and the Danish army fought a series of engagements with varying success, and the contestants eventually agreed to a partition of the kingdom between Knut and Aethelred's son and successor Edmund "Ironside." Edmund lived only a few weeks longer, and Knut was acknowledged King of England. The great fleet was disbanded, with a parting gift levied in England which amounted to 82,500 pounds. A memorial stone in Uppland, Sweden, records in terse runes the career of a soldier under the Viking chieftains, Tosti and Thorkel the Tall, and King Knut: "Ulv took in England three gelds [that is, wage payments]. That was the first which Tosti paid. Then Thorkel paid. Then Knut paid."

Knut, who had guarded his rear by marrying Aethelred's widow, Emma of Normandy, began a reconstruction of the administration which he and his father had wrecked. His brother died childless and by 1019 Knut was king of both Denmark and England. Knut's North Sea empire, which included an uncertain control over Norway, lasted only until his death in 1035. His son Harthacnut was unlucky enough to be in Denmark when his father died, and for three years a threat from Norway, newly independent under King Magnus Olafsson, pre-

Aerial view of the early 11th-century army camp at Trelleborg, Sjaelland, Denmark. Foundations of the excavated timber buildings are marked out on the grass. The reconstructed house is visible (*left*), beyond the outer camp.

vented him from traveling to claim his English throne. His illegitimate brother Harald, who had the advantage of being in England, was accordingly proclaimed king. Coming to an agreement with Magnus, Harthacnut in 1039 brought a fleet to Flanders, but an invasion of England was forestalled by the death of his brother and his own succession in 1040. Harthacnut had no children and evidently favored his half-brother Edward, surviving son of Aethelred. Edward, later known for his piety as "the Confessor," in 1042 succeeded his benefactor on the throne of England. Denmark fell into the hands of

Magnus of Norway, and it seemed for a time that England too was in danger. But the crisis passed in 1047, with Magnus' death and the succession of his uncle Harald Sigurdsson "Hardruler," who allowed his claim to England to lapse for nearly 20 years, and lost his life trying to assert his rights at Stamford Bridge near York in 1066.

The Norman dukedom. During the Danish conquest relations between England and Normandy were uncertain. Some of the earlier attacks were connived at by the Norman dukes, and the ports of the duchy were a haven for Vikings returning from raiding England. In defiance of a treaty of amity signed between Aethelred and Duke Richard II in 991, Normandy was available for the Danish army's winter quarters in 1000. But Aethelred's marriage to the duke's sister in 1002 at least provided him with a refuge, and may have established more friendly contact, and it was with some Norman assistance that Aethelred returned to claim his throne in 1014.

The duchy of Normandy had developed considerably since its formation under Rollo the Viking. The Normans had adopted Frankish religion and law, customs and political organization, and when they emerged from the obscurity of the 10th century they had become, in the words of the historian Henri Prentout, "In the forefront of French culture and civilization." Even the monasteries, burned by their ancestors at the beginning of the 10th century, at its end were being restored by the Norman aristocracy. From 1001, a year before Emma's marriage to Aethelred, Norman monasticism was reformed under direct influence of Cluny, by then the leading religious house of western Europe – a spiritual revival which helped to make the Normans respectable in the eyes of the older kingdoms.

The dukes themselves were of recent nobility; their counts and barons formed a yet newer aristocracy, and were closely linked to the ducal family by fealty and by marriage. The developing feudal customs of Francia were readily adopted, and by the middle of the 11th century the system of military tenure by knight service was all but universal. The established power of the chief vassals found its expression in Normandy, as over northern Germany, in the building of private baronial fortifications, the castles which were to play so great a role in the Norman subjugation of England. But in Normandy, unlike Germany, a series of strong dukes kept the right to licence castles firmly under their own control.

Those younger sons, who, by the custom of primogeniture in feudal land tenure, were not to inherit their paternal estates and who were unwilling to enter the church, found ready service in the wars of Normandy's neighbors. In increasing numbers during the 11th century they turned to the wars between the Christians and Arabs in Spain, and to the crumbling dukedoms of southern Italy. In 1016 a party of Norman pilgrims returning from Jerusalem was able to help the prince of Salerno and the duke of Apulia against the Saracens. Both rulers appear to

Europe c. 1050 AD. By the 11th century the kingdoms of Europe had settled into the pattern which they maintained with only minor changes throughout the Middle Ages.

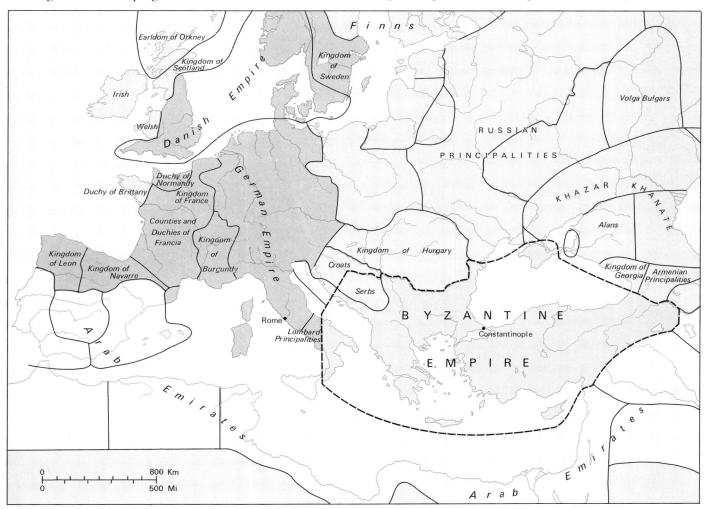

ET VENIT AD PEVENE SÆ :-

Duke William of Normandy's fleet making its way to England in 1066. The duke's ship, marked by the standard at the masthead, is a Viking warship. A scene from the tapestry worked in England between 1066 and 1077 and preserved at Bayeux, Normandy.

have requested further aid from Normandy, and the trickle of landless volunteers and adventurers became a flood. Norman mercenaries turned to banditry and then to the acquisition of estates. The Monte Cassino chronicler describes them: "Through the fields and gardens . . . happy on their horses . . . they rode up and down to seek their fortunes." By the 1050s many had carved out fiefs for themselves, and under the leadership of Robert Guiscard de Hauteville, who styled himself "By the grace of God and St Peter, Duke of Apulia and Calabria, and, with their help, hereafter [Duke] of Sicily," they founded with papal blessing the kingdom of Southern Italy and Sicily. The view of the 12th-century chronicler Jordan Fantosme was just: "The Normans are good conquerors: there is no race like them."

Epilogue. The Norman expansion into Italy and in 1066 into England was, until the brief passage of the Mongols in the 13th century, the last of the great folk movements which had swept across Europe since the fall of the Western Roman Empire. Thereafter national boundaries might shift according to the strength or weakness of individual monarchs, but the political map of Europe in 1050 is not significantly different from that of 400 years later. Throughout the 600 years of migrations we have seen the survival of the ideal of *Romanitas* among successive waves of barbarians. Now, at the end of the movements, the Roman Empire had again been renewed, to survive as a German kingdom until its abolition at the beginning of the 19th century.

Augustus, first of all the emperors, as he thought of those precious three legions which P. Quinctilius Varus lost in the forests of Germany, would surely have felt the irony.

Further Reading

Åberg, N., *Die Franken und Westgotern in der Völkerwanderung-zeit* (Uppsala, 1922).

Alcock, L., *Arthur's Britain* (Harmondsworth, 1971).

Brown, P., *The World of Late Antiquity* (London, 1971).

Bullough, D., *The Age of Charlemagne* (London, 1965).

Foote, P. G. and Wilson, D. M., *The Viking Achievement* (London, 1970).

Heer, F., *Charlemagne and his World* (London, 1975).

Hunter Blair, P., *An Introduction to Anglo-Saxon England* (Cambridge, 1966).

Krautheimer, R., *Early Christian and Byzantine Architecture* (Harmondsworth, 1967).

Lasko, P., *The Kingdom of the Franks* (London, 1971).

Maenchen-Helfen, J. O., *The World of the Huns* (Berkeley, Calif., 1973).

McEvedy, C., *Penguin Atlas of Medieval History* (Harmondsworth, 1961).

Sawyer, P., *The Age of the Vikings* (London, 1971).

Tischler, F., "Der Stand der Sachsenforschung, archäologisch gesehen," *35 Bericht, Rom.-Germ. Kommission* (1954).

Todd, M., *The Northern Barbarians 100 BC–AD 300* (London, 1975).

Trier, B., *Das Haus im Nordwestern der Germania Libera* (Münster, 1969).

Wallace-Hadrill, J. M., *The Barbarian West* (London, 1967).

Wilson, D., *The Vikings and their Origins* (London, 1970).

Acknowledgments

Unless otherwise stated all the illustrations on a given page are credited to the same source.

H. N. Abrams, Inc., New York 88 (top)
Abtei Kremsmünster, Kremsmünster 99
Aerofilms Ltd., London 40 (top), 125 (bottom)
Amgueddfa Genedlaethol Cymru, Cardiff 41 (bottom)
Ashmolean Museum, Oxford 24, 48 (bottom), 51 (top), 54
Malcolm Atkin, Norwich 33
Dick Barnard, London 38, 39 (top), 58 (top), 59 (bottom), 60 (bottom), 61 (bottom), 62 (top), 63, 107, 111 (bottom), 113 (bottom), 114 (top), 129
Bath Reference Library; by courtesy of the Society of Antiquaries, Scotland 31 (top)
Bibliothèque Nationale, Paris 36 (bottom), 102, 104 (top), 106
Janet and Colin Bord, London 37
British Crown Copyright reproduced with permission of the Controller of HMSO 52
British Library Board, London 25 (left), 30, 35
British Museum, London 64, 78, 79, 94
Camelot Research Committee; photo L. Alcock 39 (bottom)
T. C. Champion, Southampton 60 (top right)
Committee for Aerial Photography, University of Cambridge 88 (bottom), 112 (bottom)
Deutsches Archäologisches Institut, Rome 2
Devizes Museum 50 (top)
Philip Dixon 23, 25 (right), 27 (bottom), 28, 29, 56, 85 (top)
Domschatzkammer, Aachen; Foto Scala, Florence 89
Duomo, Monza; Foto Scala, Florence 110
Elsevier Archives, Amsterdam 82
Foto Marburg, Marburg 14 (top)
Foto Scala, Florence 87, 104 (bottom), 115
A. France-Lanord, Nancy 93 (right)
Ray Gardner, London 17
Richard Geiger, Keston 92
Roger Gorringe, London 32, 34, 40(bottom),42 (bottom) 44 (right), 84 (bottom), 112 (top), 113 (top right), 125 (top), 131 (top)
Robert Harding Associates, London; photo J. Pugh 42 (bottom), M. Gulliver 123
Raymond Hejdström, Visby 111 (top)
A. A. M. van der Heyden, Amsterdam 10, 69
Michael Holford Library, London 31 (bottom), 120, 126, 136
W. T. Jones, Mucking 55 (top)
A. F. Kersting, London 113 (top left)
Kunsthistorisches Museum, Vienna 70, 101
Lovell Johns, Oxford 12, 14 (bottom), 21, 36 (top), 48 (top), 65, 66, 73, 80, 105, 132 (bottom), 135

Yvonne McLean, London 45
Mansell Collection, London 16, 20 (bottom), 98
Monte Cassino Abbey; Foto Scala, Florence 91, 95, 103
Museo Archeologico, Milan; Foto Scala, Florence 109
Museo Archeologico Nazionale, Cividale del Friuli; Foto Scala, Florence 74 (top)
Museo Arqueologico Nacional, Madrid 72, 77, 97 (left)
Museo de la Real Academia de la Historia, Madrid; Foto Scala, Florence 15
Museo Nazionale, Florence; Foto Scala, Florence Jacket, 74 (bottom)
Museo Nazionale Romano; Foto Scala, Florence 9
Nationalmuseet, Copenhagen 46, 62 (bottom), 81, 134
Nottingham University Museum; photo P. Dixon 27 (top)
Oxford Illustrators, Oxford 41 (top), 49, 51 (bottom), 55 (bottom), 60 (top left), 61 (top), 61 (center), 84 (top), 85 (bottom), 86, 114 (bottom), 139–49
Picturepoint Ltd., London 20 (top), 43
Rheinisches Landesmuseum, Bonn 67, 93 (left)
Rijksdienst voor het Oudeheidkundig Bodemonderzoek, Amersfoort 122
Schleswig-Holsteinischen Landesmuseums, Schleswig 44 (left), 47, 131 (bottom)
Andrew Selkirk, London 59 (top)
Spectrum Colour Library, London 97 (right)
Statens Historiska Museum, Stockholm 132 (top)
Statens Historiska Museum, Stockholm; photo Werner Forman Archive, London 118, 119
Tesoro della Basilica di San Giovanni, Monza; Foto Scala, Florence 75
Universitetet i Bergen Historisk Museum 83
Universitetets Samling Av Nordiske Oldsaker, Oslo 22, 116
Universitetets Samling Av Nordiske Oldsaker, Oslo; photo Werner Forman Archive, London 121
University Museum of Archaeology and Ethnology, Cambridge 50 (bottom)
West Stow Environmental Archaeology Group; photo R. Darrah 57, 58 (bottom)

The Publishers have attempted to observe the legal requirements with respect to the rights of the suppliers of photographic materials. Nevertheless, persons who have claims are invited to apply to the Publishers.

The author wishes to thank his friends Patricia Borne, Dr Joan Taylor, Malcolm Todd and Professor Robert Marcus for their help and advice.

Glossary

Abbasids Arab dynasty who traced their line to Abbas, uncle of Muhammad, and who supplanted the **Umayyads** in 750.

Åberg, Nils (1888–1957) Swedish archaeologist, a pupils of Oscar **Montelius** and professor of archaeology at Stockholm. His typological studies of Bronze Age, Iron Age and migration period metalwork are fundamental to modern interpretation of European chronology and cultures.

Aethelberht (c. 550–616) King of Kent from 560, defeated by **Ceawlin** of Wessex in 568. He married Bertha, daughter of Charibert king of Paris, and during his reign Frankish influences are clear in Kentish metalwork. Through Bertha's example he accepted the Catholic mission of **St Augustine** (597) and was baptized – the first of the Anglo-Saxon kings to accept Christianity. A code of laws based on Roman style is attributed to him, and provides early evidence for custom and society in Kent.

Aethelred II (c. 965–1016) King of England 978–1016, nicknamed "Unraed" ("the ill-advised") because of his vacillating policy towards the Danish Vikings. Married Emma, daughter of Richard, duke of Normandy, to whom he fled during the invasion of King Svein of Denmark. After Svein's death (1014) he returned to his throne until his own death.

Aethelweard (? d. 998) Chronicler, who called himself an **ealdorman**, and may have been the ealdorman who arranged a treaty for Aethelred II in 994. His chronicle (from the Creation to 973) contains some otherwise unknown material for 10th-century history.

Aëtius, Flavius (c. 400–454) Roman general who was effective ruler of the west from about 430 until his assassination. His "realm" lay in Gaul, whose boundaries he maintained with the aid of Hunnic and other barbarian mercenaries, and in alliance with the Visigoths he defeated Attila's invasion of Gaul in 451.

Agilulf (d. 615) King of the Lombards, a nobleman selected by Queen **Theudelinda** as her second husband in 590. After threatening the Byzantine states he agreed to a truce, and after 605 was at peace with his neighbors in Italy. During his reign Catholics in N Italy were reestablished.

Aisled house Structure in which the weight of the roof is borne on rows of internal posts which divide the interior into a "nave" and flanking "aisles." The regular plan for north German and Scandinavian houses in the **migration period**, the type has an ancestry which runs back to the 4th or 5th millennium BC.

Akerman, John Yonge (1806–73) English antiquary, who worked as secretary to William Cobbett. Akerman had a life-long interest in the study of coins; he helped to found the Numismatic Society of London in 1836, and began the *Numismatic Journal*. He was influential as the secretary of the Society of Antiquaries of London (1848–60), and in 1855 published *Remains of Pagan Saxondum*, a synthesis of recent discoveries.

Alamanni Germanic "people," a confederation of several tribes who amalgamated in the 3rd century. About 260 they conquered the Roman frontier lands between the Rhine and Danube, and remained there, despite their defeat by the Romans in 357, until the 6th-century Frankish expansion incorporated their territory into Francia.

Alans Nomads of southeastern Russia, who migrated eastwards as their lands were taken over by the Goths during the 3rd century. The advance of the **Huns** caused a movement westwards. Some Alans joined the Huns in the 370s. A tribe of Alans crossed into Spain in 409, where they joined forces with the **Vandals**.

Alaric (d. 410) Visigoth leader who in 395 led a migration of his people into Greece and devastated the Balkans. The eastern government encouraged him to turn his attention westwards and he invaded Italy in 401 and subsequent years. From 408 to 410 he besieged Rome three times, sacking the city in 410. In an attempt to find lands for his people he marched south but failed to cross to Sicily, and died in southern Italy.

Alaric II (d. 507) King of the Visigoths, succeeded his father Euric in 484, and ruled the Catholics with toleration. In 506 he issued a code of laws abstracted from Roman practice, for the use of his Roman subjects. He was defeated and killed by **Clovis** in 507 at Vouillé.

Alboin (d. 572) King of the Lombards, succeeding his father c. 565. With **Avar** assistance he destroyed the Gepids and withdrew into Italy with his people, where he overthrew the new Byzantine state. He was murdered in 572.

Alcuin (735–804) Theologian, born at York and educated in the cathedral school. In 778, when master of the school, he was chosen by Charlemagne to found the Palace School at Aachen. He settled in Francia and from 796 to his death was abbot of Tours. He wrote theological and philosophical works and his influence was widespread in court circles.

Ammianus Marcellinus (c. 330–395) Last great Roman historian, a Greek from Antioch who served in the army, and settled in Rome in 378. His History, written in Latin for a Roman audience, spanned the years 96 AD to 378: of this the section from 353 survives and provides a detailed and apparently accurate account of events and of society in the crucial years before the barbarian movements into the empire began.

Amulet Object which is believed by its owner to have the power to ward off evil. It sometimes bears a magical inscription to ensure its efficacy.

Anastasius (c. 430–518) East Roman Emperor, who succeeded Zeno in 491. He was a careful and prudent administrator who reformed the currency, and spent much time in attempts to reconcile the irreconcilable viewpoints of theologians in the empire.

Anglo-Saxon Name given to distinguish the barbarian settlers of Britain, "the English Saxons," from their kindred still on the continent. Now generally used to define the period in England between the collapse of British power c. 550 and the Norman conquest of 1066, and applied to artifacts – Anglo-Saxon pottery, metalwork or houses.

Anglo-Saxon Chronicle Principal source for Anglo-Saxon history, compiled between 871 and c. 890, from a variety of earlier sources. Some manuscripts then produced were augmented by further annals which give variant and near-contemporary accounts of 10th- to 12th-century history.

Arbogastes (d. 394) Barbarian general, probably Frankish, who served with Theodosius the Great (380–88), and was sent by him to assist **Valentinian II**. At Valentinian's death, Arbogastes proclaimed **Eugenius**

emperor (392), first of the barbarian generals to take this step, but he and his protégé were defeated in 394 and he committed suicide.

Arcadius (383–408) Roman emperor, the eldest son of Theodosius the Great, and successor in 395 to the eastern half of the empire. His influence on events can scarcely be traced, and his government is assumed to have been controlled by his ministers.

Arianism Christian doctrine which denies the godhead of Christ the Son. In the 4th century the doctrine (founded by the priest Arius) was declared a heresy, but pockets of Arianism influenced the incoming **Goths**, and Ostrogoths, Visigoths and Vandals became Arians, in conflict with the Catholic Roman population.

Arthur (? d. c. 510) Legendary champion of the British against the Anglo-Saxon invaders. Most of the stories about him belong to the 12th century and later, and even his existence is disputed.

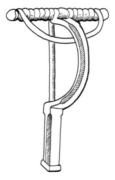
Crossbow brooch

Athaulf (d. 415) Successor of **Alaric**, who led the Visigoths out of Italy into southern Gaul in 412. In 414 he married Placidia, sister of **Honorius**, who had been captured in 410 at the sack of Rome, and in the next year retired into Spain, where he was assassinated. He is said to have intended to create a Gothic empire, but changed his mind because of his people's savagery.

Attila (c. 410–53) King of the Huns who for a short period (c. 445–53) united the nomads against the Roman Empire and invaded Gaul and Italy. He was defeated in battle by **Aëtius** in 452, and died while preparing to resume the attack. His death destroyed the Hunnic "empire," and the nomads were crushed by revolts of their German subjects.

Augustine, St [**Aurelius Augustinus**] (354–430) Church Father, who after a varied life as a teacher, philosopher and literateur, was ordained bishop of Hippo, Africa, in 395. His letters, polemics and, above all, his theological and philosophical works transformed the

Christianity of the west, and his autobiographical *Confessions* (c. 400) have inspired generations of writers. He died in the early stages of the Vandal conquest of Africa.

Augustus (63 BC–14 AD) First of the Roman emperors. Great-nephew and heir of Julius Caesar, after whose murder he rose to power, he finally (after 30 BC) made himself supreme in the Roman world. His long reign was the turning-point from the Republic to the Empire – a new constitutional arrangement whose details owe much to Augustus' own viewpoint. The armies of the Republic were whittled down and deployed along the frontiers; in the north an unsuccessful attempt to annex Germany put a halt to Roman expansion against the northern barbarians for nearly a century.

Avars Asiatic nomads, made up apparently of groups from many sources, who advanced in the 550s into Europe and set up a powerful kingdom in Hungary and southern Russia. During the 7th century their power declined as their vassals asserted their independence, and pressure by Charlemagne and by the Bulgars of the lower Danube caused their collapse in the early 9th century.

Bacaudae Celtic name of obscure meaning applied to the peasant rebels of northern Spain and Gaul from the 3rd to the 5th century. After c. 400 massive outbreaks of revolt in Armorica (NW Gaul) contributed to the breakdown of Roman power in the northern provinces.

Barrow Mound of earth heaped up over the cremated or inhumed bodies of the dead. In the **migration period** barrows vary in scale from simple low mounds some 3 feet high to the great heaps of earth, originally 30 or more feet high, which surmounted **ship-burials**.

Basilica Public meeting hall (legal or mercantile); a church modeled on such a hall. Hence used of a type of church with a broad nave and aisles, especially large urban cathedrals.

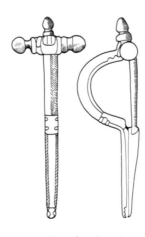
Cruciform brooch

Equal-armed brooch

Bede (673–735) English historian, who spent most of his life in the monastery at Jarrow, Northumbria, teaching Latin, Greek and Hebrew. Most of his works were biblical, but his principal composition, *The Ecclesiastical History of the English*, completed in 731, is the most valuable source for the study of the 7th century, and is arguably the greatest historical writing of the early Middle Ages in Europe.

Belisarius (d. 565) General of Justinian who campaigned against Persia (527, 540), captured Vandal Africa (533–34) and began the reconquest of Ostrogothic Italy (535).

Beorhtric (d. 802) King of the West-Saxons, who married a daughter of **Offa the Great**. He is believed to have been poisoned by his wife. During his reign the Vikings first landed in England.

Beowulf Anglo-Saxon epic poem of the early 8th century or earlier, set among the **Geats** of Sweden.

Bleda (d. c. 445) Brother of **Attila** and co-ruler of the Huns of the Danube area. Attila had Bleda murdered and assumed sole power.

Boethius, Anicius Manlius Severinus (c. 480–524). Roman senator and consul who was an important courtier of **Theodoric the Great** until suspected of treason, put in prison (where he composed his famous *On the Consolation of Philosophy*) and executed.

Boniface (680–755) Saint and missionary, born in Devon, educated at Exeter and Winchester, and in 716 went to Frisia to convert the heathen. Created bishop in 723 and archbishop in 732, he organized and reformed the new churches and the Frankish establishment. By 746 he was head of the eastern churches. Killed, with his followers, by pagans at Dokkum in Friesland.

British In prehistoric and later archaeology, the (Celtic-speaking) inhabitants of Britain in contrast to the (German-speaking) Anglo-Saxons or English.

Brooch, crossbow Plain bow-brooch, often without headplate, attributed to the 4th or early 5th century. Derived from late Roman forms, the crossbow brooch seems to be the ancestor of the more elaborately decorated brooches of the **migration period**.

Brooch, cruciform Bow-brooch with small headplate and long footplate. From the headplate protrude three knobs; the footplate normally is shaped into an animal head with eyes and nostrils. Found in Jutland and Holstein from the late 4th century, during the 5th and 6th centuries cruciform brooches spread across the North Sea to Britain.

Brooch, equal-armed Bow-brooch whose headplate and footplate are symmetrical. Found chiefly in the Elbe-Weser region and with a short-lived popularity in the first half of the 5th century.

Brooch, plate Bow-brooch with flat headplate (generally semicircular with some radiating knobs) and long, lozenge-shaped footplate. A variety of types have been distinguished, decorated with precious stones or chip-carving and distributed from the Crimea to Spain from the 4th to the 7th century.

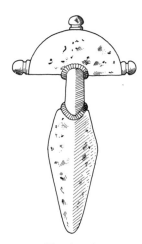

Plate brooch

Brooch, radiate General term used to refer to bow-brooches with semicircular headplate decorated with a row of radiating knobs. Two major types are the radiate brooch with straight-sided footplate (found in Frankish territories) and that with a lozenge-shaped footplate (found in Lombardic contexts).

Brooch, saucer Circular brooch, concave in section, like a modern lapel badge, generally decorated in chip-carving. Distributed in the north German lowlands and in England, and belonging to the 5th and 6th centuries.

Brooch, square-headed Bow-brooch with large square headplate, normally decorated with relief casting and carving. Comparatively plain examples from Jutland belong to the late 4th century. Elaborate 5th- and 6th-century types developed in England.

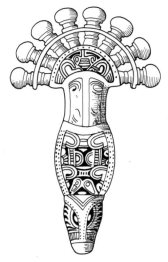

Radiate brooch of Lombard type

Browne, Sir Thomas (1605–82) Physician and author, renowned for an encyclopaedic knowledge of contemporary scientific and antiquarian theory. Knighted in 1671, as the leading citizen of Norwich. His *Hydriotaphia* (1658), a discussion of past burial customs, includes the first publication of Anglo-Saxon cremation urns.

Bulgars Asiatic nomads who remained on the shores of the Black Sea after the general withdrawal eastwards at the end of the 5th century. Little is known of their relations with the surviving **Huns** or with the **Avars**. After 679 Bulgars crossed the Danube and founded a state in the old province of Moesia which gradually became civilized.

Burgundians Germanic peoples of the Middle Rhine who were settled in the 430s near Geneva, where they established a kingdom in the Rhône valley. The expansion of the realm of the **Franks** in the 6th century led to the annexation of Burgundy, but the Burgundians enjoyed periods of comparative autonomy, and after the break-up of the Frankish Empire in the 9th century Burgundy formed an independent kingdom until 1032.

Saucer brooch

Burh, or borough Fortified position, normally used of the defended settlements constructed by Alfred and his successors as protection against the Danes.

Byre Cowshed, either a separate building for cattle or part of the farmhouse. In the three-aisled houses of prehistoric and **migration period** Europe the lower end of the house was frequently filled with stalls for animals. The type is thus frequently called a "byrehouse" or "house-and-byre" and (under the name "longhouse") is still found in Ireland, Wales and part of the continent.

Camden, William (1551–1623) English antiquary who traveled widely between 1571 and 1600 in search of archaeological material. He drew together his findings in his *Britannia*, first published in 1586, but greatly enlarged by subsequent editions during his lifetime, especially the 6th edition of 1607. In 1593 he was appointed headmaster of Westminster School, and his learning made him an influential figure in metropolitan circles. In 1622 he founded a chair of history at Oxford University, and after his death *Britannia* continued to be revised and modernized by a series of editors and translators.

Square-headed brooch

Cassiodorus, Flavius Magnus Aurelius (c. 490–c. 583) Roman senator and apologist, principal propagandist of **Theodoric the Great**, who retired from official life in 537, and after a stay (perhaps enforced?) in Constantinople founded a monastery in southern Italy which did much to preserve manuscripts of Classical authors. His historical writings copied by later writers are now lost but an edition of his official letters on behalf of Ostrogothic kings throws light on Italian history in the early 6th century.

Catch-plate Curved metal plate which holds the pin of a brooch in place, similar to that employed in a modern safety-pin.

Ceawlin (d. 593) King of the West Saxons and successor to **Cynric**. He fought against the Kentish kingdom (568) and his British neighbors, and is credited with the capture in 577 of British cities of the southwest. According to the **Anglo-Saxon Chronicle** he campaigned in the west Midlands and in South Wales, and seems to have been responsible for the rapid growth of the Saxon Kingdom of Wessex.

Celts Name given by Classical writers to prehistoric peoples of Spain, Gaul and central Europe, and extended by modern authorities to refer to the inhabitants of the British Isles, before the Roman period. The Celts shared dialects of a common language (now represented by Irish and Scottish Gaelic, Welsh and Breton) and common art forms (La Tène styles of the European Iron Age) but little else, and were gradually submerged by Roman and Germanic expansion.

Chanson de Roland Old French epic poem, in its present form dating from c. 1100, based at considerable remove on an account of the Frankish defeat of Roncevaux (778). Of considerable significance for the attitudes of 11th-century chivalry, and with immense influence on later medieval writers, its value for the events of the 8th century is minimal.

Charles the Bald (823–77) Youngest son of **Louis the Pious**. King of the West Franks who outlived his brothers and many of their heirs, to become emperor in 875.

Charles the Fat (839–87) Youngest son of **Louis the German**, king of the West Franks from 882 and crowned emperor. His reign saw the great siege of Paris by the Vikings (885), and his weakness resulted in a coup which deposed him in 887.

Charles the Simple (879–929) Son of Louis II the Stammerer, and king of France. Imprisoned by Duke Radulf of Burgundy in 923 and died in prison. Charles conceded the lower Seine to the Vikings (911), thus establishing the Duchy of Normandy.

Chaucer, Geoffrey (c. 1340–1400) Poet and courtier. The son of a London vintner, he served in the entourage of the duchess of Lancaster and rose to prominence as a royal official, knight of the shire 1386, clerk of the king's works 1389–91, and in other administrative positions. Chaucer is known now for his writings, especially his *Canterbury Tales* (1387 and later).

Chevron V-shaped pattern like that of military or police insignia. Used to describe the decoration of pottery by diagonal tooling before firing the vessel.

Claudian[us], Claudius (d. c. 404) Poet, an Alexandrine Greek who came to Rome before 395 and whose Latin eulogies in honor of courtiers led to his position as court poet of **Honorius** and propagandist of **Stilicho**. His political poems provide evidence for events about the year 400.

Clovis (c. 465–511) King of the Franks, son of Childeric, whom he succeeded in 481. Clovis' conquests made him master of much of central and eastern Gaul, and in 507 he defeated **Alaric**, king of the Visigoths, and annexed the southwest.

Columbanus, St (d. 615) Irish monk who established monasteries in Francia and in 612, with **Theudelinda**'s help, founded the Lombardic monastery at Bobbio, northern Italy.

Comites (Latin, "companions") Term used to refer to those who accompanied the emperors on their travels. In the military reorganization of the early 4th century, the name was given to high military and civil officials. Under the barbarian kingdoms *comes* became a title of nobility, usually translated "count," and like *dux* (pl. **duces**), used to represent Germanic "Graf."

Constantine III, Flavius Claudius (d. 411) Emperor who was proclaimed by the army in Britain in 407, and who crossed to Gaul where he founded an independent Gallic empire, based on the southern French town of Arles. His usurpation was legitimized in 409 by **Honorius**, hard pressed by the Visigoths, but Alaric's death allowed the Italian government to defeat and kill Constantine and disperse his followers.

Count of the Saxon Shore Commandant of the British coastal defenses, mentioned in 367, and apparently in charge of the great stone fortresses arranged around the east and southeast coasts of England, and intended to prevent sea-borne invasions.

Cynric (d. 560?) King of the West Saxons, perhaps in origin the leader of an army based in Wiltshire. He is said to have defeated the British in 552 near Salisbury, and set up an English kingdom.

Danegeld Tax on land, levied in England in 991 and subsequently (until 1084), in order to buy off Danish Vikings. Used, by analogy, to refer to similar payments of tribute on the continent or in pre-Aethelredan England.

Danelaw East Midlands and north of England: a name given (contemptuously) during the later 10th century to the area which had been conquered and settled by the Danish Vikings, and in which the kings of England allowed considerable autonomy to the Scandinavian settlers.

Dark Ages Term in occasional use to refer to the **migration period**, but unpopular because of its implication of ignorance; most appropriately used of western Scotland before c. 800, a period remarkably dark.

Diocletian (d. 316) Roman emperor, a Dalmatian soldier who was elected by the army in 284. With the aid of a military junta of his own formation he reconstructed the empire after the disasters of the 260s and 270s, and organized the civil and army administration to take account of the increasing complexities of government. In 305 he resigned his position to his deputy (and forced his co-emperor to do the same), and lived in retirement until his death.

Douglas, James (1753–1819) After serving in industry, and in the armies of Austria and Britain, Douglas took holy orders in 1780 and spent the rest of his life in a series of livings in southern and midland England. His antiquarian publications included *Nenia Britannica*, reports on his fieldwork in Kent and Sussex, which contained the examination of a large number of Anglo-Saxon burial mounds.

Duces Latin "leaders," sometimes used in the Roman army to refer to soldiers with duties beyond their normal rank. In the 4th century frontier forces were often commanded by *duces*. The name survived into the Middle Ages as an expression of nobility (hence "duke"), sometimes superior to that of the more normal **comites** ("counts").

Eadred (d. 955) Son of Edward the Elder and from 946 king of the English. He extended his control over the **Danelaw** and was responsible for the expulsion of Eirik Bloodaxe, last Danish king of York.

Ealdorman "Elder" or patriarch, used in the Anglo-Saxon kingdoms to refer to a viceroy of the king, official, noble or even ecclesiastic. Replaced by *jarl* ("earl") during the Danish occupation and gradually relegated to the title of an official in local government.

Edmund "Ironside" (c. 981–1016) Son of **Aethelred II** and for a few weeks in 1016 his successor as king of England. Edmund was famous for his military prowess against the Danish invaders. His death is said to have been through sickness, but came most opportunely for **Knut**.

Edmund the Magnificent (d. 946) Son and successor of **Edward the Elder**, who continued to expand the southern kingdom at the expense of the Danish settlers.

Edward the Confessor (d. 1066) Son of **Aethelred II**, but kept out of power by King **Knut**. In 1041–42 he was a favorite of Knut's son Harthacnut, and succeeded to the throne in 1042. Edward had close links with Normandy, and suffered from the unrest of some of his nobles, especially Earl Godwin of Wessex, whose son Harold succeeded the Confessor in 1066. Noted for his piety and finally canonized.

Edward the Elder (d. 924) King of the southern English. Son of King Alfred of Wessex, he continued his father's policy of cooperation with the Danes of the Midlands and military action when advantageous. By his death he had extended the English kingdom as far as the River Humber.

Edwin (c. 585–633) King of Northumbria; exiled after the death of his father, Edwin was approached by the Kentish missionaries while at the court of **Raedwald**. With Raedwald's help he succeeded to the throne of Northumbria in 617, and encouraged the conversion of his kingdom to Christianity. Killed in battle by Penda, king of Mercia.

Einhard (d. 840) Aristocrat educated in the monastery of Fulda. After 791 he joined the Palace School at Aachen, and became the adviser and friend of Charlemagne. He may have been clerk of the works at Aachen. After Charlemagne's death he remained influential and was made abbot of a series of houses. Between 829 and 836 he wrote his *Life of Charlemagne*, the source of much of what we know about the Frankish empire.

Emir (Amir) Arabic word meaning "commander" and used to refer to the virtually independent rulers of the conquered territories.

Eugenius, Flavus (d. 394) Western emperor 392–94, a teacher of rhetoric at Rome who was befriended by **Arbogastes**, the commander-in-chief of Frankish origin who was suspected of murdering **Valentinian II**. Eugenius was proclaimed emperor by Arbogastes, but was defeated and killed by Theodosius the Great.

Faereyinga Saga Icelandic saga, written about 1200, which gives a traditional and highly personalized account of the 9th-century settlement of the Faroe Islands.

Faussett, Bryan (1720–76) Fellow of All Souls, Oxford, and parson of livings in Shropshire and Kent. His excavations of Anglo-Saxon burials, between 1757 and 1773, were published in 1856 under the title of *Inventorium Sepulchrale*.

Federates Name given to barbarian groups or tribes who came into alliance by treaty (*foedus*) with the Roman Empire. Such peoples enjoyed their own customs and rulers, and might form virtually independent states at the edge of the empire.

Franks Germanic people settled to the east of the Rhine, who during the 5th century expanded into Belgium and northern France. Under their great king **Clovis** the Franks occupied much of Gaul, and their kingdom expanded steadily, until in the time of Charlemagne it consisted of most of western Europe

Fredegar Name given (in the 16th century) to an anonymous compiler of a major Frankish chronicle of events from the end of the Roman Empire until the establishment of the Carolingians.

Frisians Inhabitants of the Dutch coastal plain (Frisia). Frisians took part in the invasion of Britain, but have left little record of their activities there. During the 8th century Frisia was annexed by the **Franks** and remained part of the Frankish kingdom throughout the Middle Ages.

Gaiseric (d. 477) King of the **Vandals** and **Alans** from 428. In 429 he led his people from Spain into Africa, which he subdued by 439. He resisted attempts of eastern emperors to overthrow him, and with the fleet he built at Carthage he dominated the western Mediterranean, and in 455 sacked Rome.

Geats Scandinavian people living in central southern Sweden, in Götaland.

Geoffrey of Monmouth (c. 1100–55) Romantic historian, who sought patronage by his writing. His *History of the Kings of Britain* (c. 1135) enjoyed enormous popularity and introduced many of the legends of King **Arthur** to a wide audience. Created bishop of St Asaph, Wales, in 1152.

Gepids Germanic tribe of the middle Danube who led the revolt against **Attila**'s sons in the 450s. During the 6th century a series of wars against their neighbors, the Lombards, ended in decisive defeat, and the survivors were swallowed up by the **Avars** after 568.

Gibbon, Edward (1737–94) Historian, and reluctant politician. His poor health in youth concentrated his interest in literary studies, especially in the history of Rome. Lionized by the London literateurs, he was for a time a member of Parliament, but towards the end of his life lived in retirement in Lausanne, Switzerland. His chief memorial is his great survey, *Decline and Fall of the Roman Empire* (1776–88), many of whose judgments are still orthodox in the study of the Roman world.

Gildas (c. 500–71 ?) British monk said to have retired to Brittany c. 550 and revered as a saint there and in S Wales. He was called by **Alcuin** "wisest of the Britons," and his *Fall of Britain* (c. 540) is a valuable source for the situation in Britain in the first half of the 6th century.

Gododdin Poem composed in north Britain in the early 7th century, celebrating an unsuccessful attempt to drive out the English from Northumbria.

Goths Germanic peoples, divided into Ostrogoths and Visigoths. In origin both peoples may have come from the Baltic area. During the 5th century the Visigoths occupied southern Gaul and Spain, and the Ostrogoths Italy, and both set up strong barbarian kingdoms. That of the Ostrogoths succumbed to attacks by the Eastern Empire. The Visigoths were swallowed up by the expansion of the Arabs in the early 8th century.

Gratian[us], Flavius (d. 383) Roman emperor, a son of **Valentinian I**, who spent his reign (367–83) in defense of the Rhine frontier. He acquiesced in the imperial election of his brother **Valentinian II**, who controlled Italy, and remained in Gaul, where he was overthrown by **Magnus Maximus** and killed while trying to escape southwards.

Gregory I, the Great (c. 540–604) Pope 590–604. A Roman patrician who left an official career to become a monk (c. 575), and with reluctance became involved in Church administration. Famous for his reputed introduction of "Gregorian" chant. His correspondence is a mine of information about the later 6th century in Italy. In 596 he sent out the missionaries who were to convert the English to Christianity.

Grubenhaus See **sunken-floor hut.**

Hall Chief room of a house, used for ceremonial and domestic life; a (large) single-roomed house used for such ceremonial. With the decline in communal life since the Middle Ages, the term has been transferred to denote a lobby entrance.

Harald Finehair King of Vestfold (Oslo Fjord) who in the late 890s made himself master of the whole of Norway. The consolidation of his rule, until his death in the 930s, induced many Norwegians to emigrate, especially to Iceland.

Harald Harðraði (1015–66) Half-brother of King Ólaf the Saint of Norway and after Ólaf's death (1030) an exile in Novgorod and a member of the Varangian regiment of the Byzantine emperor. He returned to Norway in 1046, and in 1047 succeeded his nephew King Magnus Ólafsson. Known as *Harðraði*, "hard-ruler," he invaded England in 1066, and was killed by King Harold Godwinsson at Stamford Bridge, Yorkshire.

Harald Harefoot (d. 1040) Son of **Knut** by his mistress Aelgifu of Northampton. Elected king of northern England at his father's death (1035), and by 1037 king of all England. He died before his elder brother Harthacnut of Denmark could assert his own claim to the English throne.

Harthacnut (d. 1042) Eldest son of **Knut**, from 1035 king of Denmark, but prevented by Norwegian threat from making good his claim to his father's English throne until shortly before the death of his brother **Harald Harefoot** (1040). He died childless and was succeeded by Edward, son of his father's old adversary **Aethelred II.**

Hengest (d. 488?) Jutish mercenary leader who, according to the **Anglo-Saxon Chronicle**, was invited by **Vortigern** to settle in southeast England, together with his brother Horsa. After Horsa's death in battle (?455) Hengest established the Kingdom of Kent. A man of this name was, according to the *Fight at Finn's Burg*, a leader of "Danes" in Frisia, and may be identical with the Kentish Hengest. There is little certainty about him or his activities and other sources date his arrival in Kent to 428 (not 449).

Henslow, John Stevens (1796–1861) Botanist and geologist, founder of the Cambridge Philosophical Society and successively Cambridge Professor of Mineralogy (1822–27) and Botany (1827–61). Through the work of his most famous pupil, Charles Darwin, Henslow indirectly influenced archaeologists; his own entry into the study was less fortunate, for he believed the Anglo-Saxon urns from Kingston-on-Soar to be prehistoric.

Here Anglo-Saxon noun often translated "army" but not necessarily implying large numbers of men. Defined in the 8th century as a band of men greater than 35 in number, it is the normal term used in the **Anglo-Saxon Chronicle** to refer to the Danish "armies" of the 9th century.

Hermanaric (d. 376) Gothic chieftain in southern Russia whose kingdom was swamped by the movement of **Huns** and **Alans** westwards in the 370s. Hermanaric's defeat and suicide began the migration of Visigoths into the empire, and his memory was revered as the last of the old rulers of the Goths.

Herodotus (c. 490–c. 425 BC) Greek historian, the "father of history," from the Aegean coast of Asia Minor, who settled in the Athenian colony of Thurii in southern Italy. Herodotus traveled widely in search of historical material, and in digressions from his central theme (the Persian Wars of the 490s and 480s) he gives accounts – some mythological – of barbarian tribes far beyond the Greek world.

Hillfort Fortification on a hill, of a type well known throughout later prehistoric Europe. Excavation has shown that many such sites, believed prehistoric on the evidence of their superficial appearance, were occupied, or even constructed during the **migration period**. A group in the Rhine Valley belong to the 10th-century wars between the Magyars and the East Franks. See also **Ring fort.**

Honorius, Flavius (384–423) West Roman emperor, youngest son of Theodosius the Great

and ruler of the west from 395. During his reign Britain, Spain and parts of Gaul were lost to the empire and Rome was captured by **Alaric**. Widely recognized as one of the least effective of all the emperors.

Horsa (d. 455?) See **Hengest.**

Huns Nomadic people from Asia who during the last quarter of the 4th century destroyed the Gothic kingdoms of south Russia and caused the great migration westwards. United briefly in the 440s and early 450s by **Attila**, the Huns invaded Gaul and Italy, but were driven back to their homelands in Hungary, and soon afterwards split up into small tribal units, amalgamating with other nomadic peoples.

Ida (*floruit* c. 550) English warlord, who settled on the coast of Northumberland c. 547, built a fortress on the rock of Bamburgh, and founded the royal house of Bernicia, the northern region of Northumbria, which grew rapidly in power after his death (559?).

Immunitas Freedom from public duties or taxation, a Latin word now sometimes used to describe the precinct of a religious house so exempt.

Imperium Latin word for a command, which grew to signify the right to give orders, and so to mean supreme power, normally equivalent in the later Roman period to "empire." *Imperator*, originally "commander-in-chief," became a title used by the emperors, and came to signify "emperor." The Latin writers of the Dark Ages could use *imperium* of a single kingdom, but the word retained the connotation of a kingdom supreme among others.

Ine (d. after 726) King of West Saxons 688–726, and a vigorous upholder of his kingdom's rights, who issued a code of laws (first of the West Saxons to do so) and abdicated to go on pilgrimage to Rome, where he died.

Inhumation Name given to the burial custom by which the body was laid unburned in a grave (in contrast to *cremation*). Inhumation was demanded by Christian doctrine but was not confined to Christian peoples, for it was the custom of some of the pagan tribes of Scandinavia.

Irene (c. 752–803) Byzantine empress, wife of Leo IV (d. 780), and guardian of their son, Constantine VI. She favored the use of icons in church and proved high-handed in her advocacy. In 797 she had her son blinded and proclaimed herself *emperor*. Removed by a coup in 802, she died in exile.

Iron Age Conventional archaeological period. From the first half of the first millennium BC most areas of Europe enjoyed

cultures in which iron played some part. In areas conquered by the Romans the "Iron Age" is succeeded by the "Roman" period. Contemporary cultures *outside* the empire are described as being of the "Roman Iron Age." From c. 400 AD these periods are succeeded by the **migration period**.

Iudex Latin for "judge," the name given by Roman writers for the chief of the Visigoths.

Jerome [Eusebius Hieronymus] (c. 348–420) Church Father and Saint, born in Dalmatia and already following an official career when he entered religious life. The life of asceticism appealed to him and he traveled in the eastern deserts. A short stay in Rome (382–85) led to a commission to correct the variant texts of the Bible then current, and from 389 to his death he spent his life in theology and commentary writing. His principal works are the revised Latin translation of the Bible (the Vulgate) and his chronicle (a source for the events of the years around 400), but his correspondence preserves much curious detail.

Jómsvikinga Saga Icelandic saga written down c. 1200, which tells of the foundation of a fortified camp on the southern coast of the Baltic by a Dane from Fünen. In the camp, Jómsborg, lives a military elite under strict discipline. The saga owes much to a 12th-century nascent chivalry, but perhaps enshrines the memory of garrison camps like those of Svein Forkbeard in Denmark.

Julian[us], Flavius Claudius (332–63) Roman emperor, of the royal house of Constantine, proclaimed in 355, who fought for four years against the **Franks** and **Alamanni** (356–59). In 363 he invaded Persia and won some successes, but was killed in battle. Unlike the other 4th-century emperors Julian was pagan, and tried to promote pagan observances, and was later nicknamed "the Apostate."

Justinian[us], Flavius Petrus Sabbatius (c. 482–565) Roman emperor, nephew of the emperor Justin whom he succeeded in 527. Responsible for the reconquest of much of the western Mediterranean – Africa, Italy and part of Spain – for major reforms of Roman law, and for the great church of S. Sophia at Constantinople.

Jutes Germanic people, believed to have occupied the northern part of the Danish peninsula (Jutland) at the beginning of the **migration period**. Some of them are traditionally said to have taken part in the invasion of Britain, and have been traced in Kent and southern England.

Kemble, John Mitchell (1807–57) Philologist and historian whose studies concentrated attention on Anglo-Saxon language and history. His publications included a major edition of the poem **Beowulf** (1833) and a significant paper in 1856 in which he drew attention to the similarities in material from England and from Hannover.

Knarr Scandinavian name (otherwise, Knörr) for the heavy cargo ships used by merchants and by the settlers of the Atlantic islands.

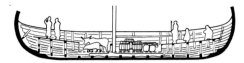

Knarr, a heavy cargo ship

Knut (Canute) (d. 1035) Younger son of Svein Forkbeard, king of Denmark. After 1016 king of England (through his father's conquest) and from 1018 king of Denmark, on the death of his elder brother. After 1030 he became king also of Norway, but his powerful North Sea empire collapsed at his death.

Landnámabók The Book of Settlements, a 12th-century compilation of traditions about the colonizers of Iceland.

Leland, John (c. 1506–52) English antiquary. Leland entered holy orders after 1522, but his interests were in the study of antiquities. Before 1530 he was appointed Library Keeper to Henry VIII, and in 1533 he became King's Antiquary. From 1534 to 1543 he traveled throughout England, making notes on the remains he saw, with the intention of summarizing these in a great work. The intention was forestalled by his insanity and early death but his notes were preserved and published as *Leland's Itineraries* in 1710, and provide source material for archaeological studies of all periods.

Lombards Germanic people who migrated southwards to occupy the Hungarian plains during the 6th century. Pressure from the **Avars** caused them to move westward, and in 568 they invaded Italy and established a kingdom in the Po valley, with virtually independent duchies in the south. The northern kingdom was annexed by Charlemagne but the duchies survived until the Norman conquest of the mid-11th century.

Louis the German (c. 805–76) Third son of **Louis the Pious** and king of the East Franks from 840 to 876.

Louis the Pious (778–840) Youngest legitimate son of Charlemagne, who succeeded to the empire in 814. His reign was disturbed by the problem of succession and by barbarian pressures, and he spent many years in civil war with his sons.

Magnus Maximus (d. 388) Roman emperor. A Spanish soldier who commanded the army in

Britain and who led his troops into Gaul where he overthrew the Emperor **Gratian**. Theodosius the Great recognized his claim to Gaul, Spain and Britain, but resisted Maximus' attempt to control Italy, and led an army which defeated Maximus, who was executed. Thinly disguised as "Prince Macsen," his memory remained a potent force in Welsh court circles until the 13th century.

Magyars Barbarian people, perhaps Finnish in origin, who migrated into southern Europe and in the early 10th century occupied Hungary, from where their horsemen raided into France, Italy, Germany and even Spain. Defeated at the battle of Lechfeld in 955, they settled down in Hungary and established a civilized Christian kingdom which survived into modern times.

Marcomanni "Border Men," a Germanic people, from the 1st century BC established in Bohemia. Major wars were fought against them from 166 to 180, but they remained a threat to the Danube frontier, and in the 6th century annexed Bavaria.

Mausoleum Tomb, strictly referring to the monumental tomb of Mausolus (d. 353 BC) at Halicarnassus, but used, by analogy, of any burial place with some pretensions to grandeur.

Mercimonium Latin noun originally meaning "merchandise," transferred to signify "market place."

Merovingians Royal family of the Frankish rulers from Childeric (d. 481) to the middle of the 8th century, a name derived from the obscure mid-5th-century Merovech, father(?) of Childeric.

Migration period (c. 400–800) Age of the folk movements. Though the German migrations outside the Roman Empire began in the 2nd century, the term is usually confined to the period of the great invasions of the 5th and 6th centuries. In northern Europe the migration period is conventionally followed by the age of the Vikings, the last of the Germanic migrations.

Montelius, Oscar (1843–1921) Swedish archaeologist who adopted the theories of evolution of Charles Darwin to the study of archaeological material. His typological studies had a profound effect on the thinking of his generation.

Namatianus, Rutilius Claudius Roman official under **Honorius** who left Rome (probably in 417) to look after his ancestral Gallic estates, apparently near Toulouse, then threatened by the impending Visigothic settlement in Aquitaine. His autobiographical poem *De reditu suo* ("On his return") describes the devastation of Italy. His account contrasts with the prevailing fatality of the Christian

historians, for he was a pagan and believed in the mission of Rome and its old gods, whom he saw as undermined by Christianity as much as by barbarian invaders.

Narses (d. 567) General of **Justinian**, at first an assistant of **Belisarius** in Italy (538), and from 550 to 554 commanding general in Italy, which he conquered in 554. Until 567 he acted as regent and administered the Italian reconstruction.

Nicaea, (first) Council of Church council held in the city of Nicaea (Iznik, Turkey) in 325, at which **Arianism** was denounced and the Nicene Creed was formulated.

Notker ("the Stammerer") (d. 912?) Author of a credulous treatise about Charlemagne, identified as a monk of St Gall, Switzerland, born c. 840 and writing in the 880s.

Nuncio Literally "messenger," the name given to ambassadors of the pope at foreign courts.

Odoacer (d. 493?) Skirian officer elected emperor in 476 in opposition to Romulus and his father Orestes. Ruled Italy until defeated and killed by **Theodoric the Great**.

Offa the Great (d. 796) English king of Mercia 757–96. During his reign the Mercian kingdom achieved its greatest extent. He was responsible for a massive border defense along his frontier with the Welsh.

Oman, Sir Charles (1860–1946) Historian and Chichele Professor of History at Oxford. A man of considerable knowledge and wide-ranging interests, with substantial publications on modern, medieval and post-Roman history.

Oratory Place for (private) prayer. From the Latin *orare*, to pray.

Orosius, Paulus Spanish churchman who fled from the **Vandals** to Africa in 414, and became an adherent of St **Augustine**. His *Historiae Adversus Paganos*, a tract tracing events from the Creation to 417 AD, relies heavily on earlier writers, but adds details of his own knowledge from contemporary history.

Ostrogoths. See **Goths**.

Otto I (the Great) (d. 973) Son of Henry the Fowler; Saxon king of Germany 936–62. From 962 emperor. In 955 he defeated the **Magyars** at the Lechfeld.

Patrick (373–c. 463) Saint and bishop. Born perhaps in Dunbarton and captured by Scotti in 389. After six years of slavery he studied under St Martin of Tours, and in 405 sailed back to Ireland, where he converted Ulster to Christianity and founded his missionary center near Armagh, where he was buried. Later, when the Irish and Roman churches were in conflict, he was made into Ireland's patron saint.

Paulinus of Pella (377–?c. 440) Gallo-Roman aristocrat, the son of a proconsul, with estates in Aquitaine, who in 414 accepted office under the brief imperial usurpation of Attalus. After Attalus' downfall, Paulinus was dispossessed and saved his life only by an appeal to the king of the **Alans**, and lived in exile in Marseilles. His poem, *Eucharisticon* (Thanksgiving), is a pessimistic account of the disasters of the early 5th century.

Pendant Ornament designed to be worn, frequently around the neck, on a strap or chain.

Pommel Protuberant knob on a sword hilt, frequently decorated with inlay or with semiprecious stones.

Sword and its pommel

Posthole Hole dug into the ground to hold the base of a post (generally packed tightly with stones or earth). Postholes and similar traces of timber emplacements are usually the only surviving remains of the buildings of the barbarians.

Procopius (c. 500–after 562) Greek historian who served with **Belisarius** in Persia, Africa and Italy (527–40). Prefect of Constantinople in 562. His *History of the Wars of Justinian* (written by c. 551) contains much of what is known of the period and preserves many details of events outside its main theme. A parallel work, the *Secret History*, retraces the same ground, but as a continuous and violent attack on Justinian's policies: it is highly unlikely that this inflammatory work was published in the emperor's lifetime.

Quadi Germanic tribe, associated, in the 2nd century and later, with the **Marcomanni**, and a constant threat to the Roman frontier of the Danube. During the 5th century some Quadi joined the **Vandals** and **Alans** in the conquest of Spain.

Radiocarbon dating Measurement of the amount of the radioactive isotope of carbon (Carbon 14) present in wood and other organic substances. The amount decreases steadily after the death of the plant or animal, and

measurement of the residue allows an estimate of the date of death. The statistical margin of error (of 2 or 3 centuries) inherent in the technique limits its value for the Middle Ages.

Raedwald (d. c. 625) King of the East Angles, who accepted Christianity at the prompting of **Aethelberht** of Kent, though continuing to worship his old gods. He was recognized as Bretwalda, "high king," of the English and placed **Edwin** on his father's throne of Northumbria. It is likely, though not certain, that the great ship-burial of Sutton Hoo, Suffolk, was the tomb of Raedwald.

Recarred (d. 601) Visigothic king, succeeded his father Leovigild in 586 and in the next year was baptized a Christian. In 589 he summoned a council at Toledo which marked the end of official **Arianism** in Spain.

Relic In church history, a personal memorial of a holy man, either clothing or other items associated with a saint, or a part of the saint's body, preserved and revered as an inspiration to piety. Relics might be displayed to pilgrims, and were collected by them and were kept safe in *reliquaries*, suitably shaped caskets, frequently ornately decorated.

Reliquary See **Relic**.

Rescue excavations Name commonly given to attempts to salvage material from archaeological sites before their destruction.

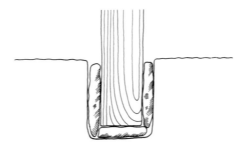

Section through a posthole

Rickman, Thomas (1776–1841) Architect. He sketched churches and wrote architectural papers, and designed many not very good churches. His archaeological contribution was his identification of Anglo-Saxon churches at a time when many of his contemporaries asserted that all buildings before c. 1050 were of wood.

Ring fort Circular, defended enclosure, typically on comparatively flat land, whose rampart consisted of a stone wall, with or without an external ditch, surrounding a small interior area. Such small defended sites are common in Ireland, west Britain and central Scandinavia.

Roland See **Chanson de Roland**.

Romanitas Roman way of life, an emotive and somewhat ill-defined ambition of rulers of the successor kingdoms from **Athaulf** to Otto III.

Romulus Augustulus (c. 455–510) Last of the emperors of the Western Empire. Son of Orestes, a Roman who had been secretary to **Attila**, he held office for a year, and was deposed in 476. Because of his youth he was allowed to live, on a state pension, in southern Italy until his death. Augustulus, "little Augustus," is a contemptuous diminutive.

Russian Chronicle Local annals, compiled in the early 12th century, which preserved detailed accounts of Swedish trade and settlement in Russia.

Sacramentary Book containing the prayers and order of ceremony used at (Catholic) church services.

Saga Old Norse word meaning a story (originally in prose) of quasi-legendary events; colloquially, a long tale. Used chiefly to describe the historical stories current in Iceland in the Middle Ages.

Salian "Salty": the name given after 350 to a branch of the Franks who settled in Holland and Belgium along the coastal plain and whose royal family, the **Merovingians**, subsequently made themselves masters of Gaul.

Salin, Bernhard (1861–1931) Swedish archaeologist and successor of **Montelius**, whose analysis of animal ornament (*Die altgermanische Thierornamentik*, 1904) is the basis of the chronology of migration period metalwork.

Salvian (c. 400–c. 470) Priest and writer, born in Trier, who became a monk at Lérins in 425 and presbyter in Marseilles about 439. He saw the barbarians, who by then had made his native province a German kingdom, as instruments of divine wrath and in his *De gubernatione dei* (440) presented this theological viewpoint, revealing incidentally much of 5th-century life in the provinces.

Saracens Originally the Arab tribes of Syria; thence, all Arabs, especially those of Spain, Italy and Palestine.

blade   handle

Sax or knife

Sax Old English *Saex*, a knife, used of the single-edged iron cleavers common in European Saxon and Anglo-Saxon graves. Continental versions have a curving back; English types (late

6th-century and later) are straight-backed with an angle near the point.

Saxons Germanic people whose homeland is located in the north German coastal plain, especially between the rivers Elbe and Weser. During the 5th-century migrations some invaded Britain, traditionally founding those kingdoms whose name ends in the suffix "-sex." Those who remained in Saxony were absorbed into the Frankish kingdom during the 8th century.

Scythians Name given (before the 5th century BC) by the Greeks to the peoples who occupied the north shore of the Black Sea. A nomadic race, probably of Asiatic origin, they remained in southern Russia until absorbed by the Goths and other immigrants in the 2nd and 3rd centuries AD. In early modern times "Scythian" was used more widely to refer to prehistoric cultures (Celtic, Germanic and Slavic) of eastern Europe.

Ship-burial Burial custom in which the body, burned or unburned, was laid within a boat or ship, usually accompanied by grave-goods, and buried beneath a mound of earth or stones.

Sidonius Apollinaris, St (c. 430–after 479) Gallo-Roman aristocrat from Lyons, son-in-law of the Emperor Avitus, and holder of official posts in Rome. Elected bishop of Clermont-Ferrand in the Auvergne in 469, he coordinated resistance to the Visigoths. After the annexation of the Auvergne by the Goths in 475, Sidonius was imprisoned, but in 476 was restored to his bishopric. His surviving works include poems and letters which throw light on society in 5th-century Gaul.

Sunken-floor hut

Smith, Charles Roach (1807–90) Antiquary. A chemist by profession, he devoted his time to the collection and arrangement of Romano-British antiquities. His acquisitions form the basis of the British Museum's Roman collection. In 1856 he published the records of Anglo-Saxon burials made by Bryan **Faussett**, under the title *Inventorium Sepulchrale*.

Solidus Roman gold coin, weighing 72 to the pound, minted from 309 as part of the reform of the currency after the collapse of the 3rd century. The prestige coin of the later empire, in which taxes and tribute were demanded, it was valued by barbarians as far as Scandinavia.

Stilicho, Flavius (d. 408) Roman general, partly of barbarian origin, who from 395 was master of the western half of the empire, as guardian of the young emperor **Honorius**. His antagonist was the Visigoth **Alaric**, whom he defeated several times in Italy, but his policies provoked a mutiny, and Honorius ordered his assassination.

Strap end Metal reinforcement (often decorated) which prevented wear and damage to the end of a strap.

Stukeley, William (1687–1765) Antiquary and physician. In 1718 he was a joint founder of the Society of Antiquaries of London, first of the national societies. Stukeley was in holy orders, but spent much of his life in the study of prehistoric antiquities; his especial interest was in Druid religion, shown in his *Stonehenge* (1740) and in a series of papers, and he identified many Anglo-Saxon relics as belonging to the prehistoric period.

Suebi Germanic people. The name was given during the 2nd century to an extensive group of tribes living to the east of the River Elbe. In the invasion of 406, the Suebi (who may by now have included a different group of tribes) crossed Gaul and founded a kingdom in Galicia, Spain, which survived until 585. The Franks, who annexed the lands to the east of the Rhine in the 6th century, continued to call these territories Suebia.

Sunken-floor hut Translation of German *Grubenhaus*, a dug-out. Used to refer to small barbarian houses which incorporate a recess cut into the subsoil, either as a cellar or as the floor surface of the building.

Svears Scandinavian people whose territory lay to the north of Stockholm, Sweden.

Swag Term used to describe the "inverted eyebrow" motif common on **migration period** pottery from north Germany, a sagging U-shaped series of incised lines.

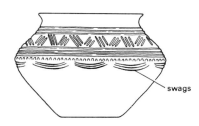

Swags on a ?4th-century pot from Norfolk

Tacitus (c. 56–c. 115 AD) Roman senator and historian of the events of the 1st century AD. Among his works is the *Germania* (of 98 AD), an ethnographical treatise in part based on obsolete information, but presenting a pungent account of the German tribes of the Rhine and Danube, which serves as the basis for the history of these peoples.

Terp German word used to refer to the mound-villages, especially of the north German coastal plain, which were raised above the surrounding marshes on artificial mounds of earth.

Theodoric the Great (c. 451–526) Ostrogothic king who, with Byzantine support, conquered Italy (489–93), and founded a Gothic kingdom. Long recognized as the greatest of barbarian kings, his realm for a time united Germans and Italians. During the reigns of his successors, Theodoric's kingdom was absorbed in the Eastern Empire.

Theodosius II (c. 401–50) Eastern Roman emperor, son of **Arcadius** who succeeded his father in 408. He was dominated by his sister and his wife until the 440s, and at all times by a series of powerful ministers. During his reign successes were achieved in wars against Persia (421–22, 441) and against John the Usurper (425), but the easterners were unsuccessful against the **Vandals** (441) and afterwards against **Attila**. The great walls of Constantinople (after 413) are named "Theodosian" for him.

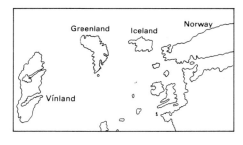

Part of the Vínland Map

Theudelinda (d. 628) Daughter of duke of the Bavarians, a Catholic who was queen of the successive Lombard kings Authari (584–90) and **Agilulf** (590–615). She corresponded with Pope **Gregory the Great** and founded the monastery of St Columbanus at Bobbio.

Typology Method of study of archaeological material, which attempts to arrange objects in a developing sequence, according to assumptions originally formulated in the field of biology.

Ulfila Bishop to the Goths, who preached the gospel to them according to the doctrine of Arius (341–48). The subsequent conversion of the Goths to **Arianism** has been attributed to Ulfila's influence, but was probably the result of contacts in the Balkans after the Gothic entry to the empire in 376. Ulfila translated the Bible into the Gothic dialect.

Umayyads First of the dynasties of Arab leaders, the descendants of a Meccan merchant who submitted to Muhammad. They seized power in 661 and maintained a system based on that of the nomadic desert tribesmen until split by internal feuds and the rise of the Persian **Abbasids** in 750.

Urn Vase, generally with rounded body and narrow neck, especially used to refer to vessels containing the cremated remains of the dead.

Valens (d. 378) Roman emperor, elevated in 364 by his brother **Valentinian I**, the western emperor, to rule the east. He was an Arian, and intolerant. He permitted the Visigoths to enter the empire, and was killed by them at Adrianople.

Valentinian I (d. 375) Roman emperor, proclaimed by the army in 364. He placed his brother **Valens** in power in Constantinople and himself took over Rome. Much of his reign was spent in the defense of the northern frontiers.

Valentinian II (d. 392) Roman emperor, a son of **Valentinian I** and his successor in Italy in 375. His reign was troubled by the usurpation of **Magnus Maximus** and the overthrow of **Gratian** in Gaul, and he fled from Italy to escape Maximus. His restoration by Theodosius the Great was shortly followed by his death, perhaps murder, at Vienne.

Valentinian III (419–55) Western Roman emperor, nephew of **Honorius** and his eventual successor in 425. Most of his reign he was dominated by his mother Placida and by the commander in Gaul, **Aëtius**, whom he murdered in 454, shortly afterwards falling victim to Aëtius' retainers.

Vandals Germanic people, perhaps originally from the Baltic area, who invaded Gaul in 406, and set up a kingdom in Spain. The majority of the Vandals migrated to Africa, where they founded a state which survived until the reconquest of the western Mediterranean under **Justinian** (535).

Varus, Publius Quinctilius (d. 9 AD) Roman general, a favorite of **Augustus** who after a successful career in Africa and Syria commanded the Rhine army, which was ambushed and destroyed in 9 AD somewhere near the middle Weser in Germany.

Viking Víkingur – Scandinavian word used to describe the seafaring raiders from Norway, Sweden and Denmark who ravaged the coasts of Europe after 800 AD. The etymology of the word is disputed; in use it signified "pirate." The noun *viking* means "pirate raid."

Villa Rural homestead in the Roman world, traditionally of courtyard form with house, workshops and farmbuildings. Normally used by archaeologists to refer to substantial establishments of the well-to-do, country houses with associated farmsteads.

Vínland Map Parchment map of the "unknown world," in the Yale University Library, published in 1965 and purporting to date to c. 1440 which shows the "island" of Vínland. It is probably a forgery.

Visigoths See **Goths**.

Vortigern (*floruit* c. 450) British prince after the withdrawal of the Roman administration, who, according to tradition, established federate Saxons in SE England (449 or earlier), apparently to ward off attacks by the Picts and other pirates. The traditional account makes this the first settling of the heathen in Britain, and Vortigern is castigated for his policy by subsequent writers.

Vosk (Danish) Disease among cattle resulting from deficiency in the mineral content of diet, and causing progressive debility, which has been held to account for migration from marginal lands in Scandinavia.

Warburton, Bishop William (1698–1779) For a time an attorney, Warburton took holy orders in 1723 and after a series of livings became bishop of Gloucester in 1759. His enormous output of published works includes treatises on philosophy, scripture and history.

Wilfrid (634–709) Saint and bishop of York. The spokesman of the Catholic Church against Celtic observance at the Synod of Whitby (664). Much of his career was spent in disputes with Northumbrian kings and with archbishops of Canterbury, and twice he visited Rome to plead his cause. Founder of the churches at Hexham and Ripon, and in 678 apostle to the Frisians.

Willibrord (c. 657–c. 738) Saint and missionary. Educated at Ripon and sent in 690 to the Frisians to complete **Wilfrid**'s mission. With Frankish support he was made archbishop of the Frisians c. 695, and founded the bishopric of Utrecht, Holland.

Wright, Thomas (1810–77) English antiquary, who spent his life editing medieval manuscripts. While an undergraduate at Cambridge he published *A History of Essex* (1831–36) incorporating archive and archaeological material. Some of his work has proved to be hasty and carelsss, but his range was impressive, including papers and volumes on medieval literature, song and language, as well as major contributions to Anglo-Saxon studies.

Index